THE DUTIES OF MAN
AND OTHER ESSAYS

THE DUTIES OF MAN
AND OTHER ESSAYS

GIUSEPPE MAZZINI

COSIMO CLASSICS

NEW YORK

The Duties of Man and Other Essays originally published by
J. M. Dent & Sons, Ltd & E. P. Dutton & Co. in 1907.

Library of Congress Cataloging-in-Publication Data
A catalog record for this book is available from the Library of Congress

Cover design by www.wiselephant.com

ISBN: 1-59605-219-8

CONTENTS

Of the seven essays contained in this volume the first
has been translated specially for this edition by Miss
Ella Noyes, the last appeared originally in the
Fortnightly Review, June 1870, from the pen of
Miss L. Martineau, the remaining five are reprinted
from " Essays by Joseph Mazzini, most of them
translated for the first time by Thomas Okey.
Edited with an Introduction by Bolton King,"
London, 1894.

INTRODUCTION

I

JOSEPH MAZZINI died on March 10, 1872. Two days later the *Times* recorded the event in these words " We have to announce to-day the death of a man who in his time has played a most singular part upon the theatre of European politics ; one whose name has for years been regarded as a symbol of Revolution, or rather Republicanism ; one in whose personal character there were many fine and noble qualities ; but still a man who was feared even more widely than he was loved, and one whose departure from the scene of action, to say the least, will be no unwelcome news to several crowned and discrowned members of the family of European sovereigns. He was the man who ever ' troubled Israel' by his ceaseless efforts in the cause of Republicanism, and now at length he is at rest. He died on Sunday at Pisa." A selection from the writings of this terror of principalities and powers is reprinted in this little book. The most timid and law-abiding citizen need not fear to turn over its pages. Two years ago the Italian people celebrated the centenary of Mazzini's birth. The King and his Ministers went in state to hear him eulogised ; commemorations were held in the government schools by order of the Minister of Instruction ; and the flags of Italy and England were wrapped around his monument.

Mazzini's name is not now as familiar to English ears as it was in the mid-Victorian period. Other days, other heroes. A Scottish university professor used sometimes to take a census of the students who had read *Sartor* as a rough test of Carlyle's place in the reading of young

Scotsmen. The results showed that Carlyle was following
the bag of meal and becoming a traditional diet. A teacher
who should number the students of our universities who had
read the *Duties of Man* would meet with a more intelligible
but not less complete ignorance of an inspiring book, and
with a knowledge of its author which never went beyond
coupling him with Garibaldi. Their fathers, who were boys
in the fifties and sixties, probably marched through the
village street shouting :

> I wish I had a penny !
> What for ? What for ?
> To buy a rope, to hang the Pope
> Instead of Garibaldi.

Boys are readier to chant the exploits of a soldier in a red
shirt than the ideas of a prophet in a black coat, and the
people are mostly boys. But that Mazzini's name will live
on among those of Italy's greatest citizens and the world's
best men, seems now beyond dispute. He has never
enjoyed the ready applause accorded to the successful
soldier, nor the sometimes sinister fame achieved by the
successful statesman. Just as in the days of his flesh he
passed along the by-ways of Europe, an exile from every
land but our own, ever conspiring and ever eluding the
authorities, so his subsequent influence has been fugitive,
secret, noiseless, but none the less real, deep, persistent.
His best compositions have had little vogue, but they are
treasured by the musicians who know. Out of print, and
unguessed at by the multitude, their teaching has inspired
some of the most unselfish activities of our time,—the
devotion of some settlement worker or East-End doctor, of
some incorruptible councillor or ardent co-operator, of some
labour leader or nationalist. But Mazzini's most precious
bequest to the world was not a bundle of essays, but a noble
life. Like Socrates he lived his philosophy, but in circumstances much more intricate and baffling than those which
beset the Athenian. The story of those circumstances is
part of the general history of Europe in the nineteenth

century. In so far as Mazzini shared in them they have been narrated for English readers most fully and judicially by Mr. Bolton King. A sympathetic memoir was written by Madame Venturi, and there are the admirable Essays of F. W. H. Myers and William Clarke. The story of the Roman Republic has been well told by Mr. R. M. Johnston.[1] Mazzini's own autobiographical notes are included in the collected edition of his writings.[2] These sources, and Mazzini's own words wherever possible, have been freely used in the short sketch which follows.

II

In the eighteenth century princes ruled over tracts of land rather than nations. The distinction was clearly seen when the French Revolution threw the people to one side and the government to the other. It is a commonplace to say that Napoleon builded better than he knew, and that instead of making France supreme in Europe he roused the slumbering spirit of nationality everywhere. Himself an Italian, pride of race united with the desire to overthrow the Austrian dominion in Italy, and led him deliberately to encourage national aspirations there. In 1800 he defeated the Austrians at Marengo, and proceeded to divide the Italian spoils among his relatives and generals. Their rule had all the unlovely features of the time—secret police, press censorship, nepotism, intrigue, plunder. Local prejudices were outraged; tens of thousands of Italians fell fighting in Spain and Russia under a foreign flag. On the other hand, the Napoleonic régime crippled feudalism, strengthened the central authority, established schools, braced the soldiery, and generally quickened the energies of the people. Napoleon fell. Scheming diplomats at Vienna parcelled out the Italian peninsula afresh between scheming kings and clerics. Austria and Piedmont became the predominant partners. The republics of

[1] To this list must now be added the important work of Mr. G. M Trevelyan : *Garibaldi's Defence of the Roman Republic.*
[2] London : Smith, Elder.

Venice and Genoa were doomed. The people, always dreading absorption by France, welcomed back the old rulers, good and bad alike. With them came the anachronisms of the old order, "the legal abuses, the feudal privileges, monasteries, ecclesiastical courts, the disabilities of Jews and Protestants." Reaction against the disturbing ideas of the Revolution led to distrust of education and the suppression of opinion. An epidemic of criticism was endangering eternal salvation. "The Liberals are sinners," declared the Duke of Modena: "pray for their repentance, but punish the unrepentant."

Meanwhile a young Genoese was pondering over forbidden French newspapers which his father kept hidden behind his innocent medical books. This inquisitive youth was Joseph Mazzini, born on June 22, 1805. Visitors to the City of Palaces will recall the house in the Via Lomellini; the Greek and Italian legends; the faded wreaths from some loyal republican club; the soiled and shabby copies of Guicciardini's *History*, Robertson's *Charles V.*, Emerson's *English Traits*; the courteous attendant who presents the stranger with a copy of the *Duties of Man*. The father was a professor of anatomy at the university, the mother a woman of strong intellect and deep affection. Both were alive to the mighty movements going on around them, and their son heard daily the republican talk of parents "whose bearing towards high or low was ever the same." He was a delicate child, and apparently never went to school. While a worthy old priest taught him the Latin declensions, the pupil was learning to revere the republics of Greece and Rome. At fourteen he matriculated at the University. He chafed at "chapels" and the innumerable formalities expected from the students. His gentle nature and acute mind won him an easy ascendency over his companions. "Simple and economical in his own habits," wrote one of them, "he always found means generously to assist the wants of those around him; indeed he carried this disposition to excess; for, not content with giving away his books

and money, he constantly bestowed even his clothes upon
the needy among his fellow-students." It was intended
that he should follow his father's profession, but he sickened
at the dissecting-room and turned to law. His real
mistress, however, was literature—"a thousand visions of
historical dramas and romances floated before my mental
eye"—and he would have served her with fine devotion
had not a more imperious rival claimed his loyalty.

The wind bloweth where it listeth. The call to Mazzini
came on a Sunday in April 1821, when he and his mother
and a friend of the family were walking in the streets of
Genoa. They were suddenly accosted by "a tall, black-
bearded man, with a severe and energetic countenance,
and a fiery glance that I have never since forgotten. He
held out a white handkerchief toward us, merely saying,
'For the refugees of Italy.' My mother and friend dropped
some money into the handkerchief, and he turned from us
to put the same request to others." The man was one
of a crowd of revolutionists who had flocked to Genoa after
a fruitless insurrection against Austria. The incident made
a deep impression on the boy of sixteen. His spirit was
crushed by the impossibility he felt of ever conceiving by
what means to free his country from the foreign yoke.
"In the midst of the noisy, tumultuous life of the scholars
around me, I was sombre and absorbed, and appeared like
one suddenly grown old. I childishly determined to dress
always in black, fancying myself in mourning for my country."
It was not easy to give up literature for politics. He read
what books in Italian, French, and English he could lay
hands on at a time when "half the masterpieces of
contemporary European literature came under the censor's
ban." He steeped his mind in the Bible and Dante Shake-
speare and Byron, Goethe and Schiller. Byron's passion
for history, his hatred of the doctrines of the Holy Alliance,
his sympathy with heroic endeavour, his exposure of the
sterility of egoism, explain the high place which Mazzini
always gave him among the world's poets. But it was
from the pages of Dante that he drew the richest nourish-

ment. Across five centuries of glory and shame, liberty and servitude, deep called unto deep in the spirits of the two men. The thought that seethed within the soul of the great Florentine was now stirring afresh in the bosom of the young Genoese—the yearning for unity, moral and political, founded upon some great organic authoritative idea, the love of country, the worship of Rome, the sublime vision of the destiny in store for her, leading the human race in holiness and truth. The pedantic critics and syllable-splitters were all astray. One had made Dante Guelph ; another Ghibelline ; nearly all proved him an orthodox Catholic. He was none of these, cried Mazzini ; he was a Christian and an Italian.

But it was no time for variant readings. The critic must give way to the apostle. He found a pulpit in a commercial paper published at Genoa, then in another at Leghorn. Both were suppressed. Three articles were written for the chief Italian review, the *Antologia*. But this was not enough for his ardent spirit. He joined the secret society of the Carbonari. It had once been the rallying-ground of enthusiastic Liberals who aimed in a vague way at independence, but it was now a declining force, and a number of unsuccessful risings had brought discredit upon it. It offered a way of usefulness, however ; but Mazzini chafed under its fantastic ritual, its negative programme, its patriotism that looked to France for deliverance. He was already dreaming of a very different society. But despotic governments dislike dreamers. Mazzini was arrested, ostensibly on the charge of introducing a recruit into the ranks of the Carbonari, really, as the Governor of Genoa told his father, because he was a thoughtful young man of talent, fond of solitary walks by night. " We don't like young people thinking without our knowing the subject of their thoughts." From his cell in the fortress of Savona he looked out upon " the sea and sky—two symbols of the infinite and, except the Alps, the sublimest things in nature." Here, with a Bible, a Tacitus, a Byron, and a friendly greenfinch for companions, he had leisure to elaborate the plan of " Young Italy."

III

The ideas of Italian unity and independence were not born with Mazzini. In the distant past there had been Dante and Rienzi. In the immediate past there had been the French Revolution, Napoleon, Romanticism—all active in the years surrounding Mazzini's birth. Romanticism has been called the starting-point of the modern political schools in Italy, the precursor alike of Young Italy and the Moderates. It was more than a mere literary revolt ; it was a propaganda of political ideas for which some of its apostles suffered the horrors of the Spielberg. Songs, plays, pamphlets, novels, were the vehicles of the new movement. Editions of Dante appeared literally by the dozen. In 1820 the *Antologia* was founded in order " to make Italy know itself." Seven years later Manzoni published his famous novel, in which the discerning could read the meaning as clearly as we now read it in *Kathleen ni Houlihan*. Wherein did Mazzini differ from these distinguished predecessors and contemporaries ? He set their ideas on fire. Where they were literary he was political ; where they were critical he was constructive ; where they were merely moral he was passionately religious.

He came out of prison with a programme, the magnificent daring of which can only be realised by those who know the Italy of the time—morselled out into a mosaic of states, divided by differences of speech and temper, honeycombed with secret associations and spies ; an aristocracy fawning on the foreign conqueror ; a common people "eating Austria with their bread," and drugged by opera, carnival, and charity ; a Church respected in proportion as one travelled away from the centre of her influence to the circumference. Out of the midst of this degradation, in it but not of it, Mazzini, young and poor, lifted up his voice : " I see the people pass before my eyes in the livery of wretchedness and political subjection, ragged and hungry, painfully gathering the crumbs that wealth tosses insultingly to it, or lost and wandering in riot and the intoxication of a brutish, angry, savage joy; and I remember that those brutalised faces bear the finger-print of God, the mark of the same mission as our own. I lift myself to the vision of the future, and behold the people rising in its majesty, brothers in one faith, one bond of equality and love, one ideal of citizen virtue that ever grows in beauty and might; the people of the future, unspoilt by luxury, ungoaded by wretchedness, awed by the consciousness of its rights and duties." He bade his countrymen unite and drive the Austrian out, heedless of help from France. "No nation reserves freedom or can long retain it which does not win it for itself. Revolutions must be made by the people and for the people." It was useless waiting for opportunities— they must be made. But it was to be war, not only on the Austrian, but on Italian ignorance, dissension, and vice— the wretched brood of oppression. Servile habits and unworthy affections must go. The nation must purify herself in order to fulfil her mission. The sole path to victory was through sacrifice—constancy in sacrifice. In the name of God and the people, he invited Italians to march through poverty, exile, and death to a free country. The second of these alternatives was to fall to his lot immediately. Released from Savona, he was offered "internment in a small town, or exile." He chose the latter, and in February 1831 said his good-byes to his family, crossed the Alps to Geneva, went thence to Lyons and Marseilles. Here, in a small room, with a handful of patriots recruited from the refugees in the town, he unfolded his plans for transforming Italy into a free, independent, republican nation. Unity was to be sought for by armed insurrection; social reform by political action and education. The aims of Young Italy were to be public; its methods, perforce, secret. To work in the open would be to march straight to the Spielberg or the scaffold. "I never saw," wrote Mazzini in after years, "any nucleus of young men so devoted, capable of such strong mutual affection, such pure enthusiasm, and such readiness in daily, hourly toil, as were those who then laboured with me. We had no office.

no helpers. All day, and a great part of the night, we were
buried in our work, writing articles and letters, getting
information from travellers, enlisting seamen, folding papers,
fastening envelopes, dividing our time between literary and
manual work. . . . We lived as equals and brothers ; we
had but one thought, one hope, one ideal to reverence. The
foreign republicans loved and admired us for our tenacity
and unflagging industry ; we were often in real want, but
we were light-hearted in a way, and smiling because we
believed in the future." The young leader united to an
indomitable spirit a striking presence. His English bio
grapher quotes a description of him as he appeared at this
time : "His long, curling black hair, which fell upon his
shoulders, the extreme freshness of his clear olive com-
plexion, the chiselled delicacy of his regular and beautiful
features, aided by his very youthful look and sweetness and
openness of expression, would have made his appearance
almost too feminine, if it had not been for his noble forehead,
the power of firmness and decision that was mingled with
their gaiety and sweetness in the bright flashes of his dark
eyes and in the varying expression of his mouth, together
with his small and beautiful moustachios and beard.
Altogether he was at that time the most beautiful being,
male or female, that I had ever seen, and I have not since
seen his equal." Thirty years later Jowett told a corre-
spondent, "Some friends of mine, who know him (Mazzini),
assure me that he has the greatest fascination of manner
they have ever met with."

The young band worked with an enthusiasm which stirred
a quick response at home. Articles, manifestoes, pamphlets
poured from their leader's fervid pen, were printed and
smuggled into Italy in barrels of pitch and bales of drapery,
and thrilled their readers with their elevated thought and
glowing prose. "Climb the hills," he bade them, "sit at the
farmer's table, visit the workshops and the artisans, whom
you now neglect. Tell them of their rightful liberties, their
ancient traditions and glories, the old commercial greatness
which has gone ; talk to them of the thousand forms of

A 224

oppression, which they are ignorant of, because no one points them out." Lodges sprang up in the chief towns of the north and centre, thousands of recruits were enrolled, and by 1833 the Austrian Government considered "Young Italy" sufficiently dangerous to declare membership thereof high treason punishable by death.

IV

For centuries Piedmont had been a buffer state, struck now by France, now by Austria. In such a position it was natural that the arts of diplomacy and war should absorb the main energies of the little kingdom. It was natural, too that patriots of all parties should look to Piedmont to lead in the struggle against Austria. Mazzini now appealed to its king to head the national movement. The character of Charles Albert offers interesting parallels to that of another potentate who in our own day has had to confront revolution. He was pathetically regarded as the leader of causes he dreaded. "Everybody," it was said, "expects a constitution from Charles Albert." In his youth he had dallied with the Carbonari, but his Liberalism was a spent sympathy. "The religious mood grew upon him ; he became a devotee, easily played on by confessor and Jesuit, timidly scrupulous to prove himself a good son of the Church and gain Papal sanction for his acts." "He stood 'between the dagger of the Carbonari and the poisoned chocolate of the Jesuits'. . . 'a strange compound of the worldly and the martyr spirit, no hero, but a perplexed, scruple-harassed man, the victim of a fatal indecision between the authority of convention and the noble promptings of his heart.'" His reply to Mazzini's appeal was to order him to be seized should he cross the frontier. The exiles then planned a rising with Genoa and Alessandria as centres, hoping to force the King to lead or abdicate, but an accident revealed the plot and a savage persecution crushed the conspiracy. There are senses in which history repeats itself with very little difference.

Forged signatures, enervating drugs, physical torture were used to force the prisoners to betray their comrades. Dreading he might succumb, Jacopo Ruffini, Mazzini's dearest friend, committed suicide in his cell. Mazzini himself was condemned to death, and the French Government decreed his banishment ; but he remained hidden in Marseilles for a year, pushing on the crusade. In the middle of July 1833 he went to Geneva to organise another insurrection, the leadership of which, contrary to his advice, was vested in an adventurer who exhausted the funds and delayed action until all chance of success was gone. The failure of the two expeditions and the strain of work, anxiety and secrecy which they involved, preyed on Mazzini's health and plunged him for a time into a black despair. The forms of his dead comrades rose up before him " like the phantoms of a crime and its unavailing remorse. I could not recall them to life. How many mothers I had caused to weep ' How many more must learn to weep, should I persist in the attempt to arouse the youth of Italy to noble action, to awaken in them the yearning for a common country ! And if that country were indeed an illusion !" Diplomatic notes poured down upon Switzerland, and Mazzini was banished from the Republic. Again he managed to elude the police, leading a hunted life, now sheltered by some Protestant pastor, now spending months in untenanted houses where in the moaning of the wind he heard Ruffini's voice calling to him. Gradually the tempest of doubt subsided. " One morning I awoke to find my mind tranquil and my spirit calmed, as one who had passed through a great danger. . . . The first thought that passed across my spirit was, ' Your sufferings are the temptations of egoism, and arise from a misconception of life.' " He searched his heart to see if it had any wicked way in it. Was there any lurking selfishness ? Material desires he had surrendered long ago, but he had clung to the affections. " I should have thought of them, as of a blessing from God, to be accepted with thankfulness, not as of something to be expected and exacted as a right and a reward. Instead of

this, I had made them a condition of fulfilling my duties.
I had not reached the ideal of love, love that has no hope in
this life. I had worshipped not love but the joys of love."
He bade a long farewell to individual hopes, dug the grave,
not of his affections, but of all the desires and ineffable
comforts of affection, so that none might ever know the Ego
buried beneath. In like manner he traced to egotism the
failure of the French Revolution and the various unsuccessful risings in Italy. Men had sought after happiness,
clamoured for their rights. A higher note must be struck.
"We fell as a political party, we must rise as a religious
party." "Life is a mission ; duty, therefore, its highest law.
. . . Each of us is bound to purify his own soul as a temple ;
to free it from egotism ; to set before himself, with a
religious sense of the importance of the study, the problem
of his own life ; to search out what is the most striking, the
most urgent need of the men by whom he is surrounded,
then to interrogate his own faculties and capacity, and
resolutely apply them to the satisfaction of that need. . . .
Young brothers, when once you have conceived and
determined your mission within your soul, let nought arrest
your steps. Fulfil it with all your strength ; fulfil it, whether
blessed by love or visited by hate ; whether strengthened by
association with others, or in the sad solitude that almost
always surrounds the martyrs of thought. The path is
clear before you ; you are cowards, unfaithful to your own
future, if, in spite of sorrows and delusions, you do not
pursue it to the end."

V

With Mazzini in Switzerland were Agostino and Giovanni
Ruffini. They lacked the heroic quality of their dead
brother, and felt acutely the strain of a conspirator's life.
For their sakes, chiefly, Mazzini decided to come to London,
and they arrived here in January 1837. Mazzini grew to
love this "sunless and musicless island," but his first
experience of a dingy lodging in a back street filled him

with longing for the Alps which he had loved "almost as a mother." More trying still was the impatience of his comrades, who could not soar to Mazzini's transcendental heights. Where all are geniuses life may be tolerable for all, but the odds are against the happiness of the family in which the genius is set solitary. Nor did a diet of potatoes and rice, with their undoubted vegetarian virtues, conduce to the harmony of the household near the Euston Road. And the maid-of-all-work had never heard of the Gospel of Duty! Much may be endured where there is money to procure better, but the exiles were in the direst poverty. Mazzini was not the man to resist the importunities of his countrymen while he had a penny left, and some of them thought that "in the name of this chimera of human brotherhood" they had a right to make themselves at home in his house. Precious souvenirs, books, clothes, began to find their way to the pawnshops, and he dragged himself from one moneylender to another, paying a ruinous rate of interest. In the daytime he found his way into "the valley of the shadow of books"—the international workshop in Bloomsbury, and under its sheltering dome began to turn out an article or two. He got to know some English families, the Carlyles among the first. In 1840 he moved to Chelsea—then a suburb of hayfields and market gardens —to be near them, and they were very kind and helpful. Mrs. Carlyle had a deep affection for him, and took him into her confidence in her domestic troubles. He repaid her with a couple of letters which are surely the noblest ever penned in such a situation.

1

LONDON, *July* 1846.

To JANE WELSH CARLYLE.

MY DEAR FRIEND,

I was yesterday almost the whole day out, and did not receive your notes, except in the evening, when it was too late to answer them. Your few words sound sad, deeply, I will not say irreparably sad ; and the worst of it is that none can help you but yourself. It is only you who can, by a calm, dispassionate, fair re-examination of the past, send back to nothingness the ghosts and phantoms that you have been conjuring up. It is only you who can teach yourself that, whatever the *present* may be, you must front it with dignity, with a clear perception of all your duties, with a due reverence to your immortal soul, with a religious faith in times yet to come, that are to dawn under the approach of other cloudless suns. I could only point out to you the fulfilment of duties which can make life—not happy—what can ? but earnest, sacred and resignated ; but I would make you frown or scorn. We have a different conception of life, and are condemned here down to walk on two parallels. Still it is the feeling of those duties that saves me from the atheism of despair, and leads me through a life every day more barren and burdensome, in a sort of calm, composed manner—such, I repeat, as the consciousness of something everlasting within us claims from every living mortal. For I now most coolly and deliberately do declare to you, that partly through what is known to you, partly through things that will never be known, I am carrying a burden even heavier than you, and have undergone even bitterer deceptions than you have. But by dint of repeating to myself that there is no happiness under the moon, that life is a self-sacrifice meant for some higher and happier thing ; that to have a few loving beings, or, if none, to have a mother watching you from Italy or from Heaven, it is all the same, ought to be quite enough to preserve us from falling, and by falling, parting, I have mustered up strength to go on, to work at my task as far as I have been able to make it out, till I reach the grave : the grave for which the hour will come, and is fast approaching without my loudly calling for it.

Awake, arise, dear friend ! Beset by pain or not, we must go on with a sad smile and a practical encouragement from one another. We have something of our own to care about, something godlike that we must not yield to any living creature, whoever it be. Your life proves an empty thing, you say. Empty ! Do not blaspheme. Have you never done good ? Have you never loved ? Think of your mother and do good—set the eye to Providence. It is not as a mere piece of irony that God has placed you here : not as a mere piece of irony that He has given us those aspirations, those yearnings after happiness that are now making us both unhappy. Can't you trust Him a little longer ? . . . How long will you remain at Seaforth ?

Does he himself propose to go anywhere? I was coming to see you on Saturday. Write if and when it does good even homœopathically to you, and be assured that to me it will always do.

Ever yours,—
Joseph Mazzini.

II

July 15th, 1846.

To JANE WEISH CARLYLE, *Seaforth.*

MY DEAR FRIEND,

I could not write yesterday, as I intended, on account of the death of Scipioni Petrucci's wife. . . . Yes; " sad at death, but not basely sad." That is what you must be, what I want you to be, and what a single moment of truly earnest thought and faith will cause you to be. Pain and joy, deception and fulfilled hopes are just, as I often said, the rain and the sunshine that must meet the traveller on his way. Bless the Almighty if He has thought proper to send the latter to you. Button or wrap your cloak around you against the first, but do not think a single moment that the one or the other have anything to do with the *end* of your journey. You know that ; but you want the *faith* that would give you strength to fulfil the task shown by the intellect. These powers will give you that too, if you properly apply to them—affection, a religious belief, and the dead. You have affection for me, as I have for you : you would not shake mine? You would not add yourself to the temptations haunting me to wreck and despair? You would not make me worse than I am by your example, by your showing yourself selfish and materialist? You believe in God ; don't you think, after all, that this is nothing but an ephemeral trial, and that He will shelter you at the journey's end under the wide wing of His paternal love? You had, have, though invisible to the eyes of the body, your mother, your father, too. Can't you commune with them? I know that a single moment of true fervent love for them will do more for you than all my talking ! Were they now what you call living, would you not fly to them, hide your head in their bosom and be comforted, and feel that you owe to them to be strong—that they may never feel ashamed of their own Jane? Why can you think them to be *dead,* gone for ever, their loving immortal soul annihilated? Can you think that this vanishing for a time has made you less responsible to them? *Can you, in a word, love them less because they are far from sight?* I have often thought that the arrangement by which loved and loving beings are to pass through death is nothing but the last experiment appointed by God to human love; and often, as you know from me, I have felt that a moment of true soul-communing with my dead friend was opening a source of strength for me unhoped for, down here. Did we not often agree about these glimpses of the link between ours and the superior life? Shall we now begin to disagree? Be strong, then, and true to those you loved, and proud, nobly proud in the eyes of those you love or esteem. Some of them are deeply, silently suffering, but needing strength too, needing it perhaps from you. Get up and work; do not set yourself apart from us. When the Evil One wanted to tempt Jesus, he led Him into a solitude.

Believe me, my dear friend, ever yours,

JOSEPH MAZZINI.

It was in these years of forced peace that Mazzini wrote some of his most important essays on Byron and Goethe; on the minor works of Dante; on Lamennais, whose *Words of a Believer*, condemned in the Pope's Encyclical as "small in size but of huge depravity," may have influenced Mazzini in writing the *Duties of Man*. In 1843 he had subjected the teaching of Carlyle to a profound criticism which is still far from commonplace, and which was highly original then. In the following year Carlyle stood staunchly by his critic in the episode of the mutilated correspondence. Mazzini discovered that his letters were being tampered with, and that English officials in high places were playing the spy for the Austrian Government. The case came up in the House of Commons, and roused general indignation. Sir James Graham made a lame defence, and charged Mazzini with promoting assassination—a charge afterwards honourably withdrawn. Carlyle pretended he knew nothing and desired to know nothing of Italian democracies and Young Italy's sorrows, of extraneous Austrian Emperors in Milan, or poor old chimerical Popes in Bologna; but there was something else he did know, as he testified in the *Times*. " I have had the honour to know M. Mazzini for a series of years, and, whatever I may think of his practical insight and skill in worldly affairs, I can

with great freedom testify to all men that he, if ever I have
seen one such, is a man of genius and virtue, a man of
sterling veracity, humanity, and nobleness of mind, one of
those rare men, numerable, unfortunately, but as units in
this world, who are worthy to be called martyr souls, who,
in silence, piously in their daily life, understand and practise
what is meant by that." The incident turned out a blessing
in disguise. It lifted Mazzini into English public life, and
brought to him and to the Italian cause a number of loyal
helpers, particularly the Ashursts, of whose daughters one
married James Stansfeld and another became Madame
Venturi, Mazzini's biographer. Among other friends were
William Shaen; Peter Taylor, Member for Leicester, the
friend of Mill and "redresser-general of unheeded wrongs";
the Chartists, Thomas Cooper and Henry Vincent; Joseph
Toynbee, the father of Arnold Toynbee; W. J. Fox, the
Unitarian orator; Joseph Cowen of Newcastle; W. J.
Linton, the engraver; and George Jacob Holyoake, the
veteran co-operator, who died but the other day. These
names recall the social wrongs and remedies of the forties : on
the one hand, bad harvests, famine, commercial crises, strikes,
unemployment; on the other, the agitations for free trade,
a free press, and the six points of the Charter. Dr. Holland
Rose has pointed out[1] that there was much in common
between the moral-force Chartists and the Italian democrat,
though the latter was at first inclined to band all English-
men as "materialist and sectarian." Residence in a country
where the industrial struggle was more fierce, more squalid,
than in his own sunnier, lazier land, deepened his sense of
the urgency of social reform. London, too, gave him the
opportunity of knowing some Italian workmen at close
quarters. He founded a political association among them,
and began the publication of a journal in which a portion
of the *Duties of Man* appeared. He befriended an un-
fortunate woman, and for years devoted a large share of his
scanty income to the education of her children. The organ-
boys attracted his notice. He was amazed to find that five

[1] *Rise of Democracy*, p. 89.

or six Italians made a practice of inducing them to leave
their rural homes in Parma and Liguria under fair promises
of food and lodging and pay. Once here they were drilled
in all sorts of beggary and deceit, and were cruelly treated.
He was able to bring some of the slave-dealers to justice in
the English courts and thereby terrify the rest. Better still,
in 1841 he opened an evening school for the boys in Hatton
Garden, and continued it for seven years—till his return to
Italy—" a holy work, holily fulfilled." "They used to come
between nine and ten o'clock at night, bringing their organs
with them. We taught them reading, writing, arithmetic,
simple geography, and the elements of drawing. On the
Sunday evenings we gathered all our scholars together to
listen to an hour's lecture upon Italian history, the lives of
our great men, the outlines of natural philosophy—any subject in short that appeared to us calculated to elevate those
unformed minds, darkened by poverty and their state of
abject subjection to the will of others. Nearly every Sunday
evening for two years, I lectured to them upon Italian history
or elementary astronomy ; a subject eminently religious, and
calculated to purify the mind, which—reduced to popular
phraseology and form—should be among the first subjects
chosen for the education of the young."

VI[1]

The failure of the expeditions organised by " Young
Italy " and the protracted exile of its chief had dissipated
the society which had set out with such radiant morning
hopes. Mazzini himself had his hours of disillusionment,
which come to every high priest of the ideal, and which
lower the level of life. He had failed to gauge the inertia
of his countrymen. He read his own shining faith into
them, and had fondly imagined that twenty millions from
the Alps to Etna were ready to strike for freedom when the
bugle called. He was impatient of men who temporised ;
he detested diplomacy, and thought the straight line was
the shortest between two given points. The Right had

[1] Cf. *The Roman Theocracy and the Republic*, 1846-49. By R. M. Johnston.

such compelling power over his own pure soul that he could not understand men who shrank from plain duties. Their slackness made him blush—"as if I were lying." These were poor qualities for a conspirator, and Mazzini was a failure in that *rôle*. He was too dogmatic in utterance, too precipitate in action, and he invariably exaggerated the strength of his own side and underrated that of the enemy.

Meanwhile a party was growing up who had imbibed much of Mazzini's teaching, but who from all the reasons which hover between prudence and cowardice was inclined to slower and less direct methods than his uncompromising democratic nature would permit. This was the party of the Moderates, led by a group of able patriotic writers of varying views. Some counselled the postponement of political insurrection and urged the establishment of schools, savings-banks, model farms and railways. Others, despairing of Unity, kindled hopes of a Federal Independence under Charles Albert and a Liberal Pontiff. Three years before the death of Gregory XVI., Gioberti, in a book which deeply moved all Italian hearts, had prophesied the coming of a reforming Pope who should mediate justly between princes and people, and assert the moral supremacy of Rome over the world. In 1846 his prophecy seemed likely of fulfilment in the advent of Pius IX. Pius had attended the conclave which was to elect Gregory's successor. So little did he, a recently elected Cardinal, anticipate the honour in store for himself, that he had brought with him a copy of Gioberti's book as a humble offering to the new Pope. One of his first acts as Pius IX. was to pardon the political prisoners and exiles, numbering some thousands in all. The enthusiasm of the populace knew no bounds. The deliverer of Italy had arrived. All things suddenly seemed possible. "To the religious, impulsive, ill-educated average Italian, a Pope's sympathy meant more than all the philosophy and idealism of Young Italy." That night, it was said, every house in Rome was illuminated, with one ominous exception—that of the Austrian Ambassador. Wild rumours attached themselves to the new pontiff—that he

was "un gran' Carbonaro," or even the secret head of
"Young Italy," whispered some.   But there were three
forces at work soon to shatter the popular idol—the Jesuits,
Metternich, and the Pope himself.   The Jesuits wielded
their secret influence far and wide, and at Rome controlled
the police and civil service.   They blocked the Pope at
every turn.   Away in Vienna, where their power was great,
Metternich had pronounced a Liberal Pope "the greatest
misfortune of the age," and openly insulted him by filling
Ferrara, a Papal city, with Austrian troops.   The Pope
himself, full of good intentions, was bewildered, one day
promising legal reforms and railway construction, the next
refusing to sanction a citizen guard, the third prohibiting
public meetings because they interrupted the studies of
youth !   The people were clamouring to go to war with
Austria.   Diplomatic negotiations, however, led Metternich
to withdraw the imperial troops from Ferrara (December 16,
1847).   But the Pope had had enough of " modern progress."
" They are mistaken, who would see in the Council of State
instituted by me," he declared at its opening ceremony,
" the realisation of their Utopias and the germ of institutions
incompatible with the Pontifical sovereignty."   The Sultan
was not the only " sick man " in Europe.

Mazzini watched this movement closely, and advised his
scattered followers to use the enthusiasm for national ends
at the sacrifice of republicanism, if necessary.   In this year
he wrote several articles to the *People's Journal*, in one
of which he foretold the coming storm.   " Europe rapidly
approaches a tremendous crisis ; a supreme contest between
peoples and their despots, which no human power can
henceforth hinder, but which the active concurrence of all
the brave and good would render shorter and less severe
and whose final result will be a new map of Europe."   The
year of revolutions arrived—1848—" when all time's sea
was foam."   From Palermo and Paris, Vienna and Berlin
came the shouts of the multitudes uprisen to reckon with
their rulers.   The King of the French escaped in a cab,
and Metternich in a cart.   The Austrian power was rapidly

crumbling in the northern towns of Italy. Mazzini hurried
to Paris and thence to Milan, where he had an enthusiastic
reception. But victory tarried. Dissensions, fomented
partly by Mazzini's presence, arose between monarchists
and republicans over the form of government to be set
up when the Austrians were routed ! The feeble indecision
and delay of Charles Albert, "the Wobbling King," led
to one disaster after another in the field, and the enemy,
under Radetzky, regained the lost ground. Ten years more
were to pass before the foreigner was finally ousted, and
then the honours were to fall to Cavour and Victor
Emmanuel.

In Rome, however, the fortunes of the Liberals were
improving so rapidly that the air of the Quirinal became
stifling. The Pope, following the ruling fashion, escaped
in a chaise to Gaeta. Rome was free. A provisional
government was set up which appealed to universal suffrage
to elect a Constituent Assembly of one hundred and fifty
members. Among the deputies elected were a general of
volunteers and his standard-bearer who had come from
the North, defeated but not beaten—Garibaldi and Mazzini.
Twenty years earlier Garibaldi had joined the ranks of
"Young Italy" at Marseilles, and then tasted of exile and
adventure in South America. The Assembly by an over-
whelming majority declared for a Republic, abolished the
hated temporal power of the Pope, but guaranteed him
liberty to exercise his spiritual office. Thus opened one
of the most moving pages in history. Mazzini had entered
the city "one evening early in March, with a deep sense
of awe, almost of worship." It is not difficult to understand
the fascination of Rome, and the desire to see her capital
of a united Italy. But with Mazzini the desire had been
a master passion which went far beyond the dream of a
political centre. Gioberti looked to a reformed Papacy ;
but in Mazzini's vision "the city of the soul" was the Temple
of Humanity sending forth a new religion of duty, sacrifice,
and brotherhood. When they cheered his first rising in
the Assembly he reiterated his faith : "These manifestations

of admiration should not be addressed by you to me, but
rather by me to you," he said; "for what little of good I
may have accomplished, or attempted, has owed its inspiration to my life's talisman, Rome. In my heart I have
said, It is not possible that the City that has already lived
two lives, should not arise to see a third. After the Rome
of conquering soldiers, after the Rome of the triumphant
Word, so I kept saying to myself, there shall come the
Rome of virtue and of example; after the City of the
Emperors, after that of the Popes, shall come that of
the People." It was a noble vision, seen by all good
men under one form or another.

Mazzini now endeavoured to unite the scattered republican
forces. Goaded by Austrian brutality, Charles Albert was
once more marching against Radetzky, but he was no match
for the old general and the Piedmontese suffered a crushing
defeat at Novara. The King abdicated in favour of his
eldest son Victor Emmanuel II, and four months later
died brokenhearted in a Portuguese monastery. In Rome
the news of Novara led to the election of Mazzini, Saffi and
Armellini as triumvirs, and from the Papal Court at Gaeta
this called forth an appeal to the Catholic Powers for "armed
intervention to free the States of the Church from the faction
of rogues." The response came from an unexpected quarter.
In the 5th Article of the French Constitution of 1848 it was
written, "France respects foreign nationalities; her might
shall never be employed against the liberty of any people!"
With what duplicity this promise was broken in "the
meanest of modern political crimes" can only be briefly
recounted here. French troops landed and marched on the
young sister-republic. Mazzini was an idealist, but he was
no coward. He would fight for a righteous principle.
There were virtues more precious than peace. A Committee
of War was formed to organise the defence under Roselli
and Garibaldi. On May 7th Ferdinand de Lesseps on
behalf of France came to terms with the Roman Republic.
He acted in good faith, but the agreement was a ruse of his
employers; and the French general Oudinot laid siege to

the city. Mazzini was the soul and strength of the defence He does not appear to have been sanguine of victory, but he was determined to leave a great republican example. "His defence of Rome raised the Italian character," wrote Jowett. Unselfish, tireless, heedless of personal comfort, with a heart soft as a child's, with a colossal belief in his divine mission, this "pestiferous conspirator" displayed to the subjects of the Pope a spiritual grandeur the like of which had rarely if ever been seen in a Vicar of Christ through all the ages of Roman christendom. "Here in Rome," he told the quarrelling deputies with unconscious irony, "we may not be moral mediocrities." "Stiffness to principles, tolerance to individuals," was to be the watchword. And nobly he obeyed it. Smaller men would have wrought their revenge on the Church which blocked Italian unity and national aspiration. A word from the Triumvir at this moment, and many a priest and church would have suffered. But when the crowd used confessional boxes to make barricades he ordered them to be taken back. He would allow no degradation of sacred symbols. "It is the duty of the government to preserve religion uncontaminated." Similarly plotters were left free and the Press hardly disturbed. After the French general had been driven back on April 30 the prisoners taken in the fight were marched to St. Peter's to be addressed in these words: "Frenchmen and Italians, in this sublime and holy spot, let us together offer our prayers to the Almighty, for the liberty of all people and for universal fraternity!" They were then escorted to the gates of the city and presented with a monster gift of cigars for their comrades beyond the walls. This was the gospel in action, neither papal nor imperial, but democratic. The Triumvir occupied a little room in the Quirinal accessible to high and low alike. He dined at a cheap restaurant for two francs a day, lived during the siege on bread and raisins, spending his slender stipend entirely on others. His only luxury was a bunch of flowers sent to him daily by an unknown hand. But the small band of heroes could not withstand the overpowering numbers of the French. The

losses were heavy, and among them dear frends of Mazzini
—Mameli the poet, Manara, the Lombard leader in the Five
Days of Milan, and many another.

Mazzini hoped for a republican rising in France which
would change the situation, but the Catholic party triumphed.
Garibaldi was brave, but vain and difficult to work with.
He sullenly refused to obey Roselli in the most critical hours
of the French attack, then roused himself to a great effort
when it was too late. On July 1st the Assembly met and
voted surrender. Mazzini, unwilling to face the mournful
fact of defeat, protested to the last. "Monarchies may
capitulate, republics die and bear their testimony even to
martyrdom." Garibaldi marched out of the city at the head of
three thousand followers, to be pursued by the enemy and to
suffer great hardship. His wife, Anita, who always accompanied him, died amid the marshes of Comacchio. Ugo
Bassi, the eloquent and fearless and gentle friar, was shot by
the Austrians in the streets of Bologna. Mazzini—one
thinks of Gordon—lingered on in Rome for some days,
almost inviting assassination. "In two short months," wrote
Margaret Fuller, one of the noble band who had nursed the
wounded through the siege, "he had grown old ; all the vital
juices seemed exhausted ; . . . but he had never flinched,
never quailed ; had protested in the last hour against surrender, sweet and calm, but full of a more fiery purpose than
ever ; in him I revered the hero, and owned myself not of
that mould."

VII

From Rome Mazzini went to Switzerland, and thence to
England, where he was to remain, except for brief intervals,
to the closing years of his life. The task of liberating and
unifying Italy passed largely into the hands of diplomatists,
with whose devious ways he had such scant sympathy that
he often judged their motives unfairly—Cavour, Louis
Napoleon, Victor Emmanuel. Mazzini had repeatedly
expressed his willingness to place unity first and the republic
second, but he found it difficult to be faithful to this con-

cession. Banished from the scene of action, without money,
and dependent on secret informers, who rarely possessed
full or accurate information, his great powers of leadership
were wasted on dark conspiracies and futile insurrections,
by which he hurt and hindered men who were working, like
himself, for a common country. Some of these men had
been ardent republicans, but had been convinced by the
disunion and failure of the Year of Revolutions that the
casual opposition of undisciplined forces would never drive
out the trained troops of the enemy. Daniel Manin, a
republican idealist with strong practical instincts backed
by a stainless life, in his defence of Venice against the
Austrians, had raised the Venetian character to heights as
heroic as those reached by the Romans under Mazzini. But
with Garibaldi and many old members of "Young Italy,"
Manin had now come to believe that the help of the
Piedmontese army with its King and Minister were indispensable to the redemption of Italy, and that the republic
must be postponed. Gioberti had awakened from his dreams
of a reformed Papacy, and had written a new book, in which
Piedmont figured as the regenerator of Italy with the help
of France. And it was to this policy that parties of all sorts
were coming. Mazzini held obstinately to the programme
of Savona, unable to imagine a profligate King and a cunning
Minister as the saviours of the nation. But "men fight to
lose the battle, and the thing they fought for comes about
in spite of their defeat, and when it comes it turns out not
to be what they meant, and other men have to fight for
what they meant under another name." The temporal
power of the Papacy ended and the unity of Italy was
achieved. A recent English historian divides the honours,
unequally, between the sword of Garibaldi and the brain
of Cavour, and says nothing of the soul of Mazzini. It is
a somewhat shallow judgment, but if it is meant to imply
that the Italy of 1870 was not what Mazzini had wished to
call into being, it may stand. "This medley of opportunists
and cowards and little Macchiavellis, that let themselves
be dragged behind the suggestion of the foreigner—I

thought to call up the soul of Italy, and I only see its corpse." The Liberalism of Cavour had triumphed. The old generation had "praised God; the new generation thought more of keeping its powder dry. The former had had its poetry, its great literary works, its appeals to history; the latter wrote leaflets and pamphlets, and spoke through the press, which had come into power since 1847. . . . The heroic idealism had gone, and rationalism and science took its place. The new spirit was matter-of-fact, thinking more of the present than the future, fearful of pitching its hopes too high, quietly, cautiously laying the foundations, determined to go on no quixotic ventures, but slowly prepare, and only fight when the odds were on its side. Mazzini flinched from no sacrifice; he was ready to surrender the present convenience and happiness of the whole community, its family life, its trade, in a desperate struggle. The new movement shrank from the terrible and impossible appeal; but it put its faith in discipline, it was willing for the sake of union to sacrifice spontaneity, to be unfair to opponents, to crush minorities."

The difference between the two protagonists could not be better illustrated than by repeating a couple of anecdotes which Mr. Myers put side by side.

"When Cavour was about six years old he was taken on a posting journey. On one stage of this journey the horses were unusually bad. The little boy asked who was responsible for the horses. He was told it was the postmaster. He asked who appointed the postmaster. He was told it was the syndic. He demanded to be taken at once to the syndic to get the postmaster dismissed."

"Mazzini as a child was very delicate. When he was about six years old he was taken for his first walk. For the first time he saw a beggar, a venerable old man. He stood transfixed, then broke from his mother, threw his arms round the beggar's neck and kissed him, crying, 'Give him something, mother, give him something.' 'Love him well, lady,' said the aged man; 'he is one who will love the people.'"

The ways of the children were the ways of the men. Who can imagine Mazzini bartering Savoy and Nice at Plombières, and negotiating the marriage of Prince Napoleon and Princess Clotilde? And in the article of death one passed away protesting his belief in God, while the other "retained a devoted priest to absolve his last hour, and made his way into heaven itself by a stroke of diplomacy."[1]

The London to which Mazzini returned after the fall of the Roman Republic was far less desolate than the London of 1837. There were now old and new friends, not a few, proud to welcome the Triumvir who had focussed in himself the fairest hopes of an aspiring people, an

> "established point of light whence rays
> Traversed the world."

The homes of the Ashursts, the Stansfelds and others were always open to him. He met many distinguished men of the time. Swinburne sang his praises. But no man was less easily seduced from the path of duty by the temptations of friendship and wealth. Nor was he the transcendentalist who turns cynic in the face of defeat. His head was still full of schemes and his days full of toil for the salvation of his country.

> Open my heart, and you will see
> Graved inside of it "Italy."

He worked incessantly to secure the "moral help" of England, and gathered into the Society of the Friends of Italy a number of the best Liberals of the day. England had

[1] F. W. H. Myers, *Essays Modern*, p. 21. For a kindlier estimate see the newly published papers of Senator Artom, Cavour's private secretary. He describes his chief's last moments in these words:

"Ou lui avait apporté le viatique à sept heures du soir, à cinq heures du matin on lui administra l'huile sainte. Quelques mots s'échappèrent encore de ses lèvres, "Italia è fatta . . . ormai la cosa va. . . . L' armonia della religione e della civiltà farà cessare le rivoluzioni in Europa." Ces phrases entrecoupés par les râles de l'agonie témoignent les grandes pensées qui occupaient cette vaste et noble intelligence à son dernier moment. Cinq minutes avant sept heures tout était fini."

indeed become his second home. His dour father had died in 1848 and his mother four years later. She had been his supreme solace through the years of loneliness and struggle —like Madame Ruffini, one of the brave mothers ' in whom Italy revived.' " My mother," he writes, " seems to me to be present, perhaps nearer than she was in her terrestrial life. I feel more and more the sacredness of duties which she recognised, and of a mission she approved. I have now no mother on earth except my country, and I shall be true to her, as my mother has been to me." She had left him a small annuity, " wisely invested with obdurate trustees," so that the money might not slip through his fingers into his public work and charity. With the aid of earnings from literary work, his income rarely rose to £200, and of this more than a third for some years went to educate the children of the poor woman he had befriended. His little room was littered with books and papers and clouded with the smoke of cheap cigars—his one luxury. When Bentham was planning Pantopticons and tabulating the Springs of Action, mice played in his study and fed from his lap. As became the apostle of a more soaring philosophy, Mazzini's pets were birds, and they flew about freely as he wrote and talked. Like most unselfish men with deep convictions, he was an inspiring talker. Music and poetry were favourite topics. Henry Sidgwick, we have recently learnt, was much impressed by him. " London is a stimulating place," he wrote to his mother in 1867 ; " one meets stimulating people. I will tell you who is one—Mazzini. I met him the other night at dinner, and he attacked me about Spiritualism, and bore down upon me with such a current of clear, eager argument—I was quite overwhelmed." No one who met him forgot his honest eyes, " readily flashing into indignation or humour, always with the latent expression of exhaustless resolution." In spite of failing health he worked on tenaciously, obstinately. " I hear you are rather un-well," he wrote to a friend. " Don't. It is absurd to be ill, while nations are struggling for liberty." Once he was arrested and imprisoned at Gaeta, where through the chinks

in the wall he saw the sea and sky as in the fortress of
Savona nearly forty years before. On his release he spent
a night secretly in Rome, and visited his mother's tomb
in Genoa. The monarchy had triumphed with the aid of
France. " He knew that the republic was afar off, that all
he could do now was quietly to educate his countrymen,
especially the working classes. He helped to organise the
friendly societies ; he advocated evening classes for workmen, circulating popular libraries, the collection of a fund
to assist societies for co-operative production ; he founded
a paper, *Roma del Popolo*, to spread his ideas. . . . He
published *From the Council to God*, and was delighted at
the success it met with in its English translation in the
Fortnightly. He was keenly interested in the English
movements for women's suffrage and against state regulation
of vice. But his chief work in these last years was to fight
the immature socialism of the time."

In his last message to the working men of Italy, he bade
them " love and work for this great, unhappy country of
ours, called to high destinies, but stayed upon the road by
those who cannot, will not know the road. This is the best
way you can have of loving me." He died in the house of
friends at Pisa, early in March 1872, and was buried beside
his mother, on one of the highest terraces in the cemetery
of Staglieno, outside his native city.

MAZZINI'S writings may be divided into literary, social, and
political. Among his earliest were " Dell' Amor Patrio di
Dante " (1826 or 1827), published in " Il Subalpino " 1837, and
contributions to the " Indicatore Genovese," founded by him
in 1828, and to the " Indicatore Livornese," also founded by
Mazzini after the suppression of the former journal, a fate
shared by the latter. His chief literary essays were composed in England, in which country he lived for many years
as an exile from 1837 : " Westminster Review " (" On the
Literary Movement in Italy," October 1837 ; " Paolo Sarpi,"

April 1838); "Apostolato Popolare," founded in 1841 by
Mazzini for the Italian working-men in England (Dante,
1841 ; Luigi Angeloni, 1842 ; Adolfo Boyer, 1842); "Monthly
Chronicle" ("Present State of French Literature," March
1839 ; Lamennais, April 1839 ; Byron and Goethe, 1839 ;
Carlyle's "French Revolution," 1843); "Foreign Quarterly
Review " ("On the Minor Works of Dante," April 1844) ;
"British and Foreign Review" ("On T. Carlyle, his Genius,
etc.," October 1843); "Revue Républicaine" ("De l'Art en
Italie"); Essay on Foscolo's Commentary of the "Divina
Commedia," 1842 ; Analytical review of the life and writings
of G. Sand, to an edition of "La Petite Fadette," 1850.

Among his Social and Political writings are : A Letter to
Carlo Alberto of Savoy, 1831 ; "Della Guerra d' Insurrezione
conveniente all' Italia," 1832, 1853 (with preface by Author) ;
"Dell' Ungheria," 1832 ; "Dell' Unità Italiana," 1833 ; Letter
to General Ramorino, 1834 : "alla Gioventù Italiana," 1834 ;
on the Encyclical of Gregory XVI., 1834 ; on the Revolutionary Initiative ("Revue Républicaine"), 1835 ; "Faith and
the Future " (written in French), 1835 ; "The Patriots and
the Clergy," 1835 ; "The Question of the Exiles" ("La
Jeune Suisse "), 1836 ; "On the Present Condition and Future
of Italy " ("Monthly Chronicle "), 1839 ; "On the Duty of
Man " (the first four chapters appeared in "Apostolato
Popolare," 1844, the remainder in "Pensiero ed Azione " and
"Unità Italiana," 1858) ; "Thoughts upon Democracy in
Europe" ("People's Journal "), 1847. Extra pages were
added by the author for the Italian Edition of his works,
published in 1865: Letter to Pius IX. on the Unity of the
Italian States, 1847 ; on his Encyclical Letter, 1850 ("L' Italia
del Popolo ") ; The Programma of the "Roma del Popolo,"
1871. His latest published writing was an essay in the
"Fortnightly " on Renan's "Réforme Morale et Intellect-
uelle," February 1874.

Editions of Works, Letters, etc. : "Scritti editi ed inediti "
(edited at first by the author, the later volumes by Saffi),
18 vols., 1861-91 ; "Life and Writings," 6 vols., 1864-70 ;
in 4 vols., 1897 ; "Prose Politiche," with preface by M.

Consigli, 1848, 1849; "Discorsi Politici," 1849; English translation of "Thoughts upon Democracy in Europe" and "On the Duties of Man," by E. A. Venturi, 1875; "Pubblicazione Nazionale delle Opere di G. M." ("La Questione d'Oriente," "Lettere Slave," "Politica Internazionale"), second edition, 1877; Inedited Letters, 1872; Letters to Daniel Stern (1864–72), 1873; French Letters (Paris), 1873; "Lettere . . . alle Società Operaie d'Italia scritte nel decennio 1861–71, etc," 1873; other letters published (Turin) 1887, (Paris) 1895; Lettere Inedite, edited by L. O. de Rosales, 1898; To A. Saffi and the Craufurd Family (1850–72), edited by Mazzatinti, 1905; Essays, republished and edited by W. Clarke 1887; Essays, Selected (Literary, Political, and Religious), edited by E. Rhys (Camelot Classics), 1887; Essays, most of them translated for the first time by T. Okey, edited by B. King, 1894 (with these is given an unpublished letter of uncertain date).

Life and Work: Simoni, 1870; Nardi, 1872; Memoir, by E. A. Venturi, 1875, 1877; Mario, 1885; Comte de Schack, 1891; Linton, "Recollections of Mazzini and his Friends," 1892; Bolton King (Temple Biographies), 1902; F. Donaver, 1903; Prefatory Memoirs to editions of Essays (see above). Mazzini himself supplied autobiographical notices to the collected edition of his Works.

TO THE ITALIAN WORKING CLASS

To you, sons and daughters of the people, I dedicate this little book, wherein I have pointed out the principles in the name and strength of which you may, if you so will, accomplish your mission in Italy; a mission of republican progress for all and of emancipation for yourselves. Let those who are specially favoured by circumstances or in understanding, and able to comprehend these principles more easily, explain and comment on them to the others, and may that spirit of love inspire them with which, as I wrote, I thought on your griefs and on your virgin aspirations towards the new life which— once the unjust inequality now stifling your faculties is overcome—you will kindle in the Italian country.

I loved you from my first years. The republican instincts of my mother taught me to seek out among my fellows the Man, not the merely rich and powerful individual; and the simple unconscious virtue of my father accustomed me to admire, rather than conceited and pretentious semi-knowledge, the silent and unnoticed virtue of self-sacrifice so often found in you. Later on I gathered from the history of our country that the true life of Italy is the life of the people, and that the slow work of the centuries has constantly tended, amid the shock of different races and the superficial transitory changes wrought by usurpations and conquests, to prepare the great democratic National Unity. And then, thirty years ago, I gave myself to you.

I saw that the Country, the United Country of free and equal men could not issue from an aristocracy

which among us has never had initiative or collective
life, nor from the monarchy which insinuated itself into
our midst in the sixteenth century in the track of the
foreigner without a mission of its own and without any
thought of unity or emancipation ; but must issue
from the people of Italy alone.   And I said so.   I saw
that it was needful for you to shake off the yoke of *hire*,
and little by little, through the means of free association,
make Labour master of the soil and of the capital of Italy ;
and before the French socialistic sects had come to
confuse the question, I said so.   I saw that Italy, such
as our souls prefigured her, could not exist until a Moral
Law, acknowledged as higher than all those now put as
intermediaries between God and man, should overthrow
the basis of every tyrannic authority, the Papacy.   And
I said so.   Nor did the furious accusations, calumnies,
and derision hurled at me ever make me betray you or
your cause or desert the banner of the future, not even
when you yourselves—led astray by the teachings of
men, idolaters rather than believers—forsook me for
those who, having trafficked in your blood, turned their
looks away from you.   The strong and sincere hand-
clasp of some of the best of you, sons and daughters of
the people, comforted me for the desertion of others and
for the many most bitter disillusionments inflicted on
my soul by men whom I had loved well and who had
professed to love me.   Not many years of life are left to
me, but the bond sealed with those few of you shall not
be broken by anything which may come until my last
day ; and perhaps will live beyond it.

Think of me as I think of you.   Let us be as brothers
in our affection for our Country.   In you essentially her
future lies.

But you will not found this future for the Country
and for yourselves, unless you rid yourselves of two
maladies which infect the well-to-do classes too much
to-day, though I hope for a short while only, and threaten
to lead Italian progress astray; Machiavelism and
Materialism.   The first, a mean travesty of the doctrine
of a great but unhappy man, leads you away from love

and from the frank, bold, and loyal adoration of truth ; the second precipitates you, through the worship of *self-interest*, into egoism and anarchy.

If you would withdraw yourselves from beneath the arbitrary rule and tyranny of men, you must adore God. And in the war which is being fought in the world between Good and Evil, you must enrol yourselves under the Banner of Good and combat Evil without truce, rejecting every dubious course, every cowardly dealing, and every hypocrisy of leaders who seek to compromise between the two. On the path of the first you will have me for comrade as long as I live.

And because these two lies present themselves to you too often in seductive guise and with the allurement of hopes which only the worship of God and of Truth can convert into *facts*, I have felt myself obliged to warn you against them by writing this book. I love you too well to flatter your passions or to indulge the golden dreams with which others try to win your favour. My voice may seem harsh and too insistent in teaching you the necessity of sacrifice and virtue towards others. But I know, and you who are good and unspoiled by false doctrine and by riches will understand before long, that every *right* you have can only spring from a *duty* fulfilled.

Farewell. Hold me now and for ever your brother.

GIUSEPPE MAZZINI.

April 23, 1860.

THE DUTIES OF MAN

THE DUTIES OF MAN

I

I WANT to speak to you of your duties. I want to speak to you, as my heart dictates to me, of the most sacred things which we know—of God, of Humanity, of the Fatherland, of the Family. Listen to me with love, even as I shall speak to you with love. My words are words of conviction matured by long years of sorrow and of observation and of study. The duties which I am going to point out to you I strive and shall strive as long as I live to fulfil, to the utmost of my power. I may make mistakes, but my heart is true. I may deceive myself, but I will not deceive you. Hear me therefore as a brother ; judge freely among yourselves, whether it seems to you that I speak the truth ; abandon me if you think that I preach what is false ; but follow me and do according to my teaching if you find me an apostle of truth. To be mistaken is a misfortune to be pitied ; but to know the truth and not to conform one's actions to it is a crime which Heaven and Earth condemn.

Why do I speak to you of your *duties* before speaking to you of your *rights* ? Why in a society in which all, voluntarily or involuntarily, oppress you, in which the exercise of all the rights which belong to man is constantly denied you, in which misery is your lot, and what is called happiness is for other classes of men, why do I speak to you of self-sacrifice and not of conquest ; of virtue, moral improvement, education, and

not of material *well-being*? This is a question which
I must answer before going further, because here precisely lies the difference between our school and many
others which are being preached to-day in Europe;
because, moreover, it is a question which rises readily
in the indignant mind of the suffering working-man.

*We are poor, enslaved, unhappy; speak to us of better
material conditions, of liberty, of happiness. Tell us if
we are doomed to suffer for ever, or if we too may enjoy
in our turn. Preach Duty to our masters, to the classes
above us which treat us like machines, and monopolise
the blessings which belong to all. To us speak of rights;
speak of the means of vindicating them; speak of our
strength. Wait till we have a recognised existence; then
you shall speak to us of duties and of sacrifice.* This is
what many of our working-men say, and follow teachers
and associations which respond to their desires. They
forget one thing only, and that is, that the doctrine
which they invoke has been preached for the last fifty
years without producing the slightest material improvement in the condition of the working-people.

For the last fifty years whatever has been done for
the cause of progress and of good against absolute
governments and hereditary aristocracies has been done
in the name of the Rights of Man; in the name of
liberty as the means, and of *well-being* as the object
of existence. All the acts of the French Revolution
and of the revolutions which followed and imitated it
were consequences of a Declaration of the Rights of
Man. All the works of the philosophers who prepared
it were based upon a theory of liberty, and upon the
need of making known to every individual his own
rights. All the revolutionary schools preached that man
is born for happiness, that he has the right to seek it
by all the means in his power, that no one has the
right to impede him in this search, and that he has
the right of overthrowing all the obstacles which he may
encounter on his path. And the obstacles were overthrown; liberty was conquered. It endured for years
in many countries; in some it still endures. Has the

condition of the people improved? Have the millions
who live by the daily labour of their hands gained the
least fraction of the well-being hoped for and promised
to them?

No; the condition of the people has not improved;
rather it has grown and grows worse in nearly every
country, and especially here where I write the price
of the necessaries of life has gone on continually rising,
the wages of the working-man in many branches of
industry falling, and the population multiplying. In
nearly every country the lot of workers has become
more uncertain, more precarious, and the labour crises
which condemn thousands of working-men to idleness
for a time have become more frequent. The yearly
increase of emigration from one country to another, and
from Europe to other parts of the world, and the ever-
growing number of beneficent institutions, the increase
of poor rates and provisions for the destitute, are enough
to prove this. The latter prove also that public attention
is waking more and more to the ills of the people;
but their inability to lessen those ills to any visible
extent points to a no less continual increase of poverty
among the classes which they endeavour to help.

And nevertheless, in these last fifty years, the sources
of social wealth and the sum of material blessings have
steadily increased. Production has doubled. Commerce,
amid continual crises, inevitable in the utter absence
of organisation, has acquired a greater force of activity
and a wider sphere for its operations. Communication
has almost everywhere been made secure and rapid,
and the price of commodities has fallen in consequence
of the diminished cost of transport. And, on the other
hand, the idea of rights inherent in human nature is
to-day generally accepted; accepted in word and, hypo-
critically, even by those who seek to evade it in deed.
Why, then, has the condition of the people not improved?
Why is the consumption of products, instead of being
divided equally among all the members of the social
body in Europe, concentrated in the hands of a small
number of men forming a new aristocracy? Why has

the new impulse given to industry and commerce produced, not the well-being of the many, but the luxury of the few?

The answer is clear to those who will look a little closely into things. Men are creatures of education, and act only according to the principle of education given to them. The men who have promoted revolutions hitherto have based them upon the idea of the rights belonging to the individual; the revolutions conquered liberty—individual liberty, liberty of teaching, liberty of belief, liberty of trade, liberty in everything and for everybody. But of what use was the recognition of their rights to those who had no means of exercising them? What did liberty of teaching mean to those who had neither time nor means to profit by it, or liberty of trade to those who had nothing to trade with, neither capital nor credit? In all the countries where these principles were proclaimed society was composed of a small number of individuals who possessed the land, the credit, the capital, and of vast multitudes of men who had nothing but their own hands and were forced to give the labour of them to the former class, on any terms, in order to live, and forced to spend the whole day in material and monotonous toil. For these, constrained to battle with hunger, what was liberty but an illusion and a bitter irony? To make it anything else it would have been necessary for the men of the well-to-do classes to consent to reduce the hours of labour, to increase the remuneration, to institute free and uniform education for the masses, to make the instruments of labour accessible to all, and to provide a bonus fund for the working-man endowed with capacity and good intentions. But why should they do it? Was not *well-being* the supreme object in life? Were not material blessings desirable before all other things? Why should they lessen their own enjoyment for the advantage of others? Let those who could, help themselves. When society has secured to everybody who can use them the free exercise of the rights belonging to human nature, it does all that is required of it. If there be any one who is unable from the fatality of his own circumstances to exercise any of these rights, he must resign himself and not blame others.

It was natural that they should say thus, and thus, in fact, they did say. And this attitude of mind towards the poor in the classes privileged by fortune soon became the attitude of every individual towards every other. Each man looked after his own rights and the improvement of his own condition without seeking to provide for others; and when his rights clashed with those of others, there was war; not a war of blood, but of gold and of cunning; a war less manly than the other, but equally destructive; cruel war, in which those who had the means and were strong relentlessly crushed the weak or the unskilled. In this continual warfare, men were educated in egoism and in greed for material welfare exclusively. Liberty of belief destroyed all community of faith. Liberty of education produced moral anarchy. Men without a common tie, without unity of religious belief and of aim, and whose sole vocation was enjoyment, sought every one his own road, not heeding if in pursuing it they were trampling upon the heads of their brothers—brothers in name and enemies in fact. To this we are come to-day, thanks to the theory of *rights*.

Certainly rights exist; but where the rights of an individual come into conflict with those of another, how can we hope to reconcile and harmonise them, without appealing to something superior to all rights? And where the rights of an individual, or of many individuals, clash with the rights of the Country, to what tribunal are we to appeal? If the right to *well-being*, to the greatest possible well-being, belongs to every living person, who will solve the difficulty between the working-man and the manufacturer? If the right to existence is the first and inviolable right of every man, who shall demand the sacrifice of that existence for the benefit of other men? Will you demand it in the name of Country, of Society, of the multitude of your brothers? What is Country, in the opinion of those of whom I speak, but the place in which our individual rights are most secure?

What is Society but a collection of men who have agreed
to bring the strength of the many in support of the rights
of each ?   And after having taught the individual for
fifty years that Society is established for the purpose of
assuring to him the exercise of his rights, would you ask
him to sacrifice them all to Society, to submit himself,
if need be, to continuous toil, to prison, to exile, for the
sake of improving it ?   After having preached to him
everywhere that the object of life is *well-being*, would
you all at once bid him give up well-being and life itself
to free his country from the foreigner, or to procure
better conditions for a class which is not his own ?
After having talked to him for years of *material* interests,
how can you maintain that, finding wealth and power in
his reach, he ought not to stretch out his hand to grasp
them, even to the injury of his brothers ?

Italian Working-men, this is not a chance thought of
my mind, without a foundation in fact.   It is history,
the history of our own times, a history the pages of
which drip with blood, the blood of the people.   Ask all
the men who transformed the revolution of 1830 into a
mere substitution of one set of persons for another, and,
for example, made the bodies of your French comrades,
who were killed fighting in the Three Days, into stepping-
stones to raise themselves to power ; all their doctrines,
before 1830, were founded on the old theory of the
rights of man, not upon a belief in his *duties*.   You cal'
them to-day traitors and apostates, and yet they were
only consistent with their own doctrine.   They fought
with sincerity against the Government of Charles X.
because that Government was directly hostile to the
classes from which they sprang, and violated and
endeavoured to suppress their rights.   They fought in
the name of the well-being which they did not possess
as much of as they thought they ought to have.   Some
were persecuted for freedom of thought ; others, men
of powerful mind, saw themselves neglected, shut out
from offices occupied by men of capacity inferior to
their own.   Then the wrongs of the people angered
them also.   Then they wrote boldly and in good faith

about the rights which belong to every man. Afterwards, when their own political and intellectual rights
had been secured, when the path to office was opened
to them, when they had conquered the *well-being* which
they sought, they forgot the people, forgot that the
millions, inferior to them in education and in aspirations,
were seeking the exercise of other rights and the
achievement of *well-being* of another sort, and they set
their minds at rest and troubled no longer about
anybody but themselves. Why call them traitors?
Why not rather call their doctrine treacherous?

There lived and wrote at that time in France a man
whom you ought never to forget, more powerful in mind
than all of them put together. He was our opponent
then; but he believed in Duty; in the duty of sacrificing
the whole existence to the common good, to the pursuit
and triumph of Truth. He studied the men and the
circumstances of the time deeply, and did not allow
himself to be led astray by applause, or to be discouraged by disappointment. When he had tried one
way and failed, he tried yet another for the amelioration
of the masses. And when the course of events had
shown him that there was one power alone capable of
achieving it, when the people had proved themselves in
the field of action more virtuous and more believing
than all those who had pretended to deal with their
cause, he, Lamennais, author of the *Words of a
Believer*, which you have all read, became the best
apostle of the cause in which we are brothers. There
you see in him, and in the men of whom I have been
speaking, the difference between the men of *rights* and
those of *duty*. To the first the acquisition of their
individual rights, by withdrawing stimulus, proves a
sufficient check to further effort; the work of the second
only ceases here on earth with life.

And among the peoples who are completely enslaved,
where the conflict has very different dangers, where
every step made towards a better state of things is
signed with the blood of a martyr, where the operations
against injustice in high places are necessarily secret and

lack the consolation of publicity and of praise, what obligation, what stimulus to constancy can maintain upon the path
of progress men who degrade the holy social war which we
carry on to a mere battle for their *rights*?   I speak, be it
understood, of the generality and not of the exceptions
to be met with in all schools of thought.   When the hot
blood and the impulse of reaction against tyranny
which naturally draw youth into the conflict have calmed
down, what can prevent these men, after a few years
of effort, after the disappointments inevitable in any
such enterprise, from growing weary?   Why should
they not prefer any sort of repose to an unquiet
existence, agitated by continual struggles and danger,
and liable to end any day in imprisonment, or the
scaffold, or exile?   It is the too common story of most
of the Italians of to-day, imbued as they are with the old
French ideas ; a very sad story, but how can it be
altered except by changing the principle with which they
start as their guide?   How and in whose name are they
to be convinced that danger and disappointment ought
to make them stronger, that they have got to fight not
for a few years, but for their whole lives?   Who shall
say to a man, *Go on struggling for your rights*, when
to struggle for them costs him dearer than to abandon
them ?

And even in a society constituted on a juster basis
than our own, who shall convince a believer in the
theory of *rights* solely that he has to work for the
common purpose and devote himself to the development
of the social *idea* ?   Suppose he should rebel; suppose
he should feel himself strong and should say to you :
*I break the social compact ; my inclinations, my faculties,
call me elsewhere*; *I have a sacred and inviolable right
to develop them, and I choose to be at war with everybody* :
what answer can you give him while he keeps to his
theory of rights ?   What right have you, because you are
a majority, to compel his obedience to laws which do not
accord with his desires and with his individual aspirations ?
What right have you to punish him if he violates them ?
Rights belong equally to every individual; the fact of living

together in a community does not create a single one.
Society has greater strength, not more rights, than the
individual. How, then, are you going to prove to the
individual that he must merge his will in the will of
those who are his brothers, whether in the Country or
in the wider fellowship of Humanity? By means of the
executioner, of the prison? Societies existing up till
now have used such means. But that is war, and we
want peace; that is tyrannical repression, and we want
education.

Education, we have said; and this is the great word
which sums up our whole doctrine. The vital question
agitating our century is a question of education. What
we have to do is not to establish a new order of things
by violence. An order of things so established is always
tyrannical even when it is better than the old. *We have
to overthrow by force the brute force which opposes itself
to-day to every attempt at improvement,* and then propose
for the approval of the nation, free to express its will,
what we believe to be the best order of things and by
every possible means educate men to develop it and act
in conformity with it. The theory of *rights* enables us
to rise and overthrow obstacles, but not to found a strong
and lasting accord between all the elements which compose the nation. With the theory of happiness, of *well-
being,* as the primary aim of existence we shall only form
egoistic men, worshippers of the material, who will carry
the old passions into the new order of things and corrupt
it in a few months. We have therefore to find a
principle of education superior to any such theory, which
shall guide men to better things, teach them constancy
in self-sacrifice and link them with their fellow men
without making them dependent on the ideas of a single
man or on the strength of all. And this principle is Duty.
We must convince men that they, sons of one only God,
must obey one only law, here on earth; that each one of
them must live, not for himself, but for others; that the
object of their life is not to be more or less happy, but
to make themselves and others better; that to fight
against injustice and error for the benefit of their brothers

is not only a *right*, but a *duty* ; a duty not to be neglected without sin,—the duty of their whole life.

Italian Working-men, my Brothers! understand me fully. When I say that the knowledge of their *rights* is not enough to enable men to effect any appreciable or lasting improvement, I do not ask you to renounce these rights ; I only say that they cannot exist except as a consequence of duties fulfilled, and that one must begin with the latter in order to arrive at the former. And when I say that by proposing *happiness, well-being*, or *material* interest as the aim of existence, we run the risk of producing egoists, I do not mean that you should never strive after these things. I say that material interests pursued alone, and not as a means, but as an end, lead always to this most disastrous result. When under the Emperors, the old Romans asked for nothing but *bread* and *amusements*, they became the most abject race conceivable, and after submitting to the stupid and ferocious tyranny of the Emperors they basely fell into slavery to the invading Barbarians. In France and elsewhere the enemies of all social progress have sown corruption and tried to divert men's minds from ideas of change by furthering the development of *material* activity. And shall we help the enemy with our own hands ? Material improvement is essential, and we shall strive to win it for ourselves ; but not because the one thing necessary for man is to be well fed and housed, but rather because you cannot have a sense of your own dignity or any moral development while you are engaged, as at the present day, in a continual duel with want. You work ten or twelve hours a day : how can you find *time* to educate yourselves ? Most of you earn hardly enough to keep yourselves and your families : how can you then find *means* to educate yourselves ? The uncertainty of your employment and the frequent interruptions in it cause you to alternate between too much work and periods of idleness : how are you to acquire habits of order, regularity, and assiduity ? The scantiness of your earnings does away with any hope of saving enough to be useful some day to your children, or to

The Duties of Man

your own old age : how are you to educate yourselves
into habits of economy? Many of you are compelled
by poverty to separate your children, we will not say
from the careful bringing-up—what sort of bringing-up
can the poor wives of working-men give their children ?—
but from the love and the watchful eye of their mothers,
and to send them out, for the sake of a few halfpence,
to unwholesome labour in factories : how, in such
conditions, can family affection unfold itself and be
ennobled ? You have not the rights of citizens, nor any
participation, by election or by vote, in the laws which
regulate your actions and your life : how should you feel
the pride of citizenship or have any zeal for the State, or
sincere affection for the laws ? Justice is not dealt out
to you with the same equal hand as to the other classes :
whence, then, are you to learn respect and love for justice ?
Society treats you without a shadow of sympathy :
whence are you to learn sympathy with society ? You
need, then, a change in your material conditions to enable
you to develop morally ; you need to work less so as to
have some hours of your day to devote to the improvement of your minds ; you need a sufficient remuneration
of your labour to put you in a position to accumulate
savings, and so set your minds at rest about the future,
and to purify yourselves above all of every sentiment of
retaliation, every impulse of revenge, every thought
of injustice towards those who have been unjust to you.
You must strive, then, for this change, and you will
obtain it, but you must strive for it as a *means*, not as an
end ; strive for it from a sense of *duty*, not only as a
right ; strive for it in order to make yourselves better,
not only to make yourselves *materially* happy. If not,
what difference would there be between you and your
tyrants ? They are tyrants precisely because they do
not think of anything but *well-being*, pleasure and
power.

To make yourselves better ; this must be the aim of
your life. You cannot make yourselves permanently less
unhappy except by improving yourselves. Tyrants will
arise by the thousand among you, if you fight only in the

name of material interests, or of a particular organisation. A change of social organisation makes little difference if you and the other classes keep the passions and the egoism of to-day; organisations are like certain plants which yield poison or remedies according to the way in which they are administered. Good men make bad organisations good, and bad men make good organisations bad. You have got to improve the classes which, voluntarily or involuntarily, oppress you to-day, and convince them of their duties; but you will never succeed in this unless you begin by making yourselves better as far as possible.

When therefore you hear men who preach the necessity of a social transformation telling you that they can accomplish it by invoking your *rights* only, be grateful to them for their good intentions, but distrustful of the outcome. The ills of the poor man are known, in part at least, to the well-to-do classes; *known* but not *felt*. In the general indifference born of the absence of a common faith; in the egoism, inevitably resulting from the continual preaching through so many years of the doctrine of material *well-being*, those who do not suffer have grown accustomed little by little to consider these ills as a sad necessity of the social order and to leave the trouble of remedying them to the generations to come. The difficulty is not to convince them, but to shake them out of inertia and to induce them, when they are convinced, to *act*, to associate themselves, to unite with you in brotherly fellowship for the purpose of creating such a social organisation as shall put an end, as far as the conditions of humanity allow, to your ills and to their own fears. Now, this is a work of faith, of faith in the mission which God has given to the human creature here upon earth; of faith in the responsibility weighing upon all those who do not fulfil that mission, and in the duty which bids every one work continually, and with self-sacrifice, for the cause of Truth. All possible theories of rights and of material *well-being* can only lead you to attempts which, so long as they remain isolated and dependent on your strength only, will not succeed, but can only bring about the worst of social crimes, a civil war between class and class.

Italian Working-men, my Brothers! When Christ came and changed the face of the world, He did not speak of rights to the rich, who had no need to conquer them ; nor to the poor, who would perhaps have abused them, in imitation of the rich. He did not speak of utility or of self-interest to a people whom utility and self-interest had corrupted. He spoke of Duty, He spoke of Love, of Sacrifice, of Faith : He said that *they only should be first among all who had done good to all by their work*. And these thoughts, breathed into the ear of a society which had no longer any spark of life, reanimated it, conquered the millions, conquered the world, and caused the education of the human race to progress a degree. Italian Working-men ! we live in an epoch like Christ's. We live in the midst of a society rotten as that of the Roman Empire, and feel in our souls the need of reviving and transforming it, of associating all its members and its workers in one single faith, under one single law, and for one purpose ; the free and progressive development of all the faculties which God has planted in His creatures. We seek the reign of God upon earth as in heaven, or better, that the earth shall be a preparation for heaven, and society an endeavour towards a progressive approach to the Divine Idea.

But every act of Christ's represented the faith which He preached, and round Him there were apostles who embodied in their acts the faith which they had accepted. Be such as they, and you will conquer. Preach Duty to the men of the classes above you, and fulfil, as far as possible, your own duties ; preach virtue, sacrifice, love ; and be yourselves virtuous and prompt to self-sacrifice and love. Declare with courage your needs and your ideas ; but without wrath, without vindictiveness, without threats. The most powerful threat, if there are any who need threats, is firm, not angry, speech. While you propagate among your companions the conception of their future destinies, the conception of a nation which will give them a name, education, work, and fair wages, together with the self-respect and vocation of men, while you kindle their spirit for the inevitable struggle for which they must prepare themselves, so that they may conquer all this in spite of all the forces of our evil government and of the foreigner, strive to instruct yourselves, to grow better, and to educate yourselves to the full knowledge and to the practice of your duties.   This is an impossible task for the masses in a great part of Italy; no plan of popular education could be realised among us without a change in the material condition of the people, and without a political revolution; they who deceive themselves into hoping for it, and preach it as an indispensable preparation for any attempt at emancipation, preach a gospel of inertia, nothing else.   But the few among you whose circumstances are somewhat better, and to whom a sojourn in foreign lands has afforded more liberal means of education, can do it, and therefore ought to do it.   And these few, once imbued with the true principles upon which the education of a people depends, will be enough tó spread them among the thousands as a guide for their path and a protection from the fallacies and the false doctrines which will come to waylay them.

II

GOD

The origin of your duties is in God. The definition of your duties is found in His law. The progressive discovery and the application of His law is the task of Humanity.

God exists. I do not need nor do I wish to prove it to you; to try to do so would seem to me blasphemy, as to deny it would seem foolishness. God exists, because we exist. God lives in our conscience, in the conscience of Humanity, in the universe which surrounds us. Our conscience invokes Him in the most solemn moments of grief and of joy. Humanity has been able to transform, to pollute, but never to suppress His holy name. The Universe manifests Him in the order, the harmony, the intelligence of its motions and of its laws. There are no atheists among you; if there were, they would deserve not curses, but tears. He who can deny God on a starry night, or beside the graves of his dearest ones, or in the presence of martyrdom, is greatly unhappy or greatly wicked. The first atheist was doubtless a man who had hidden a crime from all other men and sought by denying God to rid himself of the only witness from whom he could not hide it, and to suffocate the remorse which tormented him. Perhaps he was a tyrant who had stolen half the soul of his brothers from them with their freedom, and who tried to substitute the worship of brute force for faith in duty and in Eternal Right. After him there came now and again, from century to century, men whom philosophical aberration led to insinuate atheistic doctrines; but they were very few, and much ashamed. Then in days not long ago there came a multitude who, irritated by a false and stupid idea of God which some caste or tyrannic power had set up for its own advantage, denied God Himself; but it was for an instant only, and during that instant their need of a divinity was so great that they had to worship the goddess Reason, the goddess Nature.   To-day there are men who abhor all religion because they see the corruption in actual creeds, and do not divine the purity of those of the future; but not one among them dares to call himself an atheist.   There are priests who prostitute the name of God to venal calculations, or to fear of the powerful; there are tyrants who blaspheme it by invoking it as the protector of their tyranny.   But because the light of the sun comes to us often dimmed and clouded by foul vapours, shall we deny the existence of the sun and the vivifying power of its rays upon the universe ?   Because out of liberty wicked men sometimes produce anarchy, shall we curse liberty ?   Faith in God burns with an immortal light through all the lies and corruption with which men have darkened His name. Lies and corruption pass away, as tyrannies pass away : God remains, and the People remains, God's image upon earth.   Even as the People, through slavery, suffering, and poverty, conquers, step by step, conscience, strength, emancipation, so out of the ruins of corrupt systems of religion the holy name of God arises resplendent, surrounded by a purer, a more fervent, and more rational worship.

I do not therefore speak to you of God in order to demonstrate His existence to you, or to tell you that you ought to adore Him—you do adore Him, even without naming Him, every time that you *feel* your *life* and the *life* of the beings around you—but to tell you *how* you ought to adore Him, and to admonish you of an error which dominates the minds of many men in the classes which rule you, and, through their example, many of your minds; an error as grave and as fatal as atheism.

This error is the separation, more or less evident, of God from His work, from the earth upon which you have to fulfil one period of your existence. On the one side there are people who say to you, " True, God exists ; but all you can do is to admit His existence and to adore Him. No one can understand and explain the relation between God and men. It is a question which your conscience must debate with God himself. Think what you will about it, but do not propound your belief to your fellows, or seek to apply it to the things of this earth. Politics are one thing, religion another. Do not confound them ; leave the things of heaven to the established spiritual authority, whatever it may be, reserving to yourselves the right of refusing it credence if it seem to you to betray its mission ; let every one think and believe in his own way ; you need only occupy yourselves in common about earthly things. Materialists or spiritualists, whichever you may be, do you believe in liberty, and in the equality of man ? do you want well-being for the majority ? do you want universal suffrage ? Unite yourselves to obtain these desires ; it is not necessary for this that you should have a common understanding on questions to do with heaven."

On the other side you have men who tell you " God exists, but He is too great, too superior to all created things for you to hope to attain to Him by human works. The earth is clay. Life is but for an hour. Withdraw yourselves from the first as much as you can ; do not hold the second above its worth. What indeed are all earthly interests in comparison with the immortal life of your souls ? Think of this ; look up to heaven. What does it matter in what condition you live here below ? You are destined to die ; and God will judge you according to the thoughts which you have given, not to earth, but to Him. Do you suffer ? Bless the Lord who sends you these afflictions. Terrestrial existence is a period of trial; your earth a land of exile. Despise it and rise above it. In the midst of sufferings, of poverty, of slavery, you can turn to God, and sanctify yourselves by adoration of Him, by prayer, by scorn of worldly things, and by faith in a future in which you will have a great reward."

Of those who speak to you thus, the first *do not love* God; the second do not *know* Him.

Man is one, say to the first. You cannot divide him in two, and so contrive that he should agree with you in the principles which ought to regulate the organisation of society, while he differs from you as to his origin, his destinies, and his law of life here below. Religions govern the world. When the men of India *believed* themselves to be born, some from the head, others from the arms, others from the feet of Brahma, their divinity, they organised society by a division of mankind into castes, assigning to the first the heritage of intellectual work, to the second the business of war, to the third the servile labours, condemning themselves to an immobility which still endures and will endure while belief in this principle still exists. When the Christians declared to the world that men were all sons of God and brothers in Him, all the doctrines of the legislators and philosophers of antiquity laying down the existence of two natures in man did not avail to prevent the abolition of slavery involving a radically different organisation of society. For every advance in religious belief we can show you a corresponding social advance in the history of Humanity: but for your doctrine of indifference in the matter of religion, you can show us no other conse- quence than anarchy. You have been able to destroy, never to build up; deny this, if you can. By dint of exaggerating a principle contained in Protestantism and which Protestantism to-day feels the necessity of aban- doning—by dint of deducing all your ideas solely from the independence of the *individual*, you have arrived— where ? In commerce at anarchy—that is to say, at the oppression of the weak ; in politics at liberty—that is to say, at the derision of the weak who have neither means, time, nor knowledge to exercise their proper rights ; in morals at egoism—that is to say, the isolation and the ruin of the weak who cannot help themselves alone. But we want Association ; how is this to be securely obtained except by brothers who believe in the same guiding principle, who are united in the same faith, who take the oath in

the same name? We want education; how is this to
be given or received except in virtue of a principle
containing the expression of our common belief concerning the origin and the aim of man and of his life on
this earth? We want a common education; how is this
to be given or received, without a common faith? We
want to form a nation; how can we succeed in this,
unless we believe in a common purpose, in a common
duty? And whence can we deduce a common *duty* if
not from the idea which we form of God and of His
relation to us? Doubtless universal suffrage is an
excellent thing; it is the only legal means by which a
country may govern itself without violent crises from
time to time. But universal suffrage in a country
dominated by one faith will give expression to the
tendencies, to the will of the nation, while in a country
lacking a common belief how can it express anything
except the interests of those who are numerically
strongest and the oppression of all the rest? All
political reforms in countries without religion or indifferent to religion will last as long as it suits the caprice
or the self-interest of individuals, and no longer. The
experience of the last fifty years has taught us enough
on this point.

To the others who speak to you of *heaven*, separating
it from *earth*, you will say that heaven and earth, like
the way and the end of the way, are one thing
only. Do not tell us that the earth is clay. The earth
is God's; God created it that we might climb by it to
Him. The earth is not a sojourn of expiation and
temptation; it is the place appointed for our labour of
self-improvement, and of development towards a higher
state of existence. God created us not for contemplation, but for action; He created us in His own
image, and He is Thought and Action—nay, in Him
there is no thought which is not simultaneous action.
You say we ought to despise all worldly things, and
spurn terrestrial life, so that we may concern ourselves
only with the celestial. But what is terrestrial life if not
a prelude to the celestial, a step towards its attainment?

C 224

Do you not perceive that blessing as you do the last step of the ladder by which we must all climb, and declaring the first unholy, you cut away our path from us ? The life of a soul is sacred in every one of its stages, in the earthly stage as well as in the others which are to follow; so, then, every stage must be a preparation for the next, every temporary progress must help the continuous upward progress of the immortal life which God has kindled in each one of us, and in collective humanity which grows by the operation of each one of us.

Now, God has placed you here below upon earth ; He has surrounded you with millions of beings like yourselves, whose minds are nourished by your minds, whose improvement progresses with yours, whose life is fertilised by your life. To save you from the perils of isolation He has given you needs which you cannot satisfy by yourselves, and dominating social instincts which distinguish you from the brutes, in whom they remain dormant. He has spread about you this world which you call *material*, magnificent in beauty, and pregnant with life ; with a life which, you must never forget, reveals itself everywhere as God's visible token, but nevertheless awaits your work, depends in its manifestations upon you, and increases in power in proportion to the increase in your activity. He has placed within you inextin- guishable sympathies, pity for those who mourn, joy with those who smile, wrath against those who oppress their fellow creatures, an incessant yearning for truth ; admiration for the genius who discloses a portion of truth unknown before ; enthusiasm for those who trans- late it into action profitable to all ; religious veneration for those who, unable to make it triumph, die a martyr's death, bearing witness to it with their blood. Yet you deny, you scorn these indications of your mission lavished around you by God : you even cry anathema upon His manifestations, bidding us concentrate all our powers upon a work of inward purification which must be imperfect, nay impossible, when carried on alone.

Now, does not God punish those who strive to do this ?

Is not the slave degraded? Is not half the soul of the poor day labourer suffocated in sensual appetites, in the blind instincts which you call *material*, so long as he is doomed to spend the divine life within him in a series of physical acts unenlightened by education? Do you find a more lively religious faith in the Russian serf than in the Pole fighting the battles of his country and liberty? Do you find a more fervent love of God in the degraded subject of a Pope and of a tyrant king than in the Lombard republican of the twelfth century and the Florentine republican of the fourteenth? Wheresoever the spirit of God is, there is liberty, has been said by one of the most powerful apostles that we know; and the religion which he preached decreed the abolition of slavery; for who can understand and adore God rightly while prostrate at the feet of God's creature? Yours is not a religion; it is a sect of men who have forgotten their origin, forgotten the battle which their fathers kept up against a rotten society, and the victories which they won, transforming this world which you, O men of contemplation, despise to-day. Whatever earnest belief shall arise out of the ruins of the old worn-out creeds will transform the existing social order, because every earnest belief seeks to apply itself to all the branches of human activity; because the earth has always sought in every age to conform itself to the heaven in which it believed; because the whole story of Humanity repeats under diverse forms and in diverse degrees, varying according to the times, the saying written in the Christian prayer, *Thy kingdom come on earth, O Lord, as it is in heaven.*

Thy kingdom come on earth as it is in heaven. Let these words, better remembered and better applied than in the past, be the utterance of your faith, your prayer, O my brothers. Repeat it, and act so that it may be fulfilled. Do not heed those who try to teach you passive resignation, indifference to earthly things, submission to every temporal power even when unjust, repeating to you without understanding it this other saying, " Render unto Cæsar the things which are Cæsar's, and unto God

the things which are God's." Can they tell you anything which is not God's? Nothing is Cæsar's except
in so far as it is such in conformity with the divine law.
Cæsar—that is, the temporal power, the civil government—
is nothing but the mandatory, the executor, so far as its
powers and the times allow, of God's design; whenever
it betrays its mandate it is, I will not say your *right*,
but your *duty* to change it. Why are you here below, if
not to exert yourselves to work out the intention of God
with the means you possess and in your own sphere?
Why profess to believe in the unity of the human race,
the necessary consequence of the unity of God, if you do
not labour to realise it by combating the arbitrary divisions
and the enmities which still divide the various tribes
composing Humanity? Why believe in human liberty,
the basis of human responsibility, if we do not strive to
destroy all the obstacles which impede the first and
vitiate the second? Why speak of Brotherhood and yet
allow our brothers every day to be trampled, degraded,
despised? The earth is our field of labour; we may
not curse it, we must sanctify it. The material forces
which surround us are our instruments of labour; we
may not reject them, we must use them for good.

But this without God you cannot do. I have spoken
to you of *duties*; I have taught you that the mere
knowledge of your *rights* is not enough to guide you
permanently along the path of Progress, is not enough to
give you that progressive continuous improvement in
your conditions which you seek. Now without God
whence can we derive Duty? Without God, you will
find that whatever system of civil government you choose
to attach yourselves to has no other basis than blind,
brutal, tyrannic Force. There is no escape from this.
Either the development of human things depends upon a
law of providence which we are all charged to discover
and to apply, or it is entrusted to chance, to the circumstances of the moment and the man who knows best
how to avail himself of them. Either we ought to obey
God, or to serve men—whether one or many matters
not. If there be not a Supreme Mind reigning over all

human minds, who can save us from the tyranny of our fellow men, whenever they find themselves stronger than we? If there be not a holy and inviolable law, not created by men, what rule have we by which to judge whether an act is just or unjust? In the name of whom, in the name of what, shall we protest against oppression and inequality? Without God there is no other sovereign than Fact ; Fact before which the materialists ever bow themselves, whether its name be Revolution or Buonaparte ; Fact, which the materialists of to-day also, in Italy and everywhere, use as a justification for inactivity even when they agree in theory with our principles. Now, how shall we demand of them self-sacrifice, martyrdom, in the name of our individual opinions? Shall we transform theory into practice and abstract principle into action, on the strength of our interests alone? Do not be deceived. As long as we speak as individuals in the name of whatever theory our individual intellect suggests to us, we shall have what we have to-day, adherence in words, not in deeds. The cry which rang out in all the great revolutions—the cry of the Crusades, *God wills it! God wills it!*—alone can rouse the inert to action, give courage to the fearful, enthusiasm of self-sacrifice to the calculating, faith to those who reject with distrust all merely human ideas. Prove to men that the work of emancipation and of progressive development to which you call them is part of God's design, and none will rebel. Prove to them that the work which has to be accomplished here on earth is an essential portion of their immortal life, and all the calculations of the moment will vanish before the importance of the future. Without God you can command, not persuade ; you can be tyrants in your turn, never educators and apostles.

God wills it—God wills it! It is the cry of the People, O Brothers! it is the cry of *your* People, the cry of the Italian Nation. Do not let yourselves be deceived, you who work with sincerity of love for your nation, by those who will perhaps tell you that the Italian genius is not a political genius, and that the religious spirit has departed from her. The religious spirit never departed from Italy as long as she remained, in spite of her divisions, great and active ; but it departed from her in the sixteenth century, when Florence had fallen, and all the liberty of Italian life had been crushed by the foreign arms of Charles V. and the deceit of the Popes, and we began to lose our national character, and to live as if we were Spaniards, Germans, and French. Then our learned men began to play the buffoon to princes, and to stimulate their listless patrons by laughing at everybody and everything. Then our priests, seeing that any application of religious truth was impossible, began to traffic in holy things, and to think of themselves, not of the people whom they ought to have enlightened and protected. And then the people, despised by the learned, deceived and fleeced by the priests, banished from any influence in public matters, began to revenge themselves by deriding the learned, distrusting the priests, rebelling against all creeds, since they perceived that the old one was corrupt, and were not able to look beyond it. From that time forward we have dragged ourselves along, in abjectness and impotence, between the superstitions imposed upon us by habit, or by our governors, and incredulity. But we want to rise again, great and honoured. And we will remember the national tradition. We will remember that, with the name of God on their lips, and with the symbols of their faith in the centre of the battle, our Lombard brothers in the twelfth century vanquished the German invaders, and reconquered the liberties wrested from them. We will remember that the republicans of the Tuscan cities held their parliaments in the churches. We will remember the Florentine artisans who refused to submit their democratic liberty to the domination of the House of Medici, and by solemn vote elected Christ as head of the republic ; and the friar Savonarola preaching in the same breath faith in God and the rights of the people, and the Genoese of 1746, who, with stones for weapons, and in the name of the Virgin Mary, their patron saint, liberated their city from the German army which

occupied it ; and a whole chain of other deeds like these,
in which the religious thought protected and fertilised
the popular thought of Italy. And the religious sentiment sleeps in our people, waiting to be awakened. He
who knows how to rouse it will do more for the nation
than can be done by twenty political theories. Perhaps
it is the lack of this sentiment in the imitators of the
foreign monarchical constitutions and tactics who led
the past attempts at insurrection in Italy, as much as the
lack of an openly popular purpose, which is responsible
for the coldness with which the people have till now
regarded these attempts. Preach therefore, O Brothers,
in the name of God. He who has an Italian heart will
follow you.

Preach in the name of God. The learned will smile ;
ask the learned what they have done for their country.
The priests will excommunicate you ; say to the priests
that you know God better than all of them together do,
and that between God and His law you have no need of
any intermediary. The people will understand you, and
repeat with you : *We believe in God the Father, who is
Intelligence and Love, Creator and Teacher of Humanity*
And in this saying you and the People will conquer.

III

You live: you have therefore a law of life. There is no life without a law. Whatever exists, exists in a certain manner, according to certain conditions, and under a certain law. A law of aggregation governs minerals; a law of growth governs plants; a law of motion governs the stars; a law governs you and your life; a law as much nobler and more lofty than these, as you yourselves are higher than all other created things on earth. To develop yourselves, to act, to live according to your law, is your first, nay, your only Duty.

God gave you life: God therefore gave you the law. God is the only Law-Giver to the human race. His law is the only law which you are obliged to obey Human laws are only valid and good in so far as they conform to His law, explaining and applying it: they are bad whenever they contradict or disregard it; and it is then not only your right, but your duty, to disobey them and abolish them. He who best explains God's law and applies it to human occasions is your legitimate head: love him and follow him. But you have not, and cannot have, any *master* but God, without being false and rebellious to Him.

In the *knowledge* of your law of life, of the law of God, lies, then, the foundation of Morality, the rule of your actions and of your duties, the measure of your responsibilities; that, too, is your defence against the unjust laws which the arbitrary will of one man, or of many men, may strive to impose upon you. Without knowing this law you cannot pretend to the name or *rights* of men. All rights have their origin in a law, and as long as you are unable to invoke it you may be tyrants or slaves, but nothing else ; tyrants, if you are strong, slaves of the strong if you are weak. To be *men* you must know the law which distinguishes human nature from that of brutes, plants, minerals, and you must conform your actions to it.

Now, *how* are you to know it ?

This is the question which Humanity in all time has addressed to those who have pronounced the word *duty* : and to-day still the answers are different.

Some have answered by showing a code or a book and saying, *Within this is contained the whole moral law.* Others have said, *Let every man interrogate his own heart ; there he will find the definition of good and of evil.* Others, again, rejecting the judgment of the individual, have invoked universal opinion and declared that *where Humanity agrees in a belief, that belief is the true one.*

All are wrong. And the history of the human race has proved by unimpeachable facts the impotence of all these answers. Those who affirm that the whole moral law is to be found in a book, or in the utterances of a single man, forget that there is no code which Humanity, after believing in it for centuries, has not abandoned in order to seek and preach a better one, and that there is no reason to believe, especially to-day, that Humanity will change its way of proceeding.

Those who maintain that the conscience of the *individual* alone is the criterion of the true and the false, that is, of good and evil, need only remember that no religion, however holy, has ever existed without heretics, without dissenters by conviction, ready to face martyrdom in the name of their conscience. Protestantism to-day is divided and subdivided into a thousand sects, all founded on the rights of *individual conscience* ; all eager to make war upon each other, and perpetuating that anarchy of belief which is the true and only source of the social and political discord now tormenting the peoples of Europe. And on the other hand, the men who reject the testimony of the individual conscience, and appeal only to the common belief of Humanity, must

remember that all the great ideas which have helped
the progress of Humanity began by being opposed to
the general beliefs of Humanity, and were preached by
individuals whom Humanity derided, persecuted, and
crucified.

Each of these rules, then, is insufficient to obtain for
us a knowledge of the law of God, of Truth. Yet,
nevertheless, the individual conscience is sacred; the
general opinion of Humanity is sacred, and whoever
refuses to interrogate either the one or the other
deprives himself of an essential means of knowing the
truth. The common error till now has been the desire
to reach the truth by one of these means exclusively;
an error most fatal and decisive in its consequences,
because the conscience of the individual cannot be set
up as the only criterion of truth without falling into
anarchy, nor can the general opinion of Humanity be
invoked at any given moment as a rule from which
there is no appeal, without suffocating human liberty
and plunging headlong into tyranny.

Thus—and I give these examples to show that upon
these primary foundations the whole social edifice rests,
more than is generally supposed—thus men, falling into
the same error, have organised political society, some
solely on respect for the rights of the *individual*,
forgetting altogether the educational mission of society,
others solely upon *social* rights, sacrificing the liberty and
action of the individual.[1] And France, after her great
revolution, and England conspicuously, have taught us
how the first system leads only to inequality and
oppression of the many; Communism, if ever it
could become established fact, would show us, among
other things, how the second condemns society to
petrifaction by depriving it of all mobility and faculty
of progress.

Thus some, considering only the so-called rights of
the individual, have organised, or rather disorganised, the

[1] I am naturally speaking of countries where under a system of constitutional monarchy a certain organisation of society has been attempted.
In countries governed despotically there is no society; social rights and
the rights of individuals are equally sacrificed.

economic system by founding it solely upon the theory of unlimited *freedom of competition*; whilst the others, thinking only of *social* unity, would confide the monopoly of all the productive forces of the State to the Government ; of these two theories, the first has given us all the evils of anarchy, the second would lead to immobility and all the evils of tyranny.

God has given you the general opinion of your fellow-men, and your own conscience, to be to you two wings with which to soar towards Him. Why should you insist on cutting off one of them ? Why should you isolate yourselves, or let the world absorb you altogether ? Why should you want to suffocate the voice of the individual or of the human race ? Both are sacred ; God speaks in both. *Whenever they agree,* whenever the cry of your conscience is ratified by the general consent of Humanity, there is God, there you are sure of having the truth in your grasp ; the one is the verification of the other.

If your duties were merely negative, if they consisted solely in *not doing evil,* in not harming your fellow-man, perhaps in the state of development which even the least educated have reached to-day the voice of your conscience would be enough to guide you. You are born for good, and every time that you act directly *contrary* to the Law, every time that you commit what men call *crime,* there is something in you which accuses you, some voice of reproof which you can conceal from others, but not from yourselves. But your most important duties are positive. It is not enough *not to do* ; you must *do.* It is not enough to content yourselves with not acting contrary to the law ; you must act *according* to the law. It is not enough *not to do harm* ; you must *do good* to your brothers. Hitherto morality has too often presented itself to the majority of men in a form rather negative than affirmative. The interpreters of the Law have said, "Thou shalt not kill, thou shalt not steal" : few or none have taught them the obligations which belong to them as men, and in what way they ought to do good to their fellows and further God's design in creation.

Now, this is the chief aim of morality, and no individual, by consulting his own conscience only, may ever attain it.

The conscience of the individual speaks in accordance with his education, his tendencies, his habits, his passions. The conscience of the savage Iroquois speaks a language different from that of the civilised European of the nineteenth century. The conscience of the free man suggests to him duties which the conscience of the slave does not even suspect. Ask the poor Neapolitan or Lombard day-labourer, whose only teacher of morality has been a bad priest and to whom the only book allowed, if indeed he knows how to read, is the Austrian catechism; he will tell you that his duties are to labour industriously for any wage he can obtain in order to support his family, to submit himself blindly to the laws whatever they may be, and to do no harm to others. Should you speak to him of duties which bind him to his country and to humanity; should you say to him, "You do harm to your fellow-men by consenting to work for a wage less than the value of your work, and you sin against God and against your own soul by obeying laws which are unjust," he would answer like one who does not understand, lifting his brows in bewilderment. Ask the Italian working-man whom better circumstances or contact with men of more highly educated minds have taught a part of the truth; he will tell you that his country is enslaved, that his brothers are unjustly condemned to live in material and moral wretchedness, and that he feels it his duty to protest as far as he is able against this injustice. Why so much divergence between the promptings of conscience in two individuals of the same time and the same country? Why among ten individuals holding substantially the same creed, that which enjoins the development and the progress of the human race, do we find ten different convictions as to the manner of reducing belief to action—that is to say, as to their duties? Evidently the voice of the individual conscience is not enough in all conditions of things, and without any other guide, to reveal the law to us. Conscience can only teach us that the law

exists, not the nature of the duties which it imposes.
For this reason martyrdom has never been absent from
among men, however much egoism may have prevailed ;
but how many martyrs have sacrificed existence for
imaginary duties, for the sake of errors patent to everybody to-day !

Your conscience has need, then, of a guide, of a light
to penetrate the darkness around it, of a rule by which
to confirm and direct its instincts. And this rule is
Intellect and Humanity.

God has given *intellect* to each of you that you may
educate it to know His law. To-day poverty, the rooted
errors of centuries, and the will of your masters withhold
from you even the possibility of educating it ; and for
this reason it is necessary for you to overthrow those
obstacles by force. But even when those obstacles are
removed your individual intellect will not be enough to
teach you the law of God, if it is not supported by the
intellect of Humanity. Your life is short, your individual
faculties are weak, uncertain, and need a support. Now,
God has placed beside you a Being whose life is continuous, whose faculties are the sum of all the individual
faculties that have been exercised for perhaps four
hundred centuries ; a being which amid the errors and
the faults of individuals ever advances in wisdom and
morality ; a being in whose development God has written
and writes in every epoch a line of His law.

This Being is Humanity.

Humanity, as a thinker of the last century has said, *is
a man who is always learning.* Individuals die, but that
much of truth which they have revealed, that much of
good which they have done, is not lost with them ;
Humanity treasures it up and the men who walk over
their graves reap the benefit of it. Every one of us is
born to-day in an atmosphere of ideas and of beliefs
elaborated by the whole of bygone Humanity, and each
of us brings, even without knowing it, a more or less
important element to the life of Humanity to come.
The education of Humanity progresses as those pyramids
in the East rise, to which every passer-by adds a stone.

We pass, the wayfarers of a day, called to complete
our individual education elsewhere; the education of
Humanity shows itself only by flashes in each of us, but
is revealed slowly and progressively, continuously, in
Humanity. Humanity is the living word of God. The
spirit of God makes it fruitful and is manifested in it
from age to age ever more pure, ever more active, now
by means of an individual, now by means of a people.
From labour to labour, from belief to belief, Humanity
goes on gradually acquiring a clearer perception of its
own life, of its own mission, of God and of His law.

God incarnates Himself *successively* in Humanity. The
law of God is one, as God is one; but we only discover
it article by article, line by line, as the educative experience of preceding generations accumulates more and
more and the association of races, peoples, and individuals
grows in extent and closeness. No man, no people, no
century can presume to have discovered the whole of it;
the moral law, the law of life of Humanity, can only be
discovered in its entirety by the whole of Humanity
united in association, when all the powers, all the
faculties which constitute human nature shall be
developed and in action. But meanwhile that part of
Humanity which is most advanced in education teaches
us by its development a part of the law which we seek.
In its history we read the design of God; in its needs
our *duties*; duties which change, or rather arise, with
those needs, because our first duty is to co-operate in
lifting Humanity to that degree of improvement and of
education for which God and the times have prepared it.

Therefore, to know the law of God you must interrogate not only *your own* conscience but the conscience, the general conviction, of Humanity. Morality
is progressive, like the education of the human race and
your education is. The morality of Christianity was not
that of Pagan times; the morality of our century is not
that of eighteen centuries ago. To-day, your masters,
by separating you from the other classes, by prohibiting
all association, by imposing a double censorship upon
the press, endeavour to conceal from you your duties,

together with the needs of Humanity. And nevertheless, even before the time comes when the nation will teach you gratuitously in schools of general education the history of Humanity in the past, and its needs in the present, you will be able, if you wish it, to learn the first, in part at least, and to divine the second. The actual needs of Humanity are expressed more or less violently, more or less imperfectly, in the events which occur every day in countries where the immobility of silence is not an absolute law. Who prevents you, our brothers of the enslaved lands, from knowing them? What power of suspicious tyranny can withhold the knowledge of European events for long from the millions of men in Italy, very many of whom travel in other countries? If public associations are forbidden almost everywhere in Italy, who can prevent secret ones, if they avoid outward tokens and complicated organisations, and only consist of a fraternal chain, stretching from town to town until it touches one of the numberless points of the frontier? Do you not find at every point of the land and maritime frontier your own friends and countrymen, men whom your masters have driven out of the country because they wanted to help you, men who will be apostles of truth to you, and tell you out of their love for you that which their studies and the sad opportunities of exile have taught them concerning the tradition of Humanity and its aspirations in the present day? Who can prevent you from receiving any of the writings which your brothers print there in exile for you, if only you wish it yourselves? Read them and burn them, so that next day the inquisitors, sent by your masters, may not find them in your hands, and make them a cause of accusation against your family. Aid us with your offerings to enlarge the sphere of our mission, and to compile and print for you manuals of general history, and of the history of your country. Help us, by multiplying ways of communication, to circulate them more widely. Be assured that without instruction you cannot know your duties, and that when society does not allow you to be taught, the responsibility for every offence rests not with

you, but with it ; your responsibility begins on the day
when an opportunity of instruction is offered to you and
you neglect it ; on the day when means are presented
to you of transforming a society which condemns you
to ignorance, and you do not exert yourselves to use
them. You are not guilty because you are ignorant ; you
are guilty because you resign yourselves to be ignorant,
because, though your conscience warns you that God
has not given you faculties without imposing upon you
the duty of developing them, you allow the faculty of
thinking to sleep in your soul, because though you know
also that God would not have given you a love of truth
without giving you the means of following it, you give up
the search for it in despair and accept unquestioningly
as truth the assertions of the powers that be, and of the
priest who has sold himself to those powers.

God the Father and Teacher of Humanity reveals
His law to Humanity in space and in time.   Interrogate
the traditions of Humanity—which is the Council of
your fellow-men—not in the confined circle of one
century or of one school of thinkers, but in all the
centuries and in the majority of men past and present.
*Whenever the voice of your conscience corresponds with
that general voice of Humanity you are certain of the
truth,* certain of knowing one line of God's law.

*We believe in Humanity, the sole interpreter of God's law
upon earth;* and from the general voice of Humanity
in agreement with our conscience we deduce what I
am now going to tell you concerning your duties.

IV

DUTIES TO HUMANITY

YOUR first duties, first not in point of time but of importance—because without understanding these you can only imperfectly fulfil the rest—are to Humanity. You have duties as citizens, as sons, as husbands, as fathers—sacred, inviolable duties of which I shall presently speak at length ; but what makes these duties sacred and inviolable is the mission, the *duty*, which your nature as *men* imposes on you. You are fathers in order that you may educate *men* to worship and to unfold God's law. You are citizens, you have a country, in order that in a limited sphere, with the concourse of people linked to you already by speech, by tendencies, and by habits, you may labour for the benefit of all *men* whatever they are and may be in the future—a task which each one could ill do by himself, weak and lost amid the immense multitude of his fellow-men. Those who teach morality, limiting its obligations to duties towards family or country, teach you a more or less narrow *egoism* and lead you to what is evil for others and for yourselves. Country and family are like two circles drawn within a greater circle which contains them both ; like two steps of a ladder without which you could not climb any higher, but upon which it is forbidden you to stay your feet.

You are *men* ; that is, *rational* and *social* creatures *capable, by means of association only, of a progress* to which no one may assign limits ; and this is all that we know to-day of the law of life given to Humanity. These characteristics constitute *human nature,* which distinguishes you from the other beings around you and

which is entrusted to each of you as a seed to bring
to fruit. All your life should tend to the exercise and
the regular development of these fundamental faculties
of your nature. Whenever you suppress one of these
faculties or allow it to be suppressed wholly or in
part, you fall from the rank of men to the level of
the inferior animals and violate the law of your life,
the Law of God.

You fall to the level of the brutes and violate God's
Law whenever you suppress, or allow to be suppressed,
one of the faculties which constitute human nature in
yourself or in others. What God wills is not only that
his Law should be fulfilled in you as individuals—had
He willed this only, He would have created you solitary
—but that it should be fulfilled in the whole earth,
among all the beings whom He created in His own image.
What He wills is that the Idea of perfectibility and
of love which He has given to the world should reveal
itself in ever-increasing glory, ever more adored and
better manifested. Your earthly and individual existence
within its narrow limits of time and of capacity can
only manifest it most imperfectly and by flashes. Humanity alone, continuous through the generations and through
the general intellect fed by the individual intellect of
each of its members, can gradually unfold that divine
idea and apply or glorify it. Life, then, was given you
by God that you might use it for the benefit of
humanity, that you might direct your individual faculties
to the development of the faculties of your fellow-men,
and that you might contribute by your work some portion
to that collective work of improvement and that discovery of the truth which the generations slowly but
continuously carry on. You must educate yourselves
and educate others ; perfect yourselves and perfect others.
God is in you, without doubt; but God is likewise
in all the men who people this earth ; God is in the
life of all the generations which were, which are, and
which are to be ; and which have progressively improved,
and will continue to improve, the conception formed
by Humanity of Him, of His Law, and of our Duties.

The Duties of Man 43

You must adore Him and glorify Him wheresoever He
is. The universe is His temple. And every unresisted
and unexpiated profanation of God's temple is visited
upon all the believers. It is of little avail that you can
call yourselves pure; even could you by isolating yourselves keep your purity, you are still false to your duty
if you have corruption two steps off and do not strive
against it. It is of little avail that you worship the truth in
your hearts; if error rules your brothers in some other
corner of this earth, which is our common mother, and you
do not desire, and endeavour as far as lies in your power,
to overthrow it, you are false to your duty. The image
of God is defaced in the immortal souls of your fellow-
men. God wills that we should adore Him in His Law,
and His Law is misinterpreted, violated, denied all
around you. Human nature is false to itself in millions
of men to whom, as to you, God has entrusted the
concordant fulfilment of His design. And you, while
you remain inactive, do you dare to call yourselves
believers?

A people, Greek, Polish, Circassian, raises the banner
of the Fatherland and of Independence, fights, conquers,
or dies for it. What is it that makes your hearts beat
at the story of its battles, which makes them swell with
joy at its victories, and sorrow over its defeats? A man,
perhaps your fellow-countryman, perhaps a foreigner,
rises amid the universal silence, in some corner of the
earth, gives utterance to certain ideas which he believes
to be true, maintains them in persecution and in chains,
and dies, still constant to them, upon the scaffold. Why
do you honour him with the name of Saint and of
Martyr? Why do you respect and teach your children
to respect his memory?

And why do you eagerly read the miracles of patriotic
love recorded in Greek story, and repeat them to your
children with a feeling of pride, almost as if they were
stories of your own fathers? These deeds of the Greeks
are two thousand years old, and belong to an epoch of
civilisation which is not and never can be yours. That
man whom you call martyr died perhaps for ideas which

you do not hold, and anyhow by his voluntary death
he cut short his individual progress here below. That
people whom you admire in victory and in defeat is
a people foreign and perhaps almost unknown to you;
speaking a different language, and with a manner of life
which has no visible influence upon yours; what matters
it to you whether it is dominated by the Sultan or the
King of Bavaria, by the Russian Czar or by a government springing from the common will of the nation?
But in your heart a voice cries, "Those men of two
thousand years ago, those far-off peoples that fight
to-day, that martyr to ideas for which you would not
die, were and are your brothers: brothers not only by
community of origin and nature, but community of work
and of purpose. Those ancient Greeks passed away;
but their work did not pass away, and without it you
would not possess to-day that degree of intellectual and
moral development which you have reached. Those
peoples consecrate with their blood an idea of national
liberty for which you too are fighting. That martyr
proclaimed by his death that man must sacrifice all
things, and if needs be life also, for that which he
believes to be the Truth. It is of little importance
that he and all who seal their faith with their blood
cut short their own individual development here upon
earth; God provides elsewhere for them. But the
development of Humanity is of importance. It is of
importance that the coming generation, taught by your
combats and your sacrifices, should rise higher and grow
mightier than you in the understanding of the Law,
in the adoration of the Truth. It is of importance that
human nature, fortified by example, should become
better, and realise more and more God's will upon
earth. And wherever human nature grows better,
wherever a new truth is won, wherever a step forward
is taken on the path of education, of progress, and of
morality, it is a step, a gain, which will bear fruit sooner
or later for the whole of Humanity. You are all soldiers
of an army which moves by diverse ways, divided into
different bands, to the conquest of a single enterprise.

At present you only look to your immediate leaders;
different uniforms, different words of command, the
distances which separate the operating corps, the
mountains which conceal them from one another, make
you often forget this truth, and fix your attention exclusively upon the end which is closest to you. But
there is One above you all who sees the whole and directs
all the movements. God alone has the secret of the
battle, and will be able to gather you all together into
one camp and under one banner.

How great the distance between this belief which stirs
in our souls and which will be the basis of the morality of
the epoch now about to open, and the faith which formed
the basis of morality for the generation which we to-day
call ancient! And how close is the bond between the
idea which we form of the Divine Government and that
which we form of our duties! The first men felt God,
but without comprehending Him, without even seeking to
comprehend Him in His Law; they felt Him in His might,
not in His love; they had a confused conception of some
sort of relation between Him and the individual, but
nothing more. Little able to detach themselves from
the sphere of objects perceptible to the senses, they
embodied Him in one of these—in the tree which they had
seen struck by the thunderbolt, in the rock beside which
they had raised their tent, in the animal which first
presented itself to their eyes. This was the worship
which is called in the history of religion *fetichism*. And
at that time men knew of no bond except the *family*,
the reproduction in a certain sense of their own individuality; beyond the circle of the family there were none
but strangers, or more usually, enemies; to preserve
themselves and their family was the sole foundation of
morality. In later days the idea of God was expanded.
From objects of sense man rose timidly to the conception
of abstractions; he generalised. God was no longer
the protector of the family only, but of the association
of many families, of *cities*, of *peoples*. To *fetichism* succeeded *polytheism*, the worship of many gods. Then
morality also enlarged its sphere of action. Men recog-

nised the existence of more extended duties than those
of the family, and laboured for the increase of the *race*,
of the *nation*. Yet nevertheless Humanity was ignored.
Every nation called foreigners *barbarians*, treated them
as such, and sought by force or by fraud to conquer or to
oppress them. Every nation had foreigners or barbarians
in its midst, men, millions of men, not admitted to the
religious rites of the citizens, and looked upon as of
different nature, slaves among the free. The unity of the
human race could only be admitted as the consequence
of the unity of God. And the unity of God, divined by
a few rare thinkers of antiquity, and loudly proclaimed
by Moses (but with the fatal restriction that a single
people were God's elect) was not recognised until
towards the dissolution of the Roman Empire, through
the work of Christianity. Foremost in his teaching Christ
places these two inseparable truths: *there is one God
only ; all men are the sons of God* ; and the promulgation
of these two truths changed the aspect of the world and
enlarged the moral circle to the confines of the inhabited
earth. To the duties of man to his *family* and to his
Country they added duties to *Humanity*. Then man
learnt that wherever he found a fellow man, there was a
brother for him, a brother endowed with a soul immortal
as his own, called to ascend to its Creator, a brother to
whom he owed love, participation in his faith and the
help of counsel and of deed when needed. Then upon
the lips of the Apostles were heard sublime words, prophetic of other truths contained in germ in Christianity,
words unintelligible to antiquity, and ill understood or
disregarded by the successors of the Apostles. *For as
we have many members in one body, and all members have
not the same office ; so we, being many, are one body in
Christ, and every one members one of another.*[1] *And
there shall be one fold and one shepherd.*[2] And now, after
eighteen centuries of study and experience and toil, the
time has come for the development of these germs, for
the application of these truths not only to every individual,

[1] Paul, Ep. to Romans, ch. xii. vv. 4, 5
[2] Gospel of St. John, ch. x. ver. 16.

but to that whole sum of human faculties and powers, past and present, which is called Humanity; for the promulgation of the truth not only that Humanity is a single body and ought to be governed by a single Law, but that the first article of this Law is Progress, progress here upon earth, where we have to accomplish God's design as much as in us lies, and to educate ourselves for better destinies. The time has come to teach men that, as Humanity is a single body, we are all of us, as members of that body, bound to work for its development, and to make its life more harmonious, active, and strong. The time is come to convince ourselves that we can only rise to God through the souls of our fellow-men, and that we ought to improve and purify them even when they do not ask it of us themselves. The time has come, since that portion of God's design which He wills should be fulfilled here below can only be fulfilled by entire Humanity, to substitute for the exercise of charity towards individuals a work of *association*, aiming at the improvement of the whole, and to organise for this purpose the *Family* and the *Country*.

Other and vaster duties will reveal themselves to us in the future, as we gradually acquire a clearer and less imperfect idea of our law of life. Thus God the Father, by means of a slow but continuous religious education, guides Humanity to better things, and in this improvement each individual improves also.

We improve with the improvement of Humanity; nor without the improvement of the whole can you hope that your own moral and material conditions will improve. Generally speaking, you cannot, even if you would, separate your life from that of Humanity; you live in it, by it, for it. Your souls, with the exception of the very few men of exceptional power, cannot free themselves from the influence of the elements amid which they exist, just as the body, however robust its constitution, cannot escape from the effects of corrupt air around it. How many of you have the strength of mind to bring up your sons to be wholly truthful, knowing that you are sending them forth to persecution in a country where

tyrants and spies bid them conceal or deny two-thirds
of their real opinions ?   How many of you resolve to
educate them to despise wealth in a society where gold is
the only power which obtains honours, influence, and
respect, where indeed it is the only protection from the
tyranny and insults of the powerful and their agents ?   Who
is there among you who in pure love and with the best
intentions in the world has not murmured to his dear
ones in Italy, *Do not trust men ; the honest man should
retire into himself and fly from public life ; charity begins
at home,*—and such-like maxims, plainly immoral, but
prompted by the general state of society ?   What mother
is there among you who, although she belongs to a faith
which adores the cross of Christ, the voluntary martyr for
humanity, has not flung her arms around her son's neck
and striven to dissuade him from perilous attempts to
benefit his brothers ?   And even if you had strength to
teach the contrary, would not the whole of society, with
its thousand voices, its thousand evil examples, destroy
the effect of your words ?   Can you purify, elevate your
own souls in an atmosphere of contamination and
degradation ?

And, to descend to your material conditions, do you
think they can be lastingly ameliorated by anything but
the amelioration of all ?   Millions of pounds are spent
annually here in England, where I write, by private
charity, for the relief of individuals who have fallen into
want ; yet want increases here every year, and charity to
individuals has proved powerless to heal the evil, and the
necessity of collective organic remedies is more and more
universally felt.   When a country, in consequence of the
unjust laws which govern it, is continually threatened
with a violent struggle between oppressors and oppressed,
do you suppose that there can be a flow of capital in it
copious enough for vast, lengthy, and costly enterprises ?
Where taxes and restrictions can be imposed at the
caprice of a despotic Government, the cost of whose
armies, spies, agents, and pensioners grows with the
increasing necessity of securing itself against overthrow,
do you suppose that industries and manufactures can

have any activity or continuous development? Do
you answer that it is enough for you to organise better
the government and the social conditions of your own
country? It is not enough. No people lives to-day
exclusively on its own produce; you live by exchange,
by importation and exportation. An impoverished
foreign nation, in which the number of consumers
diminishes, is one market the less for you. A foreign
commerce upon which a bad administration brings
crises or ruin, produces crises and ruin in yours. The
failures of England and of America bring about Italian
failures. Credit nowadays is not a national but a
European institution. Moreover, in any attempt at
national reform you will have all the Governments
hostile to you, in consequence of the alliances contracted
between princes, who are the first to recognise that
the social question is a general one in the present day.
There is no hope for you except in universal reform
and in the brotherhood of all the peoples of Europe,
and through Europe of all humanity. I charge you
then, O my brothers, by your duty and by your
own interest, not to forget that your first duties—duties
without fulfilling which you cannot hope to fulfil those
owed to family and country—are to Humanity. Let your
words and your actions be for all, since God is for all,
in His Love and in His Law. In whatever land you
may be, wherever a man is fighting for right, for justice,
for truth, there is your brother; wherever a man
suffers through the oppression of error, of injustice, of
tyranny, there is your brother. Free men and slaves,
YOU ARE ALL BROTHERS. Origin, law, and goal are one
for all of you. Let your creed, your action, the banner
beneath which you fight, be likewise one. Do not say,
The language which we speak is different; tears, actions,
martyrdom form a common language for all men, and
one which you all understand. Do not say, *Humanity is
too vast, and we are too weak.* God does not measure
powers, but intentions. Love Humanity. Ask yourselves whenever you do an action in the sphere of your
Country, or your family, *If what I am doing were done*

*by all and for all, would it advantage or injure
Humanity?* and if your conscience answers, *It would
injure Humanity,* desist; desist, even if it seem to you
that an immediate advantage for your Country or your
family would ensue from your action. Be apostles of
this faith, apostles of the brotherhood of nations, and
of the unity of the human race—a principle admitted
to-day in theory, but denied in practice. Be such
apostles wherever and in whatever way you are able.
Neither God nor man can demand more of you. But
I say to you that by becoming such apostles—even to
yourselves only, when you are not able to do more—
you will advantage Humanity. God measures the
degrees of education which he allows the human race
to ascend by the number and the purity of the believers.
When you are pure and numerous, God, who numbers
you, will open for you the way to action.

V

DUTIES TO COUNTRY

YOUR first Duties—first, at least, in importance—are, as I have told you, to Humanity. You are *men* before you are *citizens* or *fathers*. If you do not embrace the whole human family in your love, if you do not confess your faith in its unity—consequent on the unity of God—and in the brotherhood of the Peoples who are appointed to reduce that unity to fact—if wherever one of your fellow-men groans, wherever the dignity of human nature is violated by falsehood or tyranny, you are not prompt, being able, to succour that wretched one, or do not feel yourself called, being able, to fight for the purpose of relieving the deceived or oppressed—you disobey your law of life, or do not comprehend the religion which will bless the future.

But what can *each* of you, with his isolated powers, *do* for the moral improvement, for the progress of Humanity? You can, from time to time, give sterile expression to your belief; you may, on some rare occasion, perform an act of *charity* to a brother not belonging to your own land, no more. Now, *charity* is not the watchword of the future faith. The watchword of the future faith is *association*, fraternal co-operation towards a common aim, and this is as much superior to *charity* as the work of many uniting to raise with one accord a building for the habitation of all together would be superior to that which you would accomplish by raising a separate hut each for himself, and only helping one another by exchanging stones and bricks and mortar. But divided as you are in language, tendencies, habits, and capacities, you cannot attempt this common work. The *individual* is too weak, and Humanity too vast. *My God*, prays the Breton mariner as he puts out to sea, *protect me, my ship is so little, and Thy ocean so great!* And this prayer sums up the condition of each of you, if no means is found of multiplying your forces and your powers of action indefinitely. But God gave you this means when he gave you a Country, when, like a wise overseer of labour, who distributes the different parts of the work according to the capacity of the workmen, he divided Humanity into distinct groups upon the face of our globe, and thus planted the seeds of nations. Bad governments have disfigured the design of God, which you may see clearly marked out, as far, at least, as regards Europe, by the courses of the great rivers, by the lines of the lofty mountains, and by other geographical conditions ; they have disfigured it by conquest, by greed, by jealousy of the just sovereignty of others ; disfigured it so much that to-day there is perhaps no nation except England and France whose confines correspond to this design. They did not, and they do not, recognise any country except their own families and dynasties, the egoism of caste. But the divine design will infallibly be fulfilled. Natural divisions, the innate spontaneous tendencies of the peoples will replace the arbitrary divisions sanctioned by bad governments. The map of Europe will be re-made. The Countries of the People will rise, defined by the voice of the free, upon the ruins of the Countries of Kings and privileged castes. Between these Countries there will be harmony and brotherhood. And then the work of Humanity for the general amelioration, for the discovery and application of the real law of life, carried on in association and distributed according to local capacities, will be accomplished by peaceful and progressive development ; then each of you, strong in the affections and in the aid of many millions of men speaking the same language, endowed with the same tendencies, and educated by the same historic tradition, may hope by your personal effort to benefit the whole of Humanity.

To you, who have been born in Italy, God has allotted, as if favouring you specially, the best-defined country in Europe. In other lands, marked by more uncertain or more interrupted limits, questions may arise which the pacific vote of all will one day solve, but which have cost, and will yet perhaps cost, tears and blood; in yours, no. God has stretched round you sublime and indisputable boundaries; on one side the highest mountains of Europe, the Alps; on the other the sea, the immeasurable sea. Take a map of Europe and place one point of a pair of compasses in the north of Italy on Parma; point the other to the mouth of the Var, and describe a semicircle with it in the direction of the Alps; this point, which will fall, when the semicircle is completed, upon the mouth of the Isonzo, will have marked the frontier which God has given you. As far as this frontier your language is spoken and understood; beyond this you have no rights. Sicily, Sardinia, Corsica, and the smaller islands between them and the mainland of Italy belong undeniably to you. Brute force may for a little while contest these frontiers with you, but they have been recognised from of old by the tacit general consent of the peoples; and the day when, rising with one accord for the final trial, you plant your tricoloured flag upon that frontier, the whole of Europe will acclaim re-risen Italy, and receive her into the community of the nations. To this final trial all your efforts must be directed.

Without Country you have neither name, token, voice, nor rights, no admission as brothers into the fellowship of the Peoples. You are the bastards of Humanity. Soldiers without a banner, Israelites among the nations, you will find neither faith nor protection; none will be sureties for you. Do not beguile yourselves with the hope of emancipation from unjust social conditions if you do not first conquer a Country for yourselves; where there is no Country there is no common agreement to which you can appeal; the egoism of self-interest rules alone, and he who has the upper hand keeps it, since there is no common safeguard for the interests of all. Do not be led away by the idea of improving your material conditions without first solving the national question. You cannot do it. Your industrial associations and mutual help societies are useful as a means of educating and disciplining yourselves; as an economic fact they will remain barren until you have an Italy. The economic problem demands, first and foremost, an increase of capital and production; and while your Country is dismembered into separate fragments—while shut off by the barrier of customs and artificial difficulties of every sort, you have only restricted markets open to you—you cannot hope for this increase. To-day —do not delude yourselves—you are not the working-class of Italy; you are only fractions of that class; powerless, unequal to the great task which you propose to yourselves. Your emancipation can have no practical beginning until a National Government, understanding the signs of the times, shall, seated in Rome, formulate a Declaration of Principles to be the guide for Italian progress, and shall insert into it these words, *Labour is sacred, and is the source of the wealth of Italy.*

Do not be led astray, then, by hopes of material progress which in your present conditions can only be illusions. Your Country alone, the vast and rich Italian Country, which stretches from the Alps to the farthest limit of Sicily, can fulfil these hopes. You cannot obtain your *rights* except by obeying the commands of *Duty*. Be worthy of them, and you will have them. O my Brothers! love your Country. Our Country is our home, the home which God has given us, placing therein a numerous family which we love and are loved by, and with which we have a more intimate and quicker communion of feeling and thought than with others; a family which by its concentration upon a given spot, and by the homogeneous nature of its elements, is destined for a special kind of activity. Our Country is our field of labour; the products of our activity must go forth from it for the benefit of the whole earth; but the instruments of labour which we can use best and most effectively exist in it, and we may not reject them without being unfaithful to God's purpose and diminishing our own strength. In labouring according to true principles for our Country we are labouring for Humanity; our Country is the fulcrum of the lever which we have to wield for the common good. If we give up this fulcrum we run the risk of becoming useless to our Country and to Humanity. Before *associating* ourselves with the Nations which compose Humanity we must exist as a Nation. There can be no association except among equals; and you have no recognised collective existence.

Humanity is a great army moving to the conquest of unknown lands, against powerful and wary enemies. The Peoples are the different corps and divisions of that army. Each has a post entrusted to it; each a special operation to perform; and the common victory depends on the exactness with which the different operations are carried out. Do not disturb the order of the battle. Do not abandon the banner which God has given you. Wherever you may be, into the midst of whatever people circumstances may have driven you, fight for the liberty of that people if the moment calls for it; but fight as Italians, so that the blood which you shed may win honour and love, not for you only, but for your Country. And may the constant thought of your soul be for Italy, may all the acts of your life be worthy of her, and may the standard beneath which you range yourselves to work for Humanity be Italy's. Do not say *I*; say *we*. Be every one of you an incarnation of your Country, and feel himself and make himself responsible for his fellow-countrymen; let each one of you learn to act in such a way that in him men shall respect and love his Country.

Your Country is one and indivisible. As the members of a family cannot rejoice at the common table if one of their number is far away, snatched from the affection of his brothers, so you should have no joy or repose as long as a portion of the territory upon which your language is spoken is separated from the Nation.

Your Country is the token of the mission which God

has given you to fulfil in Humanity. The faculties, the
strength of *all* its sons should be united for the accomplishment of this mission. A certain number of common
duties and rights belong to every man who answers
to the *Who are you?* of the other peoples, *I am
an Italian*. Those duties and those rights cannot be
represented except by one *single* authority resulting from
your votes. A Country must have, then, a single
government. The politicians who call themselves
federalists, and who would make Italy into a brotherhood
of different states, would dismember the Country, not
understanding the idea of Unity. The States into
which Italy is divided to-day are not the creation of
our own people; they are the result of the ambitions
and calculations of princes or of foreign conquerors,
and serve no purpose but to flatter the vanity of local
aristocracies for which a narrower sphere than a great
Country is necessary. What you, the people, have
created, beautified, and consecrated with your affections,
with your joys, with your sorrows, and with your blood,
is the City and the Commune, not the Province or the
State. In the City, in the Commune, where your fathers
sleep and where your children will live, where you
exercise your faculties and your personal rights, you live
out your lives as *individuals*. It is of your City that
each of you can say what the Venetians say of theirs:
Venezia la xe nostra: l'avemo fatta nu.[1] In your City
you have need of *liberty* as in your Country you have
need of *association*. The Liberty of the Commune and
the Unity of the Country—let that, then, be your faith.
Do not say Rome and Tuscany, Rome and Lombardy,
Rome and Sicily; say Rome and Florence, Rome and
Siena, Rome and Leghorn, and so through all the Communes of Italy. Rome for all that represents Italian life;
your Commune for whatever represents the *individual*
life. All the other divisions are artificial, and are not
confirmed by your national tradition.

A Country is a fellowship of free and equal men bound
together in a brotherly concord of labour towards a single

[1] Venice is our own: we have made her.

end. You must make it and maintain it such. A
Country is not an aggregation, it is an *association*. There
is no true Country without a uniform right. There is
no true Country where the uniformity of that right
is violated by the existence of caste, privilege, and
inequality—where the powers and faculties of a large
number of individuals are suppressed or dormant—where
there is no common principle accepted, recognised, and
developed by all. In such a state of things there can be
no Nation, no People, but only a multitude, a fortuitous
agglomeration of men whom circumstances have brought
together and different circumstances will separate. In
the name of your love for your Country you must
combat without truce the existence of every privilege,
every inequality, upon the soil which has given you birth.
One privilege only is lawful—the privilege of Genius
when Genius reveals itself in brotherhood with Virtue ;
but it is a privilege conceded by God and not by men,
and when you acknowledge it and follow its inspirations,
you acknowledge it freely by the exercise of your own
reason and your own choice. Whatever privilege claims
your submission in virtue of force or heredity, or any
right which is not a common right, is a usurpation and
a tyranny, and you ought to combat it and annihilate
it. Your Country should be your Temple. God at the
summit, a People of equals at the base. Do not accept
any other formula, any other moral law, if you do not
want to dishonour your Country and yourselves. Let the
secondary laws for the gradual regulation of your
existence be the progressive application of this supreme
law.

And in order that they should be so, it is necessary
that *all* should contribute to the making of them. The
laws made by one fraction of the citizens only can never
by the nature of things and men do otherwise than reflect
the thoughts and aspirations and desires of that fraction ;
they represent, not the whole country, but a third, a
fourth part, a class, a zone of the country. The law
must express the general aspiration, promote the good of
all, respond to a beat of the nation's heart. The whole

nation therefore should be, directly or indirectly, the legislator. By yielding this mission to a few men, you put the egoism of one class in the place of the Country, which is the union of *all* the classes.

A Country is not a mere territory; the particular territory is only its foundation. The Country is the idea which rises upon that foundation; it is the sentiment of love, the sense of fellowship which binds together all the sons of that territory. So long as a single one of your brothers is not represented by his own vote in the development of the national life—so long as a single one vegetates uneducated among the educated—so long as a single one able and willing to work languishes in poverty for want of work—you have not got a Country such as it ought to be, the Country of all and for all. *Votes, education, work* are the three main pillars of the nation; do not rest until your hands have solidly erected them.

And when they have been erected—when you have secured for every one of you food for both body and soul—when freely united, entwining your right hands like brothers round a beloved mother, you advance in beautiful and holy concord towards the development of your faculties and the fulfilment of the Italian mission—remember that that mission is the moral unity of Europe; remember the immense duties which it imposes upon you. Italy is the only land that has twice uttered the great word of unification to the disjoined nations. Twice Rome has been the metropolis, the temple, of the European world; the first time when our conquering eagles traversed the known world from end to end and prepared it for union by introducing civilised institutions; the second time when, after the Northern conquerors had themselves been subdued by the potency of Nature, of great memories and of religious inspiration, the genius of Italy incarnated itself in the Papacy and undertook the solemn mission—abandoned four centuries ago—of preaching the union of souls to the peoples of the Christian world. To-day a third mission is dawning for our Italy; as much vaster than those of old as the Italian People, the free and united Country which you are going to found, will be greater and more powerful than Cæsars or Popes. The presentiment of this mission agitates Europe and keeps the eye and the thought of the nations chained to Italy.

Your duties to your Country are proportioned to the loftiness of this mission. You have to keep it pure from egoism, uncontaminated by falsehood and by the arts of that political Jesuitism which they call diplomacy.

The government of the country will be based through your labours upon the worship of principles, not upon the idolatrous worship of interests and of opportunity. There are countries in Europe where Liberty is sacred within, but is systematically violated without; peoples who say, *Truth is one thing, utility another : theory is one thing, practice another.* Those countries will have inevitably to expiate their guilt in long isolation, oppression, and anarchy. But you know the mission of our Country, and will pursue another path. Through you Italy will have, with one only God in the heavens, one only truth, one only faith, one only rule of political life upon earth. Upon the edifice, sublimer than Capitol or Vatican, which the people of Italy will raise, you will plant the banner of Liberty and of Association, so that it shines in the sight of all the nations, nor will you lower it ever for terror of despots or lust for the gains of a day. You will have boldness as you have faith. You will speak out aloud to the world, and to those who call themselves the lords of the world, the thought which thrills in the heart of Italy. You will never deny the sister nations. The life of the Country shall grow through you in beauty and in strength, free from servile fears and the hesitations of doubt, keeping as its *foundation* the people, as its *rule* the consequences of its principles logically deduced and energetically applied, as its *strength* the strength of all, as its *outcome* the amelioration of all, as its *end* the fulfilment of the mission which God has given it. And because you will be ready to die for Humanity, the life of your Country will be immortal.

VI

THE Family is the Country of the heart. There is an angel in the Family who, by the mysterious influence of grace, of sweetness, and of love, renders the fulfilment of duties less wearisome, sorrows less bitter. The only pure joys unmixed with sadness which it is given to man to taste upon earth are, thanks to this angel, the joys of the Family. He who through fatality of circumstances has been unable to live the serene life of the Family, beneath the wings of this angel, has a shadow of melancholy resting upon his soul, and a void in his heart which nothing can fill; and I who write these pages for you know it. Bless God who created this angel, oh you who have the joys and consolations of the Family. Do not hold them of little account because you imagine that you can find elsewhere more ardent joys or more immediate consolation for your griefs. The Family contains an element of good rarely found elsewhere, constancy. Its affections wind themselves slowly around you, unheeded, but tenacious and enduring as the ivy round the tree; they follow you hourly, and identify themselves silently with your life. Often you are not aware of them, because they are a part of yourselves; but when you lose them you feel that an indefinable something, something intimate and necessary to your existence, is gone. You wander restless and uneasy. You may still be able to find brief joys or consolations; but not the supreme consolation, not calm, the calm of the wave upon the lake, the calm of trustful sleep, the sleep which stills the child upon its mother's breast.

The angel of the Family is Woman. Mother, wife, or sister, Woman is the caress of life, the soothing sweetness of affection shed over its toils, a reflection for the individual of the loving providence which watches over Humanity. In her there is treasure enough of consoling tenderness to allay every pain. Moreover for every one of us she is the initiator of the future. The mother's first kiss teaches the child love; the first holy kiss of the woman he loves teaches man hope and faith in life; and love and faith create a desire for perfection and the power of reaching towards it step by step; create the future, in short, of which the living symbol is the child, link between us and the generations to come. Through her the Family, with its divine mystery of reproduction, points to Eternity.

Hold the Family sacred, then, O my brothers. Hold it as an inseparable condition of life and repulse every assault which may be made upon it by men imbued with false and brutal philosophies, or by hasty thinkers who seeing it too often the nursery of selfishness and of the spirit of caste, grow angry and believe, like the barbarian, that the only remedy for its evils is to destroy it.

The Family is the conception of God, not of man. No human power can abolish it. Like the Country, and much more than the Country, the Family is an element of life.

Much more than the Country, I say. The Country, sacred to-day, will perhaps some day disappear, when every man shall reflect in his own conscience the moral laws of Humanity; but the Family will endure as long as man endures. It is the cradle of Humanity. Like every element of human life, it must be open to Progress, and its tendencies, its aspirations, must improve from epoch to epoch; but no one may ever suppress it.

To sanctify the Family more and more and to link it ever closer to the Country; this is your mission. What the Country is to Humanity, the Family must be to the Country. I have told you that the task of the Country is to educate *men*; even so the task of the family is to educate *citizens*; Family and Country are the two extreme points of the same line. And where this is not so the Family degenerates into egoism, the more disgusting and brutal the more it prostitutes that most holy thing, affection, by diverting it from its true purpose.

In the present day, egoism by force of circumstances reigns too often and too much in the Family. Bad social institutions generate it. In a society supported by spies, police, prison, and the gallows, the poor mother, trembling at every noble aspiration of her son, is impelled to teach him distrust; to say : *Beware ! the man who speaks to thee of Country, of Liberty, of the Future, and who wishes to clasp thee to his breast, is perhaps nothing else than a traitor.* In a society in which merit is dangerous, and wealth is the only basis of power, of safety, of defence against persecution and arrogance, affection impels the father to say to the youth athirst for Truth : *Beware ! in riches is thy safety ; Truth alone cannot shield thee from the power and corruption of others.* But I am speaking to you of a time when you will have founded for your sons with your sweat and your blood a Country of free men built up on merit and on the good which each of you will have done for his brothers. Till that time it is too true that you have one way only of progress open to you, one supreme duty only to fulfil : to enrol and prepare yourselves, to choose the right moment and to fight and win your Italy by insurrection. Then only will you be able to accomplish your other duties without grave and constant obstacles. And then when I shall probably be laid in the earth, you will read these pages of mine again ; the few brotherly counsels which they contain come from a heart which loves you, and they are written with sincerity and conviction.

Love and respect Woman. Do not seek only consolation in her, but strength, inspiration, a redoubling of your intellectual and moral faculties. Blot out of your mind any idea of superiority to her ; you have none whatever. The prejudice of ages has created through unequal education and the perennial oppression of the laws that *apparent* intellectual inferiority which you use to-day as an argument for maintaining the oppression.

But does not the history of all oppression teach you that those who oppress rely always for their justification upon a fact created by themselves? The feudal classes withheld education from you sons of the people almost up to our own day, and then from your want of education they drew, and still to-day draw, their arguments for excluding you from the sanctuary of the city, from the place where the laws are made, from that right to vote which initiates your social mission. The owners of the negroes in America declare the race radically inferior and incapable of education and yet persecute whoever seeks to educate it. For half a century the supporters of the reigning families have affirmed that we Italians are ill-fitted for liberty, and meanwhile by laws and by the brute force of mercenary armies they keep every way closed by which, if the disability did really exist, we might overcome it for ourselves—as if tyranny could ever be an education for liberty.

Now, we have all been, and still are, guilty of a like offence towards Woman. Put far from you even the shadow of this offence, since there is no graver offence in God's sight than that which divides the human family into two classes and imposes or allows the subjection of one to the other. Before the one God and Father there is neither *man* nor *woman*, but the *human being*, the being in whom, under the aspect of man or of woman, those characters exist which distinguish *humanity* from the order of the animals; namely, social tendency, capacity of learning, and the faculty of progressing. Wherever these characters reveal themselves, there human nature exists, and in consequence equality of rights and of duties. Like two distinct branches springing out of the same trunk, man and woman spring in differing forms from a common base, which is *humanity*. No inequality exists between them, but, as often happens with two men, a difference of tendencies, of special vocations. Are two notes of the same musical chord unequal or of different nature? Man and Woman are the two notes without which the *human* chord is not possible. Take two Peoples, one called by its peculiar gifts or by its conditions of life

to spread the idea of human association by means of
colonies, the other to preach it by the production of
universally admired masterpieces in art and literature;
are their general duties and rights different? Both these
Peoples are apostles, consciously or unconsciously, of
the same divine conception and are equals and
brothers in their mission. Man and Woman, like those
two Peoples, have distinct functions in Humanity, but
these functions are equally sacred and necessary to the
common development and are both representations of
the Thought which God has put like a soul into the
universe. Hold Woman, then, as the companion and
partaker not only of your joys and your sorrows, but
of your aspirations, your thoughts, your studies, and your
efforts for social amelioration. Hold her as your equal
in civil and political life. Be together, you and she,
the two wings of the *human* soul, lifting it towards the
ideal which we must attain. The Mosaic Bible has
said, *God created the man, and the woman from the man*;
but your Bible, the Bible of the future, shall say, *God
created Humanity, manifested in the woman and in the
man.*

Love the children whom Providence sends you; but
love them with a true, profound, stern love; not with
a nerveless, irrational, blind love, which is egoism in
you, and ruin for them. In the name of all that is
most sacred never forget that you have the charge of
the future generations, that towards these souls which
are entrusted to you, towards Humanity, and before
God, you have the most tremendous responsibility which
the human being can be sensible of. You must initiate
them not into the pleasures and greeds of life, but into
life itself, into its duties, into the moral law which
governs it. Few mothers, few fathers, in this irreligious
century, especially in the well-to-do classes, understand
the gravity and sanctity of their educational mission.
Few mothers, few fathers, think that the many victims,
the incessant struggles, and the long martyrdom of our
times are in great measure the fruit of the egoism in-
stilled thirty years ago into their children's minds by

weak mothers or careless fathers who allowed them to
get into the habit of regarding life not as a duty and
a mission, but as a search for pleasure, and an endeavour
after selfish well-being. For you, sons of labour, the
dangers are less great; most of your children learn only
too well the life of privation. And, on the other hand,
you who are compelled by your inferior social condition
to continual toil have fewer possibilities of educating
them properly. Nevertheless even you can partly fulfil
the arduous task by your example and by your word.
You can do it by your example.

"Your children will be like you, corrupt or virtuous,
according as you yourselves are virtuous or corrupt.

"How can they become honest, compassionate, and
humane if you yourselves lack uprightness, and are
without charity for your brothers? How shall they
restrain their gross appetites if they see you give way
to intemperance? How shall they preserve their natural
innocence intact if you do not fear to outrage modesty
in their presence by indecent acts and obscene words?

"You are the living model upon which their im-
pressionable nature forms itself. It depends upon you
whether your sons turn out men or brutes." [1]

And you can educate them by your words. Speak
to them of their Country, of what it was, of what it
ought to be. When at evening the smiles of the mother,
and the artless prattle of the children upon your knee,
make you forget the toils of the day, tell them over again
the great deeds of the common people in our ancient
republics; teach them the names of the good men who
loved Italy and her people, and endeavoured through
suffering, calumny, and persecution to improve her
destinies. Instil into their young hearts not hatred of
the oppressor, but an energetic resolve to resist oppression. Let them learn from your lips, and from the
tranquil approval of their mother, how beautiful it is
to follow the paths of virtue, how great to stand up as
apostles of the truth, how holy to sacrifice oneself, if
needs be, for one's brothers. Kindle in their tender

[1] Lamennais, *Livre du Peuple*, xii.

minds, while planting the germs of rebellion against
all *authority* usurped and sustained by force, reverence
for the true, the only authority, the authority of Virtue
crowned by Genius. See that they grow up hating
tyranny and anarchy alike, in the religion of a conscience
inspired but not chained down by tradition. The Nation
ought to help you in this work. And you have in the
name of your children the right to exact this from it.
Without a National Education there is no true Nation.

Love your parents. Do not let the family which
springs from you make you ever forget the family from
which you sprang. Too often indeed the new ties relax
the old, whereas they ought only to be a new link in
the chain of love which should bind together the three
generations of a family. Surround the white heads of
the mother and of the father with tender and respectful
affection till their last day. Strew their way to the
grave with flowers. Breathe over their weary souls a
fragrance of faith and immortality with the constancy
of your love. And may the affection which you keep
inviolate for your parents be a pledge of that which
your children will keep for you.

Parents, sisters and brothers, wife, children, let them
all be to you as branches growing in different order upon
the same tree. Sanctify the Family in the unity of love.
Make it a temple in which you may sacrifice together
to the Country. I do not know if you will be happy;
but I do know that if you do thus there will come to
you even in the midst of adversity a sense of serene
peace, the repose of a tranquil conscience, which will
give you strength in every trial, and will keep an azure
space of sky open before your eyes in every tempest.

VII

Preliminaries

I HAVE said to you : *You have life ; therefore you have a law of life. . . . To develop yourselves, to act, to live according to the law of life, is your first, nay, your only Duty.* I have told you that God has given you two means of knowing what is your law of life : your own conscience and the conscience of Humanity, the general conviction of your fellow-men. I have told you that whenever you interrogate your conscience, and find its voice in harmony with the great voice of the human race which history has transmitted to you, you are certain of having the eternal, the immutable truth in your grasp.

At the present day it is only with difficulty that you can properly interrogate the great voice with which Humanity speaks to you through history ; you lack really good popular books and you have no time. But the men who by their ability and conscientiousness best represent historical study and the science of Humanity in the last half-century have deduced from this voice some of the characters of our law of life. They have found out that human nature is essentially social and capable of education ; that as there is and can be but one God, there can be but one Law for the *individual* man and for *collective* Humanity ; and that the fundamental and universal character of this Law is PROGRESS. From this truth, incontestable to-day because all the branches of human knowledge confirm it, are derived all your duties to yourself, and also all your *rights*, which are summed up in one : *the right to be*

67

absolutely unfettered and to be aided, within certain limits, in the fulfilment of your duties.

You are and you feel yourselves *free*. All the sophisms of a wretched philosophy which would substitute a doctrine of I know not what fatalism for the cry of the human conscience, cannot avail to silence two invincible witnesses in favour of *liberty* ; remorse and martyrdom. From Socrates to Jesus, from Jesus down to the men who die from time to time for their Country, the Martyrs of Faith raise their voices against that slavish doctrine, crying out to you : " We too loved life ; we loved the beings who made it dear to us and who implored us to yield ; every impulse of our hearts cried to us *live!* but for the salvation of future generations we *chose* to die." From Cain down to the vulgar spy of our day, all those who betray their brothers, all the men who have set forth on the path of evil, feel in the depths of their soul self-condemnation, restlessness, a reproachful voice saying to each of them, *Why do you abandon the paths of good?*

You are *free*, and therefore *responsible.* From this moral liberty is derived your right to political liberty, your duty to conquer it for yourselves and to keep it inviolate, and the duty of others not to limit it.

You are *capable of education.* In each of you exists a certain sum of faculties, of intellectual capacities and moral tendencies, to which education alone can give life and activity, and which otherwise would remain sterile and inert, or only reveal themselves by flashes without regular development.

Education is the bread of the soul. Just as physical and organic life cannot grow and unfold without nourishment, so the moral and intellectual life needs external influences for its full development and manifestation, and must assimilate a part, at least, of the ideas, affections, and aspirations of others. The life of the individual springs up like the plant, each variety endowed with its own existence and with special characters, upon a common soil, and is nourished with the elements common to the life of all. The individual is a shoot of Humanity, and nourishes and renews its own strength in the strength of Humanity. This work of nourishment and renewal is accomplished by education, which transmits to the individual directly or indirectly the results of the progress of the whole human race. It is therefore not only because it is a *necessity* of your life, but because it is a kind of holy communion with all your fellow-men, and with all the generations which have lived, that is to say, thought and acted, before yours, that you must win education for yourselves as far as possible; a moral and intellectual education, which shall embrace and cultivate all the faculties which God has given you as seed to bring to fruit, and shall form and maintain a bond between your individual life and that of collective Humanity.

And in order that this work of education should be the more rapidly accomplished, and that your individual life should be linked more surely and intimately with the collective life of all, with the life of Humanity, God has made you essentially social beings. Every kind of lower being can live by itself, without other communion than with nature, with the elements of the physical world; you cannot. At every step you have need of your brothers; and you could not satisfy the simplest needs of life without aiding yourselves by their work. Though superior to every other being by virtue of association with your fellows, you are when isolated inferior in strength to many animals, and weak and incapable of development and of a complete existence. All the noblest aspirations of your heart, such as love of country, and also those less virtuous, such as desire of glory and of others' praise, indicate your inborn tendency to unite your life with the life of the millions who surround you. You are, then, created for *association*. It multiplies your strength a hundredfold; makes the ideas of others yours, and the progress of others yours; and raises, improves, and sanctifies your nature through the affections and the growing sentiment of the unity of the human family. The wider, the more intimate and comprehensive your association with your brothers, the further will you advance on the path of individual progress.

The law of life cannot be *wholly* accomplished except by the united work of *all*. And for every great advance, for every discovery of a portion of that law, history shows a corresponding extension of human association, a wider contact between peoples and peoples. When the first Christians came to proclaim the unity of human nature, in opposition to the pagan philosophy which admitted two human natures, that of masters and that of slaves, the Roman people had borne its eagles into the midst of all the known peoples of Europe. Before the Papacy—baleful to-day, but beneficial in the first centuries of its institution—came to announce: *the spiritual power is higher than the temporal*, the invaders, whom we call the Barbarians, had brought the Germanic and the Latin worlds into violent contact. Before the idea of liberty as applying to the peoples had started the conception of nationality which now agitates Europe and is destined to triumph, the wars of the French Revolution and of the Empire had roused and called into action an element separate till then from the rest of Europe, the Slav element.

Lastly, you are *progressive* beings.

This word PROGRESS, unknown to antiquity, will be from henceforth a sacred word for Humanity. It comprehends a whole social, political, and religious transformation.

Antiquity, the men of the old Oriental and Pagan religions, believed in Fate, in Chance, in a mysterious incomprehensible Power, the arbitrary disposer of human things, creating and destroying alternately, without men being able to understand, promote, or accelerate its action. They believed that man was powerless to found anything enduring and permanent upon our earth. They believed that the peoples were condemned to move for ever in the circle described by individuals here below; that they rose, mounted upwards to power, then descended to old age, and fatally, irrevocably perished. With the narrowest horizon of ideas and of facts before them, and without any knowledge of history beyond that of their own nation, and often of their own city, they regarded the human race solely as an aggregate of men, without any life or law of its own, and derived their ideas of it from contemplation of the individual only. The consequence of such doctrines was a disposition to accept existing *facts* without troubling or hoping to change them. Where circumstances had founded a republican form of government, the men of those times were republicans; where despotism reigned, they were submissive slaves, indifferent to progress. But since they found the human family everywhere, under a republican government and under tyranny alike, divided either into four castes, as in the East, or into two, free citizens and slaves, as in Greece, they accepted the division of castes, or the belief in two different kinds of men ; even Plato and Aristotle, the most powerful intellects of the Greek world, accepted it. The emancipation of your class would have been an impossibility among men like these.

The men who founded upon the words of Jesus a religion superior to all the beliefs of the ancient East and of Paganism, dimly foresaw, but did not grasp the holy idea contained in this word, *Progress*. They understood the unity of the human race, the unity of the law, and the perfectibility of man ; but they did not understand the power of accomplishing it which God has given to man, nor the *way* in which it must be accomplished. They limited themselves also to deducing the rule of life from the contemplation of the *individual*. Humanity as a collective body remained unknown to them. They recognised a Providence and substituted it for the blind Fatality of the ancients ; but they recognised it as the protector of the individual, not as the law of Humanity. Their mental position between the immensity of the ideal of perfectibility which they had conceived, and the sense of the brief miserable life of the individual, created a need for an intermediary term between the two, between God and man ; and not having grasped the idea of a collective humanity, they had recourse to that of

a divine incarnation; they declared that faith in this
incarnation was the only source of salvation, of strength,
of *grace* for men.

Not suspecting the continuous revelation which
descends from God upon man through Humanity, they
believed in an *immediate* and *single* revelation given at
one fixed moment, and by the *special* favour *of God.*
They perceived the link which binds men together in
God, but they did not perceive that which binds them
together here upon earth in Humanity. The succession
of the generations was of little importance to those who
did not feel how one generation acts upon another ; they
accustomed themselves therefore to disregard them, and
strove to detach man from the world and from the things
which concern Humanity as a whole, and they finished
by calling the earth, which they abandoned to the existing powers, a mere abode of expiation, putting it in
antagonism to heaven, whither man might climb by
means of grace and faith, but from which without those
means he was eternally exiled. Revelation being in their
opinion immediate and vouchsafed once only at a given
period, they concluded that nothing could be added to it,
and that the depositaries of this revelation were infallible.
They forgot that in a solemn moment, and with a sublime
intuition of the future, Jesus had said : *I have many
things to say unto you, but ye cannot hear them now.
Howbeit when he, the Spirit of truth is come, he will
guide you into all truth ; for he shall not speak of himself,
but whatsoever he shall hear that shall he speak.*[1] These
words contain a forecast of the idea of progress and of
the continuous revelation of the truth through the
medium of Humanity ; in them is found the justification
of the formula which reawakened Rome will offer to
Italy in the words "God and the People" inscribed on the
front of its republican decrees. But the men who held
the beliefs of the middle ages could not understand it.
The times were not yet ripe.

The whole edifice of the creeds which succeeded to
Paganism rests upon the foundations just indicated. It

[1] St. John, chap. xvi.

is clear that your emancipation here on earth cannot be based upon these.

Thirteen hundred years after the words of Jesus which I have quoted were spoken, a man, an Italian, the greatest of all Italians, wrote the following truths: "God is one, the Universe is God's thought; the Universe therefore is also one. All things come from God. All partake more or less of the divine nature, according to the end for which they are created. Man is the noblest of all created things. God has poured into him more of His own nature than into the others. Everything which comes from God tends towards the perfection of which it is capable. The capacity of perfection in man is unlimited. Humanity is one. God has made nothing useless; and because there is one Humanity only, there must be a single aim for *all* men, a work to be accomplished by the labour of all together. The human race must therefore work in union so that all the intellectual powers diffused in it may obtain the highest possible development in the sphere of thought and of action. There exists, then, a universal Religion for the human race."

The man who gave utterance to these thoughts was named Dante. Every city of Italy, when Italy is free and united, ought to raise a statue to him, since these thoughts contain the germ of the Religion of the Future. He wrote them in Latin and Italian books entitled *De Monarchia* and *Il Convito*, difficult to understand, and neglected in the present day even by those who call themselves scholars. But these ideas, once sown in the world of intellect, can never die. Others reap them even when they forget their origin. Men admire the oak, but who remembers the acorn from which it sprang?

The seed which Dante cast abroad has borne fruit. Tended and fertilised from time to time by some powerful intellect, it developed towards the end of the eighteenth century. The idea of Progress as the law of life, accepted and developed, verified by history, and confirmed by science, became the banner of the future. To-day there is no serious thinker who does not regard it as the pivot of his work.

We know to-day that the law of life is PROGRESS. Progress for the *individual*, progress for Humanity. Humanity fulfils that law on earth; the Individual on earth and elsewhere. One only God; one only Law. From the first moment of its existence Humanity has been gradually but inevitably fulfilling that Law. Truth has never manifested itself wholly or all at once. A continuous revelation manifests a fragment of the truth, a *word* of the Law, from age to age. Each of these *words* profoundly modifies human life upon the path towards *perfection*, and constitutes a *belief*, a Faith. The development of the religious Idea is, then, indefinitely progressive; and the successive *beliefs*, unfolding and purifying this Idea ever more and more, will one day, like columns of a temple, build up the Pantheon of Humanity, the one great religion of our earth. The men blessed by God with genius and with more than common virtue· are its apostles; the People, the *collective* sense of Humanity, is its interpreter, and accepts this revelation of Truth, transmits it from generation to generation, and reduces it to practice by applying it to the different branches and manifestations of human life.

Humanity is like a man who lives for an indefinite period and is always learning. There is not, therefore, and there cannot be, infallibility in men, or in Powers; there is not, and cannot be, a privileged *class* of depositaries and interpreters of the Law; there is not, and cannot be, a need of any *intermediary* between God and man save Humanity alone. God, by preordaining a providential design of progressive education for Humanity, and planting the instinct of progress in the heart of every man, has also put into human nature the faculties and powers necessary to fulfil it. Individual man, a free and responsible creature, is able to use or abuse them according to whether he keeps to the path of Duty, or yields to the blind seductions of Egoism; he can delay or hasten his own progress; but the providential design cannot be annulled by any human power. The education of Humanity *must* complete itself; thus we see out of the barbaric invasions which seemed to extinguish all civilised life a new civilisation arise superior to the old, and diffused over a wider zone of the earth; out of a tyranny exercised by individuals we see a more rapid development of liberty immediately issue.

The Law of Progress must be accomplished here upon earth as elsewhere. There is no antagonism between *earth* and *heaven*: and it is a blasphemy to suppose that we can, without incurring guilt, despise the work of God, the house which He has given us, and abandon it to the Powers that be, whatever their nature, to the influences of Evil, of Egoism, and of Tyranny. The earth is not a place of *expiation*; it is the place for working to realise the *ideal* of truth and justice which each of us bears implanted in his soul; it is a ladder towards that Perfection which we can only reach by glorifying God in Humanity with our works and by consecrating ourselves to translating into *fact* as much as we can of His design. The judgment which will be pronounced upon each one of us, either decreeing our upward progress upon the ladder of Perfection, or condemning us to drag ourselves once again along the course which we have already trodden with barren results or in actual sin, will be founded on the good which we have done to our brothers, upon the degree of progress which we have helped others to attain. A more and more intimate and extended association with our fellow-men is the means by which our strength will be multiplied, the field on which our duties must be accomplished, the way to realise progress in action. We must aim at making the whole of Humanity one Family, each member of which shall represent in himself the moral law for the benefit of the others. And as the perfecting of Humanity is accomplished from age to age, from generation to generation, so the perfecting of the individual is accomplished from existence to existence, more or less rapidly according to our own efforts.

These are *some* of the truths contained in that word Progress from which shall come forth the Religion of the Future. In that word alone can your emancipation be achieved.

VIII

You live. The life which is in you is not the work of Chance; the word Chance has no meaning whatever and was only invented to express the ignorance of men about certain things. The life which is in you comes from God, and reveals in its progressive development an intelligent *design*. Your life has necessarily then an *aim*, a purpose.

The *ultimate* aim for which we were created is at present unknown to us and cannot be otherwise; but this is no reason why we should deny it. Does the babe know the purpose towards which it must tend through Family, Country, Humanity? No; but the purpose exists, and we are beginning to know it for him. Humanity is God's babe; He knows the end towards which it must develop. Humanity is only just beginning to-day to understand that Progress is its law; it is only just beginning to understand, uncertainly, something of the Universe around it, and the greater part of the individuals who compose it are still quite unfit, in consequence of barbarism, slavery, or absolute lack of education, for the study of this Law and of the Universe which is necessary before we can understand ourselves. Only a minority of the men who people our little Europe are capable of developing their intellectual faculties for the purpose of acquiring knowledge. In you yourselves, most of you deprived of instruction and all subjected by necessity to a life of badly organised physical labour, those faculties lie dormant and are unable to bring their tribute to the pyramid of knowledge. How, then, can we expect to know to-day that which requires the associated work of all? Why rebel against our not having yet reached the point which will constitute the last step of our earthly Progress, when as yet only a few of us, and those disunited, are beginning even to lisp that sacred and fruitful word? Let us resign ourselves, then, to ignorance of the things which must be inaccessible to us for a long while yet, and do not let us abandon in childish anger the study of those which we are able to discover. The discovery of the truth demands modesty and self-restraint, as much as constancy. Many more souls have been lost or led astray from the right path by impatience and human pride than by deliberate wickedness. It is this truth which the ancients would teach us when they tell how the Despot ambitious of scaling the heavens could only build up a tower of confusion, and how the Giants who assailed Olympus lie blasted by thunderbolts beneath our volcanic mountains.

The important thing for us to be convinced of is, that whatever the *end* may be for which we are destined, we can only discover and attain it by the progressive development and the exercise of our intellectual faculties. Our faculties are the instruments of labour given us by God. It is necessary therefore that their development should be furthered and helped, and their exercise be free and protected. Without Liberty you cannot fulfil any of your duties ; you have therefore a right to liberty and the duty to wrest it by any means from any power whatever which denies it to you.

Without *Liberty* morality does not exist, because if there is not freedom of choice between good and evil, between devotion to the common progress and the spirit of egoism, there is no responsibility. Without Liberty no true society exists, because between free men and slaves there can be no *association*, but only dominion of some over the others. Liberty is sacred as the *individual* whose life it represents is sacred. Where there is not Liberty, life is reduced to a mere organic function. A man who allows his liberty to be violated is false to his own nature and a rebel against the decrees of God.

There is no liberty where a class, a family, or a man

assumes dominion over others in virtue of a pretended divine right, or of a privilege derived from birth or wealth. Liberty must be for all and in the sight of all. God does not delegate sovereignty to any individual; that degree of sovereignty which can be represented on our earth is entrusted by God to Humanity, to the Nations, to Society. And this also ceases and abandons the collective fractions of Humanity if they do not use it for good, for the fulfilment of the providential design. There exists, then, no sovereignty of *right* in any one; sovereignty is in the Aim, and in the actions which lead to it. The actions and the aim towards which we. are advancing must be submitted to the judgment of all. There is not and cannot be, then, any *permanent* sovereignty. That institution which we call Government is only a *Direction*; a mission entrusted to a few in order to attain more speedily the aim of the Nation ; and if they are false to this mission, the directing power entrusted to these few must cease. Every man called to the Government is an administrator of the common will; he must be *elected* and must be subject to recall whenever he misunderstands or deliberately opposes that will. There cannot exist, then, I repeat, a class or family which holds the power by its own right, without a violation of your liberty. How can you call yourselves free in the presence of men who possess the power to command you without your consent ? The republic is the only legitimate and logical form of government.

You have no master but God in heaven and the People on earth. When you have discovered a line of the Law, of God's will, you must bless it and obey it. When the People, the collective body of your fellows, declare that they hold a certain belief, you must bow your head and abstain from every act of rebellion.

But there are things which constitute your individual being and are essential to human life. And over these not even the People has any right. No majority, no collective force can rob you of that which makes you *men*. No majority can decree a tyranny and extinguish or alienate its own liberty. Against a people who would commit such suicide you cannot use force, but the right of protest by whatever means circumstances may suggest to you lives and will live in each of you eternally.

You ought to have liberty and everything that is indispensable for the moral and material nourishment of life.

Personal liberty; liberty of locomotion; liberty of religious belief; liberty of opinion on all subjects; liberty of expressing opinion through the press or by any other peaceful method; liberty of association so as to be able to cultivate your own minds by contact with the minds of others; liberty of trade in all the productions of your brains and hands: these are all things which no one may take from you—except on certain rare occasions which it is not necessary to mention now—without grave injustice, without arousing in you the duty to protest.

No one has the right, in the name of society, to imprison you or to subject your person to restraint or to espionage, without telling you why with the least possible delay, and conducting you promptly before the judicial authority of the country. No one has the right to impede you by passports or other restrictions from passing from one part to another of your native land. No one has any right of persecution or intolerance or exclusive legislation over your religious opinions: nothing except the great pacific voice of Humanity has the right to interpose itself between God and your conscience. God has given you thought; no one has the right to restrain it, or to forbid the expression of it, which is the communion of your soul with the soul of your brothers, and the only way of progress which we have. The press must be absolutely free; the rights of the intellect are inviolable, and any preventive censorship is tyranny; society may only punish the offences of the pen, such as the inculcation of crime and openly immoral teaching, as it punishes other offences. Punishment decreed by a solemn public judgment is a consequence of human responsibility, while every intervention *beforehand* is a negation of liberty. Peaceful *association* is sacred, like thought; God planted the tendency in you as a perennial means of progress, a pledge of that unity which the human family is destined one day to attain; no power has any right to impede or limit it. The duty of each of you is to use the life which God gave you, to preserve and develop it; each of you, then, owes to life a debt of labour, the sole means of its material sustenance. Labour is sacred. No one has the right to forbid it or fetter it or make it impossible by arbitrary regulations : no one has the right to restrain free traffic in its products ; your native land is your market, from no part of which you may be shut out.

But when you have obtained the recognition of these liberties as sacred—when you have finally established the state upon the votes of all and in such a manner that all the ways which can lead to the development of human faculties shall be open to the *individual*—then, remember that still above each of you stands the great aim which it is your duty to attain : the moral perfection of yourself and of others, an ever more intimate and wider communion between all the members of the human family, so that at some future day it shall recognise one Law only.

"Your task is to form the universal family, to build the City of God, and by a continuous labour gradually to translate His work in Humanity into fact.

"When you love one another as brothers and treat each other reciprocally as such, and each one, seeking his own good in the good of all, shall identify his own life with the life of all, his own interests with the interests of all, and shall be always ready to sacrifice himself for all the members of the common family, and they equally ready to sacrifice themselves for him, most of the ills which weigh to-day upon the human race will vanish like the thick mists gathered upon the horizon vanish at the rising of the sun ; since it is His will that Love shall unite little by little, and ever more closely, the scattered elements of Humanity and order them in a single body, and Humanity be one, as He is one." [1]

[1] Lamennais, *Livre du Peuple*, iii.

Do not let these words, spoken by a man who lived and died like a saint and who loved the people and their future with an immense love, ever be out of your minds, O my brothers. Liberty is only a *means*: woe to you and to your future if you ever accustom yourselves to regard it as an end. Your individual being has duties and rights which may never be given up to any one; but woe to you and to your future if the respect which you owe to what constitutes your *individual* life should ever degenerate into a fatal *egoism*! Your Liberty is not the negation of all authority; it is the negation of all authority which does not represent the collective purpose of the Nation, and which presumes to establish and support itself upon any other foundation than that of your free and spontaneous consent. The doctrines of casuists have in these latter times perverted the sacred conception of Liberty; some have reduced it to a mean immoral *individualism*—have said that the Ego is everything and that the one aim of human labour and social organisation ought to be the satisfaction of its desires; others have declared that *all* government, *all* authority, is an inevitable evil, but that it must be restricted and fettered as much as possible; that Liberty has no limits, that the sole task of every society is to promote it indefinitely; that a man has the right to use and abuse Liberty, provided that his action does not result directly in evil to others; and that a government has no mission beyond that of *preventing* one individual from *injuring* another. Reject these false doctrines, O my brothers; it is they who delay Italy even now upon the road of her future greatness. The first has generated the egoism of class; the second turns society, which ought, if well ordered, to represent your collective purpose and life, into nothing more than a soldier or police officer charged to maintain an apparent peace. Both debase *Liberty* into *Anarchy*; they abolish the idea of collective moral improvement; abolish the mission of education and of Progress which Society ought to take upon itself. If you should understand Liberty in this way you would deserve to lose it, and sooner or later you would lose it.

Your Liberty will be sacred so long as it develops under the ruling influence of the Idea of Duty and of Faith in the common perfectibility. Your Liberty will flourish, protected by God and by men, so long as you regard it not as the right to use and to abuse your faculties in any direction which it pleases you to choose, but as the right to *choose freely and according to your special tendencies a means of doing good.*

IX

EDUCATION

Goᴅ has made you capable of education. It is therefore your duty to educate yourselves as far as in you lies,
and your right that the society to which you belong
should not *hinder* you in your work of education, but
should help you in it and *supply* you with means of
education when you lack them.

Your liberty, your rights, your emancipation from
unjust social conditions, the life-work which each of you
has to fulfil here on earth, depend upon the degree of
education which it is given you to obtain. Without
education you cannot choose rightly between good and
evil; you cannot acquire a knowledge of your own
rights; you cannot obtain that share in political life without which you will never succeed in emancipating yourselves; you cannot define your own life-work to yourselves. Education is the bread of your souls. Without
it your faculties lie numb and unfruitful, as the vital
power which dwells in the seed lies sterile if it is cast into
untilled soil and lacks the benefit of irrigation and the
care of a diligent husbandman.

At the present day you either have no education or else
only bad or inadequate instruction, given you by men
and powers which represent nothing except themselves
and observe no guiding principle. The best of them
believe that they have done all that is required of
them if they have opened upon the territory which
they govern a certain number of schools, unequally
distributed, in which your children may receive some
degree of elementary teaching. This teaching consists
principally of reading, writing, and arithmetic.

Such teaching is called *instruction*; and differs from *education* as much as our organs differ from our life. Our organs are not life; they are only its instruments and its means of manifesting itself; they do not rule or direct it, and they are equally the means of action for the most saintly or the most corrupt life. In the same way instruction provides the means of putting into practice what is taught by education, but cannot take the place of education.

Education is addressed to the *moral* faculties; *instruction* to the *intellectual*. The first develops in man the knowledge of his duties; the second makes him capable of fulfilling them. Without *instruction*, *education* would be too often ineffective; without *education* *instruction* would be a lever lacking a fulcrum. You can read; what does that amount to if you cannot tell which books contain error, which the truth? You are able by writing to communicate your thoughts to your brothers; what is the use if your thoughts only express egoism? *Instruction*, like riches, can be a source of either good or evil according to the intention with which it is used. Consecrated to the general progress it is a means of civilisation and of liberty; used only for personal advantage it becomes a means of tyranny and corruption. In Europe to-day *instruction* unaccompanied by a corresponding degree of moral *education* is a very grievous evil; it keeps up the inequality between class and class of the same people and inclines the mind to calculation, to egoism, to compromises between justice and injustice and to all false doctrine.

The distinction between the men who offer you more or less *instruction*, and those who preach *education* to you, is deeper than you suppose, and I must devote a few words specially to the subject.

Two schools of thought divide the camp of those who fight for liberty against despotism. The first declare that *sovereignty* resides in the *individual*; the second maintains that it belongs to *society* only, and rules by means of the expressed will of the majority. The first imagines that it has fulfilled its peculiar mission when it has proclaimed the *rights* believed to be inherent in human nature, and has safeguarded liberty; the second looks almost exclusively to *association*, and deduces the *duties* of each individual from the compact which constitutes that *association*. The first does not see beyond what I have called *instruction*, because *instruction* tends in fact to give facilities of development to the individual faculties, but without any general direction; the second understands the necessity of an *education* which is for it the manifestation of the *social* programme. The first leads inevitably to moral anarchy; the second tends to forget the rights of liberty, and runs a risk of leading to the despotism of the majority.

To the first of these schools that generation of men belonged who were called in France *doctrinaires*, who betrayed the hopes of the people after the Revolution of 1830, and by proclaiming *liberty of instruction* and nothing else, perpetuated the governing monopoly in the hands of the *middle class*, which possesses more means of developing its individual faculties; the second is unfortunately only represented to-day by sects and powers belonging to antiquated beliefs, and hostile to the dogma of the future, Progress.

Both these schools err through too narrow and exclusive aims.

The truth is this: All sovereignty is in God, in the moral law, in the providential design which governs the world—and which is gradually revealed by the inspirations of men of virtuous genius, and by the natural tendency of Humanity in the different epochs of its existence—in the purpose which we have to attain, and the mission which we have to fulfil. There is no sovereignty in the individual, there is none in society except in so far as the one and the other conform to that design, to that law, and direct themselves towards the attainment of that purpose. An individual who rules is either the best interpreter of the moral law and governs in its name, or a usurper to be overthrown. The mere vote of a majority does not constitute sovereignty, if it is evidently adverse to the supreme moral law, or deliberately closes the way to future progress. Social good, liberty, progress; outside these three terms there can be no sovereignty.

Education teaches in what social welfare consists.

Instruction secures for the individual the free choice of means of obtaining a continuous progress in the conception of social welfare.

It is of first importance to you that your sons should be taught what are the ruling principles and beliefs which guide the lives of their fellow-men in their own times and in their own country; what the moral, social, and political programme of their nation is; what the spirit of the legislation by which their deeds will have to be judged; what degree of progress Humanity has already attained, and that which it has yet to attain. And it is important to you that they should feel themselves from their earliest years united in the spirit of equality and of love for a common aim, with the millions of brothers that God has given them.

The Education which shall give your children this sort of teaching can come only from the Nation.

The moral teaching of to-day is mere anarchy. Left exclusively to the parents, it is nil where poverty and the necessity of an almost incessant material toil deprive them of time for educating their children themselves, and of means of providing other teachers; it is bad where egoism and corruption have perverted and contaminated the family. When means exist the young ones are imbued with superstitious or materialistic ideas, with tendencies towards Liberty or towards cowardly resignation, towards aristocracy or reaction against aristocracy, according to whether a layman or priest is chosen for the instructor by the paternal inclination. Taught thus, how can they when they are grown to manhood associate themselves in brotherly union for a common task, and represent in their own persons the unity of the country? Society calls upon them to further the development of a common idea into which they have never been initiated. Society punishes them for violation of laws of which they are still ignorant, and the spirit and scope of which are never taught by society to the citizen. Society desires of them co-operation and sacrifice for an end which no teacher has unfolded to them at the opening of their lives as citizens. Strange to say, the Doctrinaire School which I have mentioned above recognises the right to rule and teach the young in each *individual*, but not in the *association* of all, not in the Nation. Their cry, *Liberty of teaching*, disinherits the country of its right of moral direction. They declare the uniformity of the monetary system and of weights and measures to be of first importance; but the uniformity of the principles on which the national life must be founded and developed is nothing to them. You should not let yourselves be beguiled by this cry which almost all the modern supporters of Constitutional Governments repeat one after the other.

Without National Education, from which alone a national conscience can issue, a Nation has no moral existence.

Without National Education common to all the citizens, equality of *duties* and of *rights* is a formula devoid of meaning; the knowledge of duties and the capacity of exercising rights are left to the chance of fortune or to the arbitrary will of those who choose the teachers.

The men who proclaim their opposition to uniformity of education invoke liberty. Whose liberty? That of the fathers or of the children? The liberty of the children is violated, in their system, by the paternal despotism; the liberty of the younger generations is sacrificed to the old; the liberty of progress becomes an illusion. Individual beliefs, perhaps false and hostile to progress, are alone transmitted to the child, and with the weight of the paternal authority, at an age when inquiry into them is impossible. Later on, the destiny which chains most of you to material labour the whole day long will prevent the young soul, already impressed with these beliefs, from comparing them with others and modifying them. In the name of that lying liberty, the anarchical system, of which I now speak, tends to found and perpetuate the worst of all despotisms, a *moral caste*.

What this system advocates should be properly called arbitrary will, not *Liberty*. True Liberty cannot exist without equality, and there can be no equality among those who do not proceed from one basis, from a common principle, from a uniform sense of Duty. Liberty cannot be exercised outside that sense of Duty. I told you a few pages back that true Liberty does not consist in the right to choose *evil*, but in the right to choose between the paths which lead to *good*. The *liberty* invoked by these false philosophers is an arbitrary right given to the father to choose evil for the son. What ? If a father threatened to mutilate or injure in any way the body of his child, society would interfere, invoked by public opinion; and shall the *soul*, the mind of this being be of less account than the body ? Shall not society protect it from the mutilation of its faculties, ignorance, and from the perversion of the moral sense, superstition ?

That cry of liberty of teaching served a useful purpose at the time when it first arose, and is useful also in the present day whenever moral education is the monopoly of a despotic Government, of a retrograde caste, or a priesthood antagonistic by the nature of its dogmas to Progress. It was a weapon against tyranny, an imperfect but indispensable watchword of emancipation. Let it serve you wherever you are slaves. But I am speaking to you of a time when religious faith shall write the word Progress on the doors of the temple, and every public institution shall repeat this word in various forms ; when National Education shall at the conclusion of its teaching dismiss the pupils with these words : *To you, destined to live under a common compact with us, we have taught the fundamental bases of this compact, the principles in which your Nation believes to-day. But remember that the first of these principles is Progress. Remember that your mission as a man and as a citizen is to improve the mind and the heart of your brothers, wherever you can. Go, examine, compare, and if you*

discover a truth superior to what we believe we possess,
publish it boldly and you will have the blessing of your
Country. Then, but not before, renounce that cry of
liberty of teaching as unequal to your needs and fatal
to the unity of the Country. Ask, and exact, the
establishment of a system of free national education,
compulsory for all.

It is the duty of the Nation to communicate its
programme to every citizen. Every citizen ought to
receive in its schools moral teaching, a course in the
history of nationalities, including a rapid survey of the
progress of Humanity, and in the history of his own
country, a popular exposition of the principles which
direct the legislation of the country, and the elementary
instruction about which there is no dispute. Every
citizen ought to learn in these schools equality and
love.

This programme once transmitted to the citizens,
Liberty regains its rights. Not only the teaching of the
family, but every other is sacred. Every man has
an unlimited right to communicate his own ideas to
others ; every man has the right to hear them. Society
ought to protect, to encourage, the free expression of
thought in every form, and to throw open every way for
the development and modification of the social programme in the direction of Good.

X

GOD has made you social and progressive beings. It is your duty, then, to associate yourselves and to progress as much as is possible in the sphere of activity in which you are placed by circumstances, and it is your right to demand that the society to which you belong shall not impede you in your work of association and of progress, but shall *help* you in it and *supply* you with the means of *association* and of progress if you lack them.

Liberty gives you the power of choosing between good and evil, that is, between duty and egoism. *Education* must teach you how to *choose*. *Association* must give you the means with which to put your choice into practice. *Progress* is the *end* which you must have in sight when you choose and is at the same time, when visibly achieved, the proof that you were not mistaken in your choice. When a single one of these conditions is betrayed or neglected, neither the *man* nor the *citizen* exists, or he exists only in an imperfect state, arrested in his development.

You must fight, then, for all these things and especially for the right of Association, without which liberty and education would be useless.

The right of Association is as sacred as religion, which is the association of souls. You are all sons of God; you are therefore brothers, and is it not a crime to restrict association, *communion* between brothers?

The word *communion*, used deliberately here, was spoken to you by that Christianity which men proclaimed in the past as the immutable truth, but which is in fact one step only in the ascending series of the religious manifestations of Humanity. And it is a holy word. It taught men that they were a single family of equals in God, and it united master and slave in the same thought of salvation, in the same hope, and the same love of heaven.

It was an immense advance on earlier times when people and philosophers believed the souls of citizens and of slaves to be of different nature. This mission was enough for Christianity. The *communion* was the symbol of the equality and the brotherhood of souls ; it remained for Humanity to expand and develop the truth hidden in that symbol.

The Church could not and did not do it. Timid and uncertain in its beginning, allied with princes and temporal powers later, and imbued by self-interest with an aristocratic tendency alien to the spirit of its Founder, it wandered from the right way and retrograded so far as to diminish the value of the communion by limiting it for laymen to communion in bread alone and reserving for priests communion in the *two kinds*.

Thenceforward the cry of all who felt the right of the whole human family to an unrestricted communion, without distinction between ecclesiastics and laymen, was, *Communion in both kinds for the people ; the chalice for the people !* In the fifteenth century this cry was the cry of insurgent multitudes and the prelude, sanctified by martyrdom, of the religious reform. A holy man, John Huss of Bohemia, leader of this movement, perished in the flames kindled by the Inquisition. Most of you to-day are ignorant of the history of these old struggles, or think they were only fanatical struggles over purely theological questions. But when history, popularised by National Education, has taught you that every step forward in religious thought brings a corresponding progress in civil life, you will understand the true value of these conflicts, and honour the memory of these martyrs as your benefactors.

We owe to them and to the martyrs who preceded them our knowledge to-day that there is no privileged class between God and man ; that the best among us in virtue and in knowledge of divine and human things may and ought to counsel and direct us on the right path, but without a monopoly of power or any class supremacy; and that the right of communion is equal for all.   What is holy in heaven is holy on earth.   And the communion of men in God brings as its consequence the association of men in the earthly life.   From the religious association of souls springs the right of association in the faculties and works which convert *thought* into *reality*.

Consider Association, then, as your duty and your right.

Some who would limit the citizen's right to association will tell you that the true association is the State, the Nation ; that you are and ought to be all members of it, and that therefore any partial association between you is either adverse to the State, or superfluous.

But the State, the Nation, only represents the association of the citizens in those things and those aims which are common to *all* the men who compose it.   There exist aims and ends which do not embrace *all* the citizens, but only a certain number of them.   And as the aims and ends common to all constitute the Nation, so the aims and ends common to *some* of the citizens ought to constitute the *special* association.

Moreover—and this is the fundamental basis of the right of association—association is the guarantee of Progress.   The State represents a certain sum and set of principles in which the universal body of citizens are agreed at the time of its foundation.   Suppose that a new and true principle, a new and reasonable development of the truths which give life to the State, is revealed to some of the citizens ; how can they spread the knowledge of it without association ?   Suppose that in consequence of scientific discoveries, of new communications opened between one people and another, or from some other cause, a *new* interest becomes apparent to a certain number of men belonging to the State ; how can those who are first aware of it make a place for it among the long-existing interests, except by uniting their individual means and strength ?   Inertia and content with the condition of things already existing and sanctioned by the common consent of mankind are habits of mind too natural in men to allow a single individual to shake them and overcome them. But the association of a minority which grows every day can do it. Association is the method of the future. Without it the State would remain stationary, enchained to the degree of civilisation already reached.

The object of association should be *progressive*, not *contrary* to the truths established for ever by the universal agreement of Humanity and of the Nation. An association instituted for the purpose of facilitating the robbery of other people's property, an association which makes polygamy obligatory on its members, an association which preaches the dissolution of the Nation or the establishment of Despotism, would be illegal. The Nation has a right to say to its members : " We cannot tolerate the spread of doctrines in our midst which violate that which constitutes human nature, Morality, or the Country. Go forth and establish among yourselves, beyond our confines, the association which your tendencies suggest.

Association must be peaceful. It ought to have no other arms than the written or spoken Word. Its purpose must be to persuade, not to compel.

Association must be *public*. Secret associations are weapons of lawful warfare when Liberty and Country do not exist, but are unlawful and may be dissolved by the Nation when Liberty is a recognised right and the Country protects the development and inviolability of thought. Even as association ought to open the way to Progress, so it ought also to be subject to the examination and judgment of all.

And finally association must respect in others the rights which spring from the essential conditions of human nature. An association which, like the mediæval corporations, should violate the liberty of labour, or should tend directly to restrict liberty of conscience, might justifiably be repressed by the Nation through its government.

Outside these limits liberty of association among citizens is as sacred and inviolable as Progress, to which it gives life. Any government which should attempt to restrict it would betray its social mission; it would be the *duty* of the people, first to warn it, and, when all pacific means had been exhausted, to overthrow it.

And these, O my Brothers, are the principal grounds upon which your Duties are based, the sources from which your Rights spring. An infinite number of special questions may arise in your civil life; but it is not the scope of this work to foresee, or help you to solve, them. The sole intention of my work is to point out to you the *principles* which, like torches for your path, should guide you in dealing with these questions, and which, if sincerely applied, will always supply you with a means of solving them. And this, I think, I have done.

I have pointed to God as the source and pledge of equality among men; to the moral law as the source of every *civil* law, and the standard by which you must judge the conduct of those who make the laws; to the people, to you, ourselves, the universal body of citizens who form the nation, as the sole legitimate interpreter of the law, and the source of all political power.

I have told you that the fundamental character of the law is Progress; progress unlimited and continuous from age to age; progress in every branch of human activity, in every manifestation of thought, from religion down to industry and the distribution of wealth.

I have pointed out to you what your *duties* are to Humanity, to the Country, to the Family, and to yourselves. And I have deduced these duties from the characters which constitute the *human* creature, and which you are under an obligation to develop. These characters, inviolable in every man, are: liberty, capability of education, social tendencies, capacity, and the necessity of progressing. And from these essential characters, without which a human being is neither a man nor a citizen, I have deduced your duties, your rights, and the general nature of the government which you ought to seek for your country. Do not ever forget

these principles. Keep watch so that they may never
be violated. Incarnate them in yourselves, and you will
be free and will progress.

The work which I have undertaken for you would,
then, be complete, if a tremendous obstacle to your
fulfilment of these duties and the exercise of these rights
did not arise out of the very heart of society as it is now
constituted; namely, the inequality of *means*.

For the fulfilment of duties, and for the exercise of
rights, three things are necessary: time, intellectual
development, and an assured material existence.

Now, very many of you in the present day do not
possess these elements of progress. Their life is a
constant and uncertain struggle to gain the means of
sustaining material existence; it is not a question for
them of *progressing*, but of *living*.

There exists, then, a profound and radical evil in
society as it is organised to-day. And my work would
be useless if I did not define this evil, and point out to
you the way to correct it.

The *Economic* question will therefore be the subject of
the final portion of my work.

XI

I

MANY, too many of you, are poor. For three-fourths at least of the men who belong to the working-classes, whether agricultural or industrial, life is a daily struggle to gain the means indispensable to existence. They work with their hands ten, twelve, sometimes fourteen hours a day, and yet by this assiduous, monotonous, severe labour they barely earn the necessaries of *physical* existence. To point out to them the duty of progress, to speak to them of intellectual and moral life, of political rights, of education, is, in the actual state of society, sheer irony. They have neither the *time* nor the *means* for progress. Worn out, exhausted, half-stupefied by a life spent in a round of petty mechanical toils, they learn in it a dumb, impotent, often unjust rancour against the class of men who employ them ; they seek forgetfulness of their present sufferings and of the uncertainty of the morrow in the excitement of strong drink, and lay themselves down to rest in places more fitly described as dens than as rooms, to awake next day to the same dull exercise of their physical powers.

This is a terrible condition, and it must be altered.

You are *men*, and as such you have faculties, not only physical, but intellectual and moral, which it is your duty to develop ; you ought to be *citizens*, and as such you ought to exercise for the general benefit rights which demand a certain degree of education and a certain amount of time.

It is clear that you ought to work *less* and earn *more* than you do to-day.

We who are all sons of God and brothers in Him one to another are called to form one single large family. In this family there may exist inequalities resulting from different aptitudes, different capacities, inclination to different kinds of work. But one principle ought to rule it. *Whoever is willing to give for the good of all that much of work of which he is capable ought to obtain enough recompense to enable him to develop his own special life more or less in all the aspects which define it as human.*

This is the *ideal* which we ought to study how to approach more nearly from century to century. Every change, every revolution, which does not bring us one step nearer to it, which does not achieve a *social* advance in correspondence with the *political* advance, which does not further by one degree the material improvement of the poorer classes, violates God's design, and debases itself to a war of factions, each seeking unlawful dominion; it is a lie and an evil.

But how far can we realise this ideal to-day? And *how* and by what means can we realise it?

Some of your more timid friends have sought the remedy in the *morality* of the working-man himself. Founding savings-banks or other like institutions, they have said to the working-men; *Bring your wages here; save; abstain from all excess in drink and other things; free yourselves from want by self-denial.* And these are excellent counsels, since they seek the moral reform of the working-man, without which all reforms would be useless. But they do not solve the question of poverty, nor do they take any account of *social* duty. Very few of you *can* save anything out of your wages. And those very few can only by slow and patient accumulation provide in part for their old age. But economic reform must have in view provision for the period of manhood, for the development and full expansion of *life* when it is active and strong and can help efficaciously towards the progress of the Country

and of Humanity.   With regard to material welfare, the
question is how to *increase* wealth and production ; and
the counsels of which I have spoken do not indicate
how this is to be done either.   Moreover society, which
lives by the labour of the sons of the people and
demands of them a tribute of blood whenever danger
threatens it, has a sacred debt towards them.   Other
thinkers there are, not enemies of the people, but only
indifferent to them and to the cry of suffering which
rises from the hearts of the men of labour, and fearful
of any important innovation.   These, attached to a so-
called school of *economists* who fought meritoriously and
successfully all the battles for liberty of industry, but
without taking into consideration the necessity of *progress*
and of *association* as inseparable from human nature,
maintained, and still maintain, like the philanthropists
of whom I have just spoken, that every one can, even
in actual conditions, build up his own independence
by his own activity.   They declare that any change
in the system of labour would turn out superfluous
or harmful, and that the formula *Every one for himself
and liberty for all* is sufficient to create little by little
an approximate equilibrium of ease and comfort among
the classes that constitute society.   Freedom of internal
trade, freedom of commerce among the nations, a gradual
reduction of custom duties, especially upon raw materials,
general encouragement given to great industrial enterprises, to the multiplication of ways of communication
and to all machinery that increases production—this
is as much as society can do according to the economists ; any further intervention on its part would be,
according to them, a source of evil.

   If they were right the disease of poverty would be
incurable ; and God forbid, O my Brothers, that I
should ever be persuaded to agree with them, and fling
as an answer to your sufferings and your aspirations
this despairing, atheistical, immoral conclusion.   God
has decreed for you a better future than that contained
in the remedies of the economists.

   These remedies only aim, in fact, at a possible and

temporary increase in the *production* of wealth, not at
its more equal *distribution*. While the *philanthropists*
contemplate the *man* alone, and endeavour to make
him more moral without troubling themselves to increase
the general wealth by giving him any opportunity of
improving his material conditions, the *economists* think
only of increasing the sources of *production* without
concerning themselves about the *man*. Under the
exclusive régime of liberty which they preach, and which
has more or less regulated the economic world in the
times nearest to us, the most unimpeachable documentary
evidence shows us an increase of productive activity
and of capital, but not of universally diffused prosperity.
The poverty of the working-classes remains unchanged.
Freedom of competition for those who possess nothing,
for those who are unable to save anything from their
daily wages, and therefore have nothing with which to
start any commercial undertaking, is a lie, just as political
freedom is a lie for those who from want of education,
instruction, opportunities, and time cannot exercise its
rights. Increased facilities of trade, improvements in
the means of distribution and exchange, might little by
little emancipate labour from the commercial tyranny
of the intermediate class between the producer and
consumer; but cannot avail to emancipate it from the
tyranny of *capital*, or give the means of labour to those
who lack them. And for want of an equal distribution
of wealth, a juster division of products, and a progressive
increase in the number of consumers, capital itself is
diverted from its true economic purpose, and remains
in part stationary in the hands of a few instead of
spreading itself wholly in circulation. It is used for
the production of superfluous objects and luxuries, and
for the satisfaction of fictitious needs, instead of being
concentrated on the production of objects of first
necessity for existence, and is risked in perilous and
often immoral speculations.

In the present day *capital*—and this is the curse of
our actual economic society—is the despot of labour.
The three classes which to-day form society in its

economic sense are—*capitalists*, that is, the possessors of the means and implements of labour, namely, lands, factories, ready money, and raw material; *contractors*, that is, the heads and initiators of labour, commercial men, who represent or ought to represent intellect; and *working-men*, who represent manual labour. Of these the first class only is master of the field; it is his to promote, delay, or accelerate the labour at will, and to direct it towards certain ends. And his share in the profits of the work and the value of the production is comparatively determined; the location of the instruments of labour does not vary except within known and narrow limits; and time up to a certain point at least is his since he is not under the domination of absolute want. The share of the second is uncertain; it is dependent on their intellect and activity, but particularly on circumstances, on the greater and less development of competition, and on the flow and ebb of capital in consequence of events out of the reach of calculation. The share of the last class, the *working-men*, is a wage determined before the work is done, and without regard to the greater and lesser profits which result from the enterprise; and the limits within which the wage varies are determined by the relation which exists between the labour *offered* and the labour *required*—in other words, between the working population and the *capital*. Now, as the former tends to increase, and to an extent which generally surpasses, even if by only a little, the increase of the latter, wages tend, where other causes do not intervene, to decrease. And time is not in the hands of the working-man. Financial and political crises, the sudden application of new machinery to different branches of industrial activity, irregularities in production, and its frequent excessive accumulation in a single direction—an evil inseparable from a short-sighted competition—the unequal distribution of the labouring population on certain points and in certain branches of activity, and many other causes disturbing to labour deprive the working-man of the free choice of his conditions. His alternatives are absolute want, or the acceptance of any terms which may be offered to him.

Such a state of things, I repeat, contains the germs of a malady which must be cured. But the remedies proposed by the *economists* are ineffectual for this purpose.

And nevertheless, there is a progress in the condition of the classes to which you belong; an historical, continuous progress, which has overcome very different obstacles. You were once *slaves*; then you were *serfs*; now you are *wage-earners*. You have freed yourselves from slavery, from serfdom; why should you not free yourselves from the yoke of *wages*, and become free producers, master of the whole value of what you produce? Why should you not by your own doing and the assistance of society, which has sacred duties towards its members, peacefully accomplish the greatest and most beautiful revolution that can be conceived—a revolution which should make labour the economic basis of human fellowship, the fruits of labour the basis of property, and should thus gather together under one single law of equilibrium between production and consumption, without distinction of classes, and without the tyrannic predominance of one of the elements of labour over another, all the children of our common Mother, our Country?

II

A sense of social duty towards the working-classes, such as I have been pointing out, had been slowly growing in men's minds—thanks chiefly to the republican propaganda—and thus insuring the popular revolution of the future, when in the last thirty years certain schools of thinkers arose, in France especially, mostly good men and friends of the people, but carried away by an excessive love of system and by individual vanity. Under the name of *socialism* these men introduced exclusive and exaggerated doctrines, often antagonistic to the wealth already gained by other classes, and economically impossible. By terrifying the masses of the lower middle-class, and producing distrust between the different orders of citizens, they threw the social question into the background and split up the republican camp in two. In France the first effect of this distrust and terror was a more easy triumph for the *coup d'état*.

I cannot now examine one by one with you these different systems, which were called Sansimonism, Fourierism, Communism, or some other name. Founded almost all of them upon *ideas* good in themselves and accepted by all who belong to the Faith of Progress, their promulgators spoiled or frustrated them by the false or tyrannic methods by which they proposed to apply them. And it is necessary that I should briefly point out to you in what their errors consisted, because the promises held out to the people by these systems are so dazzling that they might easily allure you, and you would run a risk by embracing them of retarding that future emancipation which you will certainly obtain, and before long. It is true—and this should be enough to awaken a strong doubt in your minds—that when circumstances called any of these men to power they did not even attempt a practical application of their own doctrines ; giants of audacity in their writings, they retreated when confronted by the reality of things.

If you examine these systems attentively some day and remember the fundamental ideas which I have been pointing out to you, and the characters inseparable from human nature, you will find that they all violate the Law of Progress, the manner in which this is fulfilled in humanity, and one or other of the faculties which form the Man.

Progress is accomplished step by step, through laws which no human power can break, by *development*, by the perpetual *modification* of the elements which manifest the activity of life. Men have often in certain epochs, in certain countries, and under the influence of certain prejudices and certain errors, given the name of elements, of conditions of social life, to things which have no root in nature, but only in the conventions and customs of a mistaken society, and which disappear after that particular epoch or beyond the boundaries of those particular countries. But you can discover what are the true elements inseparable from human nature, by interrogating—as I told you elsewhere—the instincts of your souls and then testing by the traditions of all ages and of all countries these instincts of yours, whether they be such as have been always the instincts of Humanity. And those things which an inborn voice (and the great voice of Humanity) indicates as constituent elements of life have to be modified, and developed continuously from epoch to epoch, but can never be abolished.

Among these elements of human life, besides religion, liberty, association and others mentioned in the course of this work, property is also one.

The *principle*, the origin, of property is rooted in human nature itself, and represents the necessities of that material life which it is the duty of the individual to maintain. As by means of religion, science, liberty, the *individual* is called to transform, to improve, and to govern the *moral* and *intellectual* world, so also he is called to transform, to improve, and to govern the *physical* world by means of material *labour*. And property is the *token* of the fulfilment of that mission and represents the amount of *work* by which the individual has transformed, developed, and increased the productive forces of nature.

Property is therefore eternal in its *principle*, and you find it existing and protected throughout the whole existence of Humanity. But the methods by which property is governed are subject to change, and destined, like every other manifestation of human life, to obey the law of Progress. Those who, finding property already established in a particular form, declare that form to be inviolable and oppose all attempts to transform it, deny Progress itself; one need only open two volumes of history dealing with two different epochs, to find in both a change in the constitution of property. And those who, because they find it badly constituted at a certain epoch, declare that it must be abolished, and wiped out of the social system, deny an element of human nature; and could they ever have their way they would only succeed in retarding Progress by mutilating Life. Property would inevitably reappear a short time after and probably in the same form which it had at the time of its abolition.

Property is badly constituted at the present day because its actual distribution originated, generally speaking, in conquest; in the violence by which in remote times certain invading peoples possessed themselves of lands and fruits of labour not their own. Property is badly constituted because the basis of the division between proprietor and workmen of the fruits of a work accomplished by both together does not rest upon a just and equal rate, proportioned to the work itself. Property is badly constituted because by conferring on those who possess it political and legislative rights which are denied to the working-men, it tends to be the monopoly of a few and inaccessible to the greater number. Property is badly constituted because the system of taxation is badly constituted and tends to maintain a privilege of wealth in the proprietor, while oppressing the poorer classes and depriving them of every possibility of saving. But if, instead of correcting evils and slowly modifying the constitution of property, you sought to abolish it, you would suppress a source of wealth, of emulation, and of activity, and you would be like the savage who to gather the fruit cuts down the tree.

It is not necessary to abolish property because only a *few* possess it now ; but the way must be opened for the many to acquire it.

We must go back to the *principle* which makes it legitimate, and so arrange that *labour* alone shall be able to produce it.

Society must be directed towards a more equable basis of remuneration between the proprietor or capitalist and the working-man.

The system of taxation must be altered, so that it shall not touch incomes which only suffice for existence and shall leave the poor man the power of accumulating savings and of thus gradually acquiring property. And to bring this to pass, the privileges conceded to property must be suppressed and *all* must be allowed to contribute to the work of legislation.

Now, all these things are possible and just. By educating yourselves and organising yourselves to demand them insistently and to resolve to have them, you could obtain them; but by seeking the abolition of property you would seek an impossibility, you would do an injustice to those who have gained it by their own labour, and you would diminish production instead of increasing it.

III

The abolition of individual property is nevertheless the remedy proposed by many of the *socialistic* systems of which I am speaking, and especially by Communism. Others go further; and finding the religious conception, the conception of government, and the conception of country falsified by religious errors, by class privilege, and by the egoism of dynasties, they demand the abolition of all religion, all government, and all nationality. This is the proceeding of children or of barbarians. Would it not be as reasonable, since maladies are often engendered by corrupt air, to seek the suppression of every respirable gas?

But you need no confutation from me of the error of those who in the name of liberty wish to found *anarchy* and to abolish *society* so as to leave only the *individual* and his rights. My whole work is directed against that wicked dream, which denies progress, duties, human brotherhood, the solidarity of nations, everything that you and I venerate. But the design of those who, confining themselves to the economic question, demand the abolition of individual property and the establishment of communism, touches the opposite extreme, denies the *individual*, denies *liberty*, closes the way to progress, and, so to speak, petrifies society.

The general formula of communism is as follows: the possession of all the means of production, that is, lands, capital, machinery, and all instruments of labour, etc., shall be concentrated in the State; the State shall assign his share of work to each, and shall adjust the recompense, some say, with absolute equality, and others say in proportion to his needs. Such an existence, were it possible, would be a life of beavers, not of men. The liberty, the dignity, the conscience of the individual would all disappear in an organisation of productive machines. Physical life might be satisfied by it, but moral and intellectual life would perish, and with it emulation, free choice of work, free association, stimulus to production, joys of property, and all incentives to progress. Under such a system the human family would become a herd needing nothing more than to be led to a sufficient pasture. Which of you would resign himself to such a system?

Equality is thus secured, they say. How?

Equality in the distribution of labour? It is impossible. Work is of different kinds, and cannot be reckoned by its duration or by the amount performed in an hour; but by the difficulty, by the lesser or greater unpleasantness of the work, by the expenditure of vitality which it involves, by the benefit which it confers on society. How can you reckon the equality between an hour passed in a coal mine, or in purifying the corrupt water of a marsh, and an hour spent in a spinning factory? The impossibility of such a calculation has suggested to some of the founders of these systems the idea of making every one perform in turn a certain amount of labour in every branch of useful industry; an absurd remedy which would make good production impossible, while it could not succeed in suppressing the inequality between the weak and the strong, between the man of intellectual capacity and one slow of intellect, between the man of lymphatic temperament and the man of nervous temperament. Work easy and agreeable to one is laborious and difficult to another.

Equality in the distribution of products? It is impossible. Either equality would have to be absolute and would constitute an immense injustice, as it would not distinguish between the different needs resulting from difference of organism, nor between the powers and capacities acquired from a sense of duty, and those received, without any merit, from nature. Or else the inequality must be relative and calculated according to different needs ; and not taking account of individual production, it would violate those rights of property which ought to belong to the labourer as the fruit of his labour.

Then who would be the judge to decide upon the needs of every individual ? The State ?

Working-men, my Brothers, are you disposed to accept a hierarchy of lords and masters of the common property —masters of the mind in consequence of an exclusive education, masters of the body from possessing the power of *determining* your work, your capacity, and your needs ? Is not this a return to ancient slavery ? Would not these masters, representing such great interests, be carried away by the theory of *interests* and be seduced by the immense power concentrated in their hands into founding again the hereditary dictatorship of the ancient castes ?

No ; communism would not produce equality among the men of labour ; it would not increase production— which is the great necessity of the present day—because as soon as the means of life are secured human nature —in the average man at least—is satisfied and the incentive to an increase of production, to be diffused among all the members of society, becomes so small that it is not enough to stimulate his faculties ;[1] production would not be improved ; there would be no incitement to progress in invention ; nor could progress ever be assisted by the uncertain and unintelligent collective direction of the general organisation. For the evils which afflict the sons of the people the only remedy of Communism is protection from hunger. Now, cannot this be done, cannot the working-man's right to life and to work be secured without upsetting the

[1] It has been calculated that if, in a hundred thousand workmen, one workman should produce a hundred francs' worth in the year more than the average production, he would receive for himself a thousandth part of a franc every year, three centimes every thirty years. Who can call this a spur to production ?

whole social order, without rendering production sterile, impeding progress, abolishing the liberty of the individual, and chaining him down in a tyrannic organisation ?

IV

The remedy for your present condition cannot be found in any arbitrary general organisation built up according to the plan of some particular mind, contradicting the universally adopted bases of civil existence and established all at once by means of decrees. We are not here below to create Humanity, but to continue it ; we can and we must modify its constituent elements and order them better, but we cannot suppress them. Humanity rebels and always will rebel against any such attempt. Time spent over these illusions would therefore be time wasted. Nor can the remedy be found in an increase of wages imposed by the governing authority without other changes which would increase capital. An increase in the money spent on wages—that is, an increase in the cost of production—would involve a rise in the price of products, a diminution of consumption, and consequently less employment for the working-man.

It is not to be found in anything that would annul *liberty*—consecration of labour and spur to effort ; nor in anything which would diminish capital—instrument of labour and of production.

The remedy for your present condition is the *union of capital and labour in the same hands.*

When Society shall recognise no distinction beyond that of *producers and consumers*, or rather when every man shall be a *producer* and a *consumer*—when the entire fruits of labour, instead of being distributed between that series of middle-men who, beginning with the capitalist and descending to the retail seller, often heighten the price of the product 50 per cent., shall be retained by labour—the *permanent* causes of poverty will disappear from your midst. Your future lies in your emancipation from the exactions of capital, arbiter to-day of a production in which it has no actual share.

I speak of your *material* and *moral* future. Look round you. Wherever you find *capital* and *labour* united in the same hands—wherever the profits of labour are divided between all who labour, in proportion to the increase of those profits and to the amount by which each workman has helped in the collective work—you find a decrease of poverty and at the same time an increase of morality. In the Canton of Zurich, in the Engadine, and in many other parts of Switzerland where the peasant is the proprietor, and land, capital, and labour are united in the same individual—in Norway, in Flanders, in Eastern Frisia, in Holstein in the German Palatinate, in Belgium, in the Island of Guernsey on the English coast—there may be seen a prosperity comparatively superior to that of all the other parts of Europe where the land does not belong to the cultivator. A race of husbandmen noted for honesty, dignity, and independence, and for their frank and sincere manners, people these countries. The habits of the miners of Cornwall in England and of the American whalers who trade with China, among whom participation in the profits of the enterprise obtains, are recognised by official documents to be better than those of workers subject to the system of payment by a predetermined rate of wages.

Association of labour, division of the profits of labour—that is, of the profits resulting from the sale of the products—among the labourers, in proportion to the amount and the value of the work accomplished : this is the social future. In this is contained the secret of your emancipation. You were *slaves* once ; then *serfs* ; then *wage-earners* ; before long you shall be, if you will it, free producers and brothers in *Association*.

Association, free and voluntary, and organised on certain bases by yourselves, among men who know, love, and esteem one another; not compulsory association, imposed by the governing authority and ordered without regard for individual affections and ties, and treating men as so many machines for production, rather than as beings of free and spontaneous will.

Association administered in a spirit of republican

brotherhood by your own delegates and from which you shall be able to withdraw yourselves if you wish ; not subject to the despotism of the State and of a hierarchy arbitrarily constituted and ignorant of your needs and aptitudes.

Association of *groups* formed according to your own tendencies, not, as the authors of the systems to which I have called your attention would have, of all the men belonging to a given branch of industrial or agricultural activity.

The concentration of *all* the individuals in the State, or even in a single city, engaged in the same craft, in one *single* productive society, would lead again to the old tyrannical monopoly of the Corporations. It would make the producer arbiter of prices to the injury of the consumer, would give a legal form to the oppression of minorities, would deprive a dissatisfied workman of every possibility of getting work, and would suppress the necessity of progress by extinguishing all rivalry in work, all stimulus to invention.

Association has been attempted in the last twenty years, first timidly and in unfavourable circumstances in France, then in England and in Belgium, and has been crowned with success wherever it was undertaken with energy, resolve, and the spirit of self-sacrifice. It contains the secret of an entire social transformation, a transformation which, in virtue of your traditions and of the initiative in social progress which you have always possessed, should be accomplished first in Italy. And this transformation, emancipating you from the slavery of wages, would at the same time give new life to production, to the advantage of all classes, and would improve the economic condition of the country. Under the present system the aim of the capitalist is usually to amass as much wealth as he can in order to retire from the arena of work ; under the system of *association* you would tend instead to secure the *continuity* of work, that is, of production. At present the head, the director of the work, who owes his fortune not to any special aptitude, but to his possession of capital, is often improvident, rash, or incapable; an association directed by delegates, watched over by all its members, would not run any risks from such defects. To-day labour is often directed towards the production of *superfluities*, not *necessaries*; in consequence of capricious and unjust inequality in the payment workers abound in one branch of activity and are wanting in another; the working-man limited to a *fixed* wage has no motive for devoting to his work all the zeal of which he is capable and all the activity with which he might increase or improve his output. Association, it is evident, would remedy this and other causes of irregularity and of inferiority in production.

Liberty to withdraw oneself, without doing harm to the *association*; equality of all members in the election of an executive appointed for a given time—or better, subject to removal; freedom of admission, subsequently to the foundation of the association, without the obligation of putting in capital, but with permission to supply it, for the good of the common fund, by a deduction from the profits of the first years; *indivisibility and perpetuity of the collective capital*; remuneration for all, equal to the *necessities* of life; distribution of the tools and instruments of labour, according to the quantity and quality of each one's work,—these are the general principles upon which you must found your associations if you are willing to do a work involving present sacrifice but future gain for the class to which you belong. Each of these principles, that especially which concerns the perpetuity of collective capital—the pledge of your emancipation and your link with future generations—needs a chapter to itself. But a special study of working-men's associations does not enter into the plan of my present work. Perhaps if God allows me yet a few years of life I shall do it separately, out of my love for you. Meanwhile be sure that these rules which I have laid down for you here are the fruit of deep and earnest study, and deserve your attentive consideration.

But the capital? The capital with which to start the *association*; where is it to come from?

This is a grave question; and I cannot treat of it here as I should wish. But I will point out to you briefly your own duty and the duty of others.

The primary source of that capital must be in yourselves, in your savings, in your spirit of self-sacrifice. I know the position of most of you; but to some the good fortune of regular or better-paid employment affords the possibility of collecting, by the careful economy of eighteen or twenty combined together, the small sum sufficient for starting the work on your own account. And the consciousness of fulfilling a solemn duty and of deserving your desired emancipation ought to sustain you in this economy. I could tell you of industrial associations, now financially powerful, which were started here in England by the payment of a penny a day by a certain number of working-men. I could repeat to you many stories of sacrifice heroically endured in France and elsewhere by bands of working-men, who are now possessors of considerable capital.[1] There is scarcely any difficulty which a firm will, sustained by the

---

[1] In the year 1848 the delegates of some hundreds of working-men who had united for the purpose of founding an Association for the manufacture of pianofortes were led by the want of the large capital necessary for the undertaking to ask the Government for a subvention of 300,000 francs. The Government Commission refused to grant it. The Association broke up, but fourteen of the working-men decided to defy every obstacle and to re-establish it by their own unaided efforts. They had neither money nor credit; they had faith.

A few of them brought to the new Society materials and tools to the value of about 2,000 francs. But a floating capital was indispensable. Each of the associates contributed, not without difficulty, ten francs. A few working-men who had no direct interest in the Society added their small offerings to this slender capital. And on March 10, 1849, the sum of 229 francs and 50 centimes having been collected, the Association was declared constituted.

This common fund was barely sufficient for the start, and for the small daily expenses indispensable to a manufacturing business. Nothing remained for wages, and more than two months passed without the workers receiving a single halfpenny of pay. How did they live during this critical time? As working-men do live during interruptions of work, helped by the working-man who is fortunate enough to have work—selling, pawning one by one their household goods and utensils.

Some work having been executed, the price was paid on May 4, 1849. That day was for the Association what a victory is at the beginning of a war; and they celebrated it. When the debts had been paid, and the money owed them collected, there remained for every member the sum of 6 francs and 61 centimes. It was agreed that each should keep 5 francs as wages and devote the rest to a fraternal dinner. The fourteen members,

consciousness of doing good, may not overcome. Each
of you might contribute by means of your savings a
little something to the small primary fund, in money or
in material or in implements. You might be able, if
your conduct were such as to win confidence and
esteem, to collect small loans from relations or fellow
workmen, who would become merely shareholders in the
association, and would not receive interest on their loans
except on the profits of the enterprise. In many of your
industries, in which the price of the raw material is very
little, the capital required to start work independently is
inconsiderable. If you are determined to get it you will
find a way. And it will be better for you if the formation of this small capital is all your own, gained by the
sweat of your brow, or through the credit which you
have acquired by working well. As those nations best
preserve freedom who have conquered it with their blood,
so your associations will draw a larger and *steadier*
profit from the capital collected by long hours of work
and by economy than from that derived from any other
source. This is the nature of things. The Working-men's

most of whom had not tasted wine for a year, met together with their
families at a common feast, the cost of which was 16*d*. per family.
For a whole month yet, the wages were not more than 5 francs a week.
In June a baker, a music-lover or speculator, proposed to buy a piano and
pay for it in bread. The proposal was accepted and the price agreed on at
the rate of 480 francs. This was good fortune for the Association, which
was now sure of having at least the first necessary of life. The value of
the bread was not calculated in the wages. Each had as much as he wanted,
and for the married ones as much as their families needed.
Little by little the Association, composed of very capable workmen, over-
came all the obstacles and privations which it had had to encounter in the first
period. Its books present the best testimony of the progress made For
the month of August, 1849, the weekly earnings of each man rose to 10, 15,
20 francs, and this sum did not represent the whole profits ; every member
paid into the common fund a larger sum than he kept.
The books of the Society on December 30, 1850, gave the following
results. There were 32 members at this time. The establishment paid a
rent of 2,000 francs, and the premises were already too small for the work.

Value of tools and plant, 5,922 francs 60 cents.
Goods and raw material, 22,972 francs 28 cents.
In hand, notes for 3,540 francs.
Outstanding credits, nearly all good, 5,861 francs 90 cents.

The balance therefore was 39,317 francs 88 cents. Out of this the Society
only owed 4,737 francs 80 cents to a few creditors, and 1,650 francs to eighty
friendly working-men of the same trade who had made loans to the
Association in the first period. Actual balance, 32,950 francs 2 cents.
The Association has continued to flourish ever since.

Associations, founded in Paris in 1848 with the aid of Government subsidies, prospered very much less than those which formed their original capital by their own sacrifices.

But although I counsel you to self-sacrifice because I love you truly and do not with servile adulation flatter or make light of any possible weaknesses in you, that does not lessen the duty of others. The men whom circumstances have provided with wealth must understand this ; they must understand that emancipation is a part of the Providential Design, and that it will be inevitably accomplished, either with them or against them. Many of these men, and especially those of republican faith, do understand this ; and among these, if you give them proofs of determined will and honest intelligence, you will find help in your enterprises. They can—and as soon as they perceive that the desire for association is not the caprice of an hour, but the faith of a majority among you, they will—give you facilities for obtaining credit, either by advances, or by founding banks which will give credit on the security of the future work of a collective body of working-men, or perhaps by admitting you to a share in the profits of their undertakings, an intermediate stage between the present and the future by which you might be able to obtain the small amount of capital necessary for an independent association. In Belgium more than elsewhere institutions such as I have described already exist under the name of *Banks of Anticipation*, or of *People's Banks*. In Scotland many banks will give credit to any man of known probity who pledges his honour and offers as his security another man of equally proved honesty. And the admission of the workmen to a share in the profits is a plan adopted with singular success by several employers.

XII

CONCLUSION

BUT the State, the Government—an institution legitimate only when founded upon a mission of *education*
and of progress not yet understood—has a solemn debt
towards you, a debt which it will easily fulfil if ever there
is a really National Government, the Government of a free
and united People. The Government will then be able
to bestow assistance of many kinds upon the People, which
will solve the social problem without spoliation, without
violence, without laying hands on the wealth previously
acquired by the citizens, without rousing that antagonism
between class and class which is unjust, immoral, and
fatal to the nation and which visibly retards the progress
of the French in the present day.

Powerful assistance might be given in the following
ways :—

The exercise of moral influence in favour of the
associations by the publicly manifested approval of the
Government agents, by frequent discussion of their
fundamental principle in the Representative Assembly,
and by legislation granted to all voluntary associations
formed upon the basis described above.

Improvement in ways of communication and abolition
of whatever now hinders the free transport of produce.

The institution of public storehouses and depôts, which
when the approximate value of the consigned goods had
been ascertained would grant to the associations a document
or bond similar to a bank bill and admissible for circulation and discount, so as to make it possible for the
association to continue its work without being strangled
by the necessity of an immediate sale at any price.

The concession of public works to the associations upon the same terms as those granted to individual enterprise.

Simplification of judicial forms, which in the present day are ruinous and often inaccessible to the poor man.

Legislative facilities granted for the sale and transfer of landed property.

A radical change in the system of taxation by the substitution of a single tax on incomes for the present complicated and costly system of direct and indirect taxation. And sanction given to the principle that *life is sacred*; and that since without life neither work, nor progress, nor fulfilment of duties is possible, taxation must not begin until an income exceeds the sum of money *necessary* for the maintenance of life.

But there are other means. The secularisation or appropriation of ecclesiastic possessions—a step which there is no advantage in discussing now, but which is inevitable when once the nation assumes a mission of education and of collective progress—will place in the hands of the State a vast sum of wealth. Now suppose that to this is added the value represented by land fertile and capable of cultivation, but hitherto unreclaimed, the value represented by the profits of the railways and of other public undertakings, of which the administration should be centred in the State: the value represented by the landed property belonging to the Communes,[1] the value represented by *collateral* inheritances, which beyond the fourth degree ought to revert to the State, and the value of other sources of wealth which it is unnecessary to enumerate. Suppose that with all this immense accumulation of wealth a NATIONAL FUND was formed, to be consecrated to the intellectual and economic progress of the whole country. Why should not a considerable part of this fund be transformed, with the necessary precautions to prevent its being squandered,

[1] This property belongs *legally* to the Commune, *morally* to the needy members of the Commune. It is not meant that it should be taken from the Communes, but that it should be consecrated to the poor of each commune by being constituted under the direction of elective Communal Councils the inalienable *capital* of agricultural Associations.

into a fund of credit, to be distributed at a rate of
interest of one and a half or of two per cent. to the
voluntary working-men's associations, formed according
to the principles indicated above and offering the security
of *morality* and of *capacity* ?   That capital ought to be
sacred to the work of the future also and not of a single
generation only.   But the vast scale of the operations
would ensure compensation for inevitable losses from
time to time.

The distribution of this *credit* ought to be carried out,
not by the Government nor by a Central National Bank,
but by *local Banks administered by elective Communal
Councils* and with the supervision of the Central Government.   Without lessening the actual wealth of the
various classes, and without allowing one class alone to
monopolise the revenue from the taxation which is levied on
all the citizens, and ought therefore to be devoted to the
benefit of *all*, the series of measures suggested here, by
diffusing credit, increasing and improving production, compelling a graduated diminution in the rate of interest and
trusting to the zeal and the interest of all the producers
to insure the progress and continuity of work, would
replace the limited sum of wealth now concentrated in a
few hands and ill-directed, by the rich *nation*, manager of
its own production and its own consumption.   And this,
Italian Working-men, is your future.   You can hasten it.
Win your Country !   Establish a popular Government
which shall represent its collective life, its mission, its
thought.   Organise yourselves in a vast universal League
of the People, so that your voice shall be *the voice of
millions and not of a few individuals only*.   You have
Truth and Justice on your side : the Nation will listen
to you.

But beware !   Believe the words of a man who has
studied for thirty years the course of events in Europe,
and has seen the holiest and most useful enterprises fail,
at the moment of success, through the immorality of
men : you will not succeed except by *growing better yourselves* ; you will not win the exercise of your rights except
by *deserving* them, through self-sacrifice, industry, and

love. If you seek them in the name of a duty fulfilled
or to be fulfilled, you will obtain them, but if you seek
them in the name of egoism or of some right to *well-
being* taught you by materialists, you will only achieve
momentary triumphs, followed by tremendous disillusionments. Those who speak to you in the name of
well-being, of material happiness, will betray you. They
also seek their own well-being, and to obtain it they will
unite with you, as with an element of strength, while they
have obstacles to overcome ; but as soon as they have
obtained well-being by your aid, they will abandon you
that they may enjoy their acquisition in tranquillity. This
is the history of the last half-century, and the name of
this half-century is *materialism*.

And it is a history of sorrow and of blood. I have
seen them—the men who denied God, religion, the
virtue of duty and of self-sacrifice, and spoke only in the
name of the right to *happiness* and *enjoyment*—fighting
boldly with the words People and Liberty on their lips,
and mingling themselves with us men of the new faith,
who rashly received them into our ranks. As soon as an
opportunity was offered to them, through a victory or a
cowardly compromise, of securing comfort and pleasure
for themselves, they deserted us, and became our bitter
enemies the day after. A very few years of danger and
privation were enough to weary them. Being unconscious
of a law of duty, and without faith in a mission imposed
upon men by a Power supreme over all, why should
they have persisted in sacrifice until the end of life ?
And with deep grief I have seen the sons of the people,
who had been educated in materialism by such philosophers as these, prove false to their mission, false to the
future, false to their country and to themselves, beguiled
by the stupid, immoral hope of perhaps finding material
well-being in the caprices and the interests of tyranny.
I saw the working-men of France stand by, indifferent
spectators of the *coup d'état* of the 2nd of December,
because all social questions had been reduced for them
to a question of *material* prosperity, and they deluded
themselves into the belief that the *promises*, artfully

circulated among them by the man who had extinguished
the liberty of their country, would become facts. To-day
they lament their lost liberty, and have not acquired
the promised *well-being*. No ! I tell you with profound
conviction, that without God, without belief in a Law, without morality, without the power of self-sacrifice, and by
straying from the right path in the wake of men who have
neither faith, nor worship of truth, nor the life of
apostles, nor anything beyond the vanity of their own
systems, you will never succeed. You may bring about
insurrections, but never the true, the great Revolution
which you and I invoke ; that Revolution, if it is not
an illusion of egoists, spurred on by revenge, is a work
of religion.

To improve yourselves and others—this must be the
first aim and the supreme hope of every reform, of every
social change. The lot of a *man* is not altered by reno-
vating and embellishing the house in which he lives ;
where only the body of a slave breathes, and not the soul
of a man, all reforms are useless ; the neat dwelling,
luxuriously furnished, is a whited sepulchre, nothing
else. You will never induce the society to which you
belong to substitute the system of *association* for that
of wages, except by proving that your association will be
an instrument of improved production and of collective
prosperity. And you can only prove this by showing
yourselves capable of founding and maintaining the
association by honesty, mutual kindliness, capacity for
sacrifice, and love of work. To progress you must show
yourselves *capable* of progressing.

Three things are sacred : Tradition, Progress,
Association. "I believe"—thus I wrote twenty years
ago—" in the immense voice of God which the centuries
transmit to me through the universal tradition of
Humanity ; and it tells me that the Family, the Nation,
and Humanity are the three spheres within which the
human *individual* has to labour for the common *end*, for
the moral perfecting of himself and of others, or rather
of himself through others and for others. It tells me
that property is designed to manifest the *material* activity

of the individual, the part which he takes in the transformation of the physical world, as the right to *vote* ought to manifest the part which he takes in the administration of the political world. It tells me that the merit or demerit of the individual before God depends upon his use of these rights in those spheres of activity. It tells me that all these things, being elements of human nature, are transformed and modified continuously as they approach ever more nearly to the ideal which our souls dimly apprehend, but that they can never be destroyed ; and that the dreams of *communism*, of the abolition and absorption of the individual in the social *whole*, have never been more than accidental and transitory phenomena in the life of the human race, appearing in every great intellectual and moral crisis, and are incapable of realisation except upon a minute scale, as in the Christian Convents.   I believe in the eternal progress of the life in God's creatures, and in the progress of Thought and of Action, not only in the man of the past, but in the man of the future.   I believe that it is not of so much importance to *determine* the form of future progress, as to open, by means of a truly religious education, every path of progress to men and to render them capable of accomplishing it.   And I believe that man cannot be made better, more worthy of love, more noble, more divine—which is our aim and *end* upon earth— by heaping upon him physical enjoyments and by setting before him as the object of life that irony which is called *happiness*.   I believe in Association as the sole means which we possess of accomplishing Progress, not only because it multiplies the action of the productive forces, but because it brings into closer relations all the various manifestations of the human soul, and puts the life of the *individual* into communion with the *collective* life.   And I know that *Association* can never be fruitful unless it exists among *free individuals*, among *free* nations capable of realising their solemn mission.   I believe that man ought to be able to eat and live without having all the hours of his existence absorbed by material labour ; that he ought to have time for developing his superior faculties.   But

I listen with terror to those voices which tell us : *man's aim in life is self-preservation; enjoyment is his right,* because I know that such maxims can only create egoists and that they have been in France and elsewhere, and threaten to be in Italy, the destruction of every noble idea, of all martyr spirit, and every pledge of future greatness.

"That which saps the vitality of Humanity in the present day is the want of a common faith, of a thought shared by all and reuniting earth and heaven, the Universe and God. Lacking this common faith, man has bowed down before lifeless matter, and has consecrated himself to the adoration of the idol Self-Interest. And the first priests of that fatal worship were the kings, princes, and evil governments. They invented the horrible formula : *every one for himself*; they knew that thus they would create egoism, and that between the egoist and the slave there is but one step."

Italian Working-men, my Brothers, shun this step. On shunning it depends your future.

A solemn mission is yours : to prove that we are all sons of God and brothers in Him. You can only do this by improving yourselves and fulfilling your Duty.

I have pointed out to you, to the best of my power, what your Duty is. And the chief and most essential duty of all is to your Country. To secure the freedom and unity of your Country is your duty; and it is also a necessity. The encouragement and the measures of which I have spoken can only be the work of a Free and United Country. The amelioration of your social condition can only result from your participation in the political life of the nation. Without the franchise you will never find true representatives of your aspirations and needs. Without a popular government which, seated in Rome, shall formulate the *Italian Compact*, founded upon the common consent of the nation, and directed to the *progress* of *all* the citizens of the State, there is no hope of better things for you. That day in which, following the example of the French *socialists*, you should separate the *social* from the *political* question and should say : *We can emancipate ourselves whatever may be the form of constitution which rules the Country*, you would yourselves seal the perpetuity of your social servitude.

And I will point out to you, in bidding you farewell, another Duty, not less solemn than that which obliges us to found a Free and United Nation.

Your emancipation can only be founded on the triumph of one principle, the unity of the Human Family. To-day, half of the human family, the half from which we seek inspiration and consolation, the half to which is entrusted the first education of our children, is, by a singular contradiction, declared civilly, politically, and socially unequal, and is excluded from this unity. It is for you who seek your emancipation, in the name of religious truth, to protest in every way and upon every occasion against this negation of unity.

The *emancipation of woman* should be always coupled by you with the *emancipation of the working-man.* It will give your work the consecration of a universal truth.

INTERESTS AND PRINCIPLES

INTERESTS AND PRINCIPLES

I

January 6th, 1836.

THERE is a charge too often brought against those who, like us, love to dwell on political generalities, and insist at length on principles; the charge, that we pay little attention to material interests, that we are apt to sacrifice or neglect *facts* for what they are pleased to call *abstract theories*.

We are told: " You are dreamers. What use to us are all your discussions about principles which can only mature slowly, and which you can only address to a small minority of intellects ? At the present moment we want facts, and facts alone. Come down from the lofty sphere where we are not disposed to follow you, to the firm ground of practical work. Leave generalities ; descend to particulars. Speak of what we can see, and what is palpable to the senses. Face the question of material interests ; would you forsooth profess to make the masses progress by virtue of mere abstractions ? Yonder are people dying for lack of food ; men who are hungry and athirst, men who have not wherewith to clothe themselves in winter. All your theories of a social polity, of Humanity, of a unifying and religious faith, will never renew their strength, never clothe their nakedness. Proclaim those needs openly. Teach the proletariat its rights. Uncloak one by one the crimes, the injustice, the infamy of our rulers. Denounce every act of authority that injures any interest whatever, that infringes a single right. Fight, Fight. Shout Liberty in the ears of the People. Revolt is the principle of the century. Then guide it. In the stormy atmosphere

that surrounds us, amid the political tempest that pursues
and presses upon us on all sides, do not cheat yourselves
into thinking that your message of peace, your weak
speech of religion and love, will be heeded. Let the
Future and its Faith alone. The Present demands all
our thought. Consecrate yourselves to it, and do not
come and weary us with your mysticism and spiritualistic
beliefs."

They who speak thus are convinced that it is enough
to crush us if they call us *dreamers*.

And nevertheless those very men are attacked by discouragement; they are silent—or if they speak, they curse.
A hundred times they have thought to achieve their
purpose; as often have they been compelled to start
afresh. All they say has been already said; all they
do has been already done,—but never to any purpose.

All the war of criticism, all the opposition of *detail* and
of practical reform that they urge on us to-day has been
experimented to the uttermost in France. And where is
France to-day? She has fallen headlong from one wreck
to another: from the Revolution to the Empire; from
the Empire to the Bourbon Monarchy; from Charles X.
to Louis Philippe. What has she gained by the change?
What difference can you see between the censorship of
the first Restoration and the September Press Laws? [1]

The blood-stained wounds of the proletariat have been
exposed. A thousand times have men counted the
victims of the deep social inequality that insults the
Cross of Christ.

We know now the sweat and tears that the rich man's
bread costs the poor. Yes, and the poor man, the workman, has learnt to plead his cause before the tribunal of
frightened Europe, his indictment, summarised in two
words, terrible in their energy—*Death or Work*. A
people of workmen has protested against the present
division of labour, against the greed of the privileged
classes. What has been the result? What has been

---

[1] A series of violently repressive laws against the freedom of the press,
known in French History as the Laws of September, carried by the De
Broglie Ministry in September 1835. See Louis Blanc's *Histoire de Dix
Ans*, Vol. IV. c. xi. p. 312.

done? Have any remedies been tried, or any great improvements made? To the producer's cry of *Death or Work*, the unproductive and speculative class replied— *Death*. The cannon has thundered. All this opposition, so intrepid, so indefatigable in the petty skirmishes for interests and rights, looked on at the butchery with their arms at rest. Not in all France did a single cry answer the cry of anguish of the Lyons workmen.[1] Why is this?

Thanks to the writers of a whole century,—thanks to the martyrs of many centuries,—Liberty and Equality as *principles* are to-day admitted in the series of social axioms. Independence is universally recognised as the fairest jewel in a People's crown. The right not to be oppressed, or maimed, or tortured by the tyranny of the few, or by foreign invasion, is enshrined in the hearts of all as a sacred imprescriptible right. But does this advance us further? Not only in Italy, and Poland, and Germany, but everywhere, material interests are openly violated; and yet we all are conscious of our rights. Ask whom you will in those unhappy countries. You will everywhere encounter hatred of the Russian and the Austrian; a clear desire for freedom; the consciousness of right that would justify insurrection; the conviction of the real advantages that would result for future generations. And yet they suffer in silence; they bow their necks to the yoke; they do not strive to break it. Why is this?

Because between oppression and insurrection it is necessary to pass through gendarmes, prisons, and the gallows. Because to face all that, the consciousness of the *fact* is not enough; they must feel their *duty* to destroy it. Because the mere *conviction* does not suffice to begin a struggle: that must break forth as the manifestation of a *faith*.

There were men who preached insurrection to those peoples; who said to them, " You have material interests; those interests are trodden under foot; see that

<hr />

[1] Arbitrary suppression of the Workmen's Associations of Lyons by the military forces, April 1834. See Louis Blanc's *Histoire de Dix Ans*, Vol. IV. c. v. pp. 196–201.

you provide a remedy. You have rights; those rights
are violated; see that you assert free play for them."
For this they conspired. But tyranny was watching.
It shed their blood before the conspiracy was ripe; it
sent a few heads rolling at the conspirators' feet. Then
they stepped back. A single chance of death outweighed
a thousand chances of success. They said, " Our rights
are valuable, and we should dearly wish to win them;
but first of all rights is the right to live. The interest
of our own life surpasses all other possible material
interests. It embraces and outweighs them all. Without life we can have neither rights, nor well-being, nor
riches, nor material improvement. Why should we
hazard our life for an uncertain stake? Where should
we find a recompense?" Such were their words; and
if we refuse to leave the circle of material calculations,
we must own they are consistent. Two-thirds at least
of popular Revolutions only benefit the succeeding
generation. The generation that made them is nearly
always condemned to mark with its own dead the road
of progress for its successor. Itself can never enjoy the
result of its travail.

Now, what theory of material interests, what proof of
individual rights, could argue a law of self-sacrifice, or
martyrdom, if martyrdom be the goal that awaits us?
Analyse, compare, phrase by phrase, all the doctrines
of the utilitarians; you will never harmonise with them
the sacrifice of life. Martyrdom is folly to a People that
has no stimulus outside material interests; to their intelligence Christ has lost all meaning.

For us, we maintain that there has never been a single
great Revolution that has not had its source outside
material interests. We know of riots, of popular insurrections, but of none that has been crowned with
success, or transformed into a Revolution.

II

Every Revolution is the work of a *principle* which has
been accepted as a basis of faith. Whether it invoke

Nationality, Liberty, Equality, or Religion, it always fulfils itself in the name of a Principle, that is to say, of a great truth, which, being recognised and approved by the majority of the inhabitants of a country, constitutes a common belief, and sets before the masses a new *aim*, while Authority misrepresents or rejects it. A Revolution, violent or peaceful, includes a negation and an affirmation: the negation of an existing order of things, the affirmation of a new order to be substituted for it. A Revolution proclaims that the State is rotten; that its machinery no longer meets the needs of the greatest number of the citizens; that its institutions are powerless to direct the general movement; that popular and social thought has passed beyond the vital principle of those institutions; that the new phase in the development of the national faculties finds neither expression nor representation in the official constitution of the country, and that it must therefore create one for itself. This the Revolution does create. Since its task is to increase and not diminish the nation's patrimony, it violates neither the truths that the majority possess, nor the rights they hold sacred; but it reorganises everything on a new basis; it gathers and harmonises round the new principle all the elements and forces of the country; it gives a unity of direction towards the new *aim*, to all those tendencies which before were scattered in the pursuit of different aims. Then the Revolution has done its work.

We recognise no other meaning in Revolutions. If a Revolution did not imply a general reorganisation by virtue of a social principle; if it did not remove a discord in the elements of a State, and place harmony in its stead; if it did not secure a moral unity; so far from declaring ourselves Revolutionists, we should believe it our duty to oppose the revolutionary movement with all our power.

Without the purpose hinted at above, there may be riots, and at times victorious *insurrections*, but no Revolutions. You will have changes of men and administration; one caste succeeding to another; one dynastic

branch ousting the other. This necessitates retreat ; a
slow reconstruction of the past, which the insurrection
had suddenly destroyed ; the gradual re-establishment
under new names of the old order of things, which the
people had risen to destroy. Societies have such need
of unity that if they miss it in insurrection they turn
back to a restoration. Then there is new discontent,
a new struggle, a new explosion. France has proven
it abundantly. In 1830 she performed miracles of
daring and valour for a negation : she rose to destroy,
without positive beliefs, without any definite organic
pupose, and thought she had won her end when she
cancelled the old principle of legitimacy. She descended
into that abyss which insurrection alone can never fill ;
and because she did not recognise how needful is some
principle of reconstruction, she finds herself to-day, six
years after the July Revolution, five years after the days
of November, two years after the days of April, well
on her way to a thorough restoration.

We cite the case of France because she is expected
to give political lessons, hopes, and sympathies ; and
because France is the modern nation in which theories
of pure reaction founded on suspicion, on individual
right, on liberty *alone*, are most militant, therefore the
practical consequences of her mistakes are shown most
convincingly. But twenty other instances might be
cited. For fifty years, every movement which, in its
turn, was successful as an *insurrection*, but failed as a
revolution, has proven how everything depends on the
presence or absence of a principle of reconstruction.

Wherever, in fact, individual rights are exercised without the influence of some great thought that is common
to all ; wherever individual interests are not harmonised
by some organisation which is directed by a positive
ruling principle, and by the consciousness of a common
aim, there must exist a tendency for some to usurp
others' rights. In a society like ours, where a division
into *classes*, call them what you will, still exists in full
strength, every right is bound to clash with another
right, envious and mistrustful of it ; every interest

naturally conflicts with an opposing interest: the land-
lord's with the peasant's; the manufacturer's or capitalist's with the workman's. All through Europe—since
equality, however accepted in theory, has been rejected
in practice, and the sum of social wealth has accumulated in the hands of a small number of men, while the
masses gain but a mere pittance by their relentless toil
—it is a cruel irony, it gives inequality a new lease of
life, if you establish unrestricted liberty, and tell men
they are free, and bid them use their rights.

A social sphere must have its centre; a centre to
the individualities which jostle which each other inside
it; a centre to all the scattered rays with diffuse and
waste their light and heat. Now, the theory which
bases the social structure on individual *interests* cannot
supply this centre. The absence of a centre, or the
selection among opposing interests of that which has
the most vigorous life, means either anarchy or privilege
—that is, either barren strife or the germ of aristocracy,
under whatever name it disguises itself: this is the parting of the ways which it is impossible to avoid.

Is this what we want when we invoke a Revolution,
since a Revolution is indispensable to reorganise our
nationality? Do we want to condemn ourselves to
ceaseless eddying in the whirlpool where France and
Europe have tossed for half a century? Do we want
to be always making and unmaking, and be still in
a provisional dispensation, be still uncertain of the
morrow? Do we want strife, or peace and harmony?
This is the whole question.

For us there is no doubt. To find a centre for all
the many interests we must rise to a region above them
all, independent of them all. To close a provisional
dispensation and organise a peaceful future, we must
reconnect that centre with something, eternal as Truth,
progressive as its development in the sphere of facts.
To prevent the clash of individualities we must find an
aim common to all, and direct ourselves towards it. To
make it easier for all to reach it we must consolidate
and associate the forces of all. What else is *association*

but a conception that makes for unity? And how can such a conception be understood without a *principle* around which it may revolve?

We are, therefore, driven to the sphere of *principles*. We must revive belief in them ; we must fulfil a work of faith. The logic of things demands it.

III

Principles alone are constructive. Ideals are never translated into facts without the general recognition of some strong belief. Great things are never done except by the rejection of individualism and a constant sacrifice of self to the common progress. Now, self-sacrifice is the sense of Duty in action. And the sense of Duty cannot spring from individual interests, but postulates the knowledge of a superior, inviolable Law. Every law rests on a principle : otherwise it is arbitrary and its violation is *permissible*. This principle must be freely accepted by everybody : otherwise the law is despotic and its violation is a *duty*. The application of principle lies in a life in conformity with law. To discover, to study, to preach the *principle* which shall be the basis of the social law of the country and of the times in which he lives, should be the aim of every man who directs his thought to any political organisation. *Faith* in that principle is the parent of effective and lasting work. The isolated and barren knowledge of *individual interests* can only lead to the isolated and barren knowledge of *individual right*. And the knowledge of individual right will, where that right is denied, lead in its turn to discontent, opposition, strife, sometimes insurrection, but insurrection which, like that of Lyons, results only in a bitterer hostility between the classes which compose society. Whenever, therefore, we desire to do one of those great deeds called Revolutions, we must always return to the knowledge and preaching of principles. The true instrument of the progress of the peoples is to be sought in the *moral* factor.

But do we, therefore, neglect the *economic* factors,

material interests; the importance of industrial victories, and the labours that won them? Do we preach principles for principles' sake, faith for faith's sake, as the romantic school of literature to-day preaches *art for art's sake.*

God forbid! We do not suppress the *economic* factor: we believe, on the contrary, that it is destined in the society of the future to admit an ever-increasing extension of the principle of *equality*, and to incorporate the fruitful principle of *association.* But we subordinate the economic to the *moral* factor, because if withdrawn from its controlling influence, dissociated from principles, and abandoned to the theories of individualism which govern it to-day, it would result in brutish egotism; in perpetual strife between men who should be brothers; in the expression of the *appetites* of the human species, whilst it ought rather to represent on the ascending curve of progress the material translation of man's activity, the expression of man's industrial mission.

No, we do not neglect material interests: on the contrary, we reject as imperfect and irreconcilable with the needs of the age every doctrine which does not include them, or regards them as less important than they really are. We believe that to every stage of progress there should be a corresponding positive improvement in the material condition of the people; and this successive improvement, in a certain manner, verifies for us the progress made. But we maintain that material interests cannot be developed alone, that they are dependent on principles, that they are not the *end and aim* of society; because we know that such a theory is destructive of human dignity; because we remember that when the *material* factor began to hold the field in Rome, and duty to the people was reduced to giving them *bread* and *public shows*, Rome and its people were hastening to destruction; because we see to-day in France, in Spain, in every country, liberty trodden under foot, or betrayed precisely in the name of commercial interests and that servile doctrine which parts material well-being from principles.

We do not forget the services rendered to the cause of progress by the political school of the *Rights of Man*, nor the importance of the economic teachings, which towards the end of the eighteenth century assailed the absurd and immoral *restrictive system* under which governments committed the industrial development of the nation to customs officers, as they committed its moral development to censors and constabulary.[1] In an age when the rights of individuals were systematically violated, these teachings were indispensable, and without them we should not now be where we are. But to-day we have passed beyond them; we cannot stand still within their limits without denying the new tendencies which aim at reconstruction. The peoples hailed the destructive work of the past century because they hoped that a new organisation would take the place of the old one; but since then they have been disillusioned again and again, and now they will not stir unless rekindled by a new organic programme. The *individual* is sacred: his interests, his rights, are inviolable. But to make them the only foundation of the political structure, and tell each individual to win his future with his own unaided strength, is to surrender society and progress to the accidents of chance and the vicissitudes of a never-ending struggle; to neglect the great fact of man's nature, his *social* instinct; to plant egotism in the soul; and, in the long run, impose the dominion of the strong over the weak, of those who have over those who have not. The many abortive attempts of the last forty years prove this.

When, therefore, we preach almost exclusively those *principles* which seem to us to derive from the actual condition of human knowledge, we purpose following the way which leads to the material as well as the moral future of the nations. When we insist on the need of raising on those principles a structure of belief, in the place of dead or dying creeds, we shall be responding to a prayer of the peoples, often ill-expressed, more

[1] *Birri*; armed Italian police with a military organisation somewhat similar to the Royal Irish Constabulary.

often ill-understood, but which has been revealed in many forms most dissociated and dissimilar, and is the historical secret of the nineteenth century. And when we say: "Rise to the sphere of principles; guide the peoples, now wandering in darkness, to the law of Progress, to Humanity, to God; awake again the moral sense, the sentiment of Duty in men whom others would fain convert into calculating-machines; show a great purpose to the young, so easily assailed to-day by discouragement and doubt; give to men by enthusiasm, and religion, and love, a new moral existence, since the old one of privilege and inequality is dust and ashes,"— when we say this, we are convinced that every other method of treating public questions is an illusion, or a lie; that political *forms* considered in isolation and by themselves are, as the ancients said of law, spiders' webs that imprison little insects, but which are torn through by big ones; that the *spirit* alone gives importance to *forms*; that institutions are a *dead letter*, ineffectual and impotent, whenever the breath of popular progress, and brotherhood, and association does not inspire them; that all written declarations are futile where men have surrendered themselves to individualism, and organised themselves on a basis of inequality, and therefore naturally tend to elude such declarations, and rather seek in them a weapon of defence against others; convinced that no other method can profit the cause of Humanity, the great interests of the People, and Labour, and Nationality, and moral growth—the only things which merit our sacrifices and our labours.

Instil into a People's soul, or into its teachers and writers, one single principle, and it will be worth more to that People and Country than a whole system of interests and rights addressed to each individual; or a war to the death against the acts of a corrupt government.

If by dint of example you can root in a nation's heart the principle which the French Revolution proclaimed but never carried out, that *the State owes every member the means of existence or the chance to work for it*, and add a fair definition of existence, you have prepared the triumph of right over privilege; the end of the monopoly of one class over another, and the end of *pauperism* [1]; for which at present there are only palliatives, Christian charity, or cold and brutal maxims like those of the English school of political economists.

When you have raised men's minds to believe in the other principle: that *society is an association of labours*, and can, thanks to that belief, deduce both in theory and practice all its consequences; you will have no more castes, no more aristocracies, or civil wars, or crises. You will have a *People*.

And when the gospel of the brotherhood of all the men of a nation has made the soul a sanctuary of virtue and love; when the great conception of Nationality is no more dwarfed to mean proportions; when it seeks as a basis for its rights something more than mere material interest, interest that always has its rivals; when the mother repeats its pure and holy doctrine to the child at her knee, at those hours of morn and even when woman, angel-grown, teaches her offspring heavenly truths as axioms and principles immutable—then only will you have a nation such as you can never have from sophists who would found a godless Nationality. For Nationality is belief in a common origin and end, and if set up to-day by one interest it can be overthrown to-morrow by another interest more daring and more powerful.

And so it must ever be. Principles, which some would relegate among abstractions, by their nature lie so near material interests, and what is called the *economic factor*, that they involve its practical triumph as an inevitable consequence. The sphere of principles includes and embraces them all. But all material progress is the infallible result of all moral progress. We cease to waste our strength in a petty war, nor try to defeat interests in detail and without guarantee

[1] In text, *mendicita*—mendicity. A phase of the social problem in Continental nations analogous to pauperism in England.

of permanent success; we strive instead to reach the common source and plant ourselves in the key of the position. The effects of our exertions may appear more slowly, but they are more certain, and alone are durable. The work of faith, the moral work, advances insensibly, like the movement of the hand on the clock, but it alone is called to mark the solemn hours of the nations.

A newspaper is not a work of legislation : it operates indirectly only. A newspaper does not clothe the naked poor, or give bread to the starving: it preaches and insists that this should be done. Now, how shall we work on the reader's mind? How convince him, not only of the existence of the decease but of the need of a remedy? How communicate to him the spirit of activity, the power of self-sacrifice, which are necessary to overcome obstacles? A newspaper, generally speaking, is written for the well-to-do classes, and these classes, comfortable in their prosperity, have never experienced privation or suffering; they see at times the misery of the poor, but easily accustom themselves to consider it as a sad social *necessity*, and leave to future generations the care of finding a remedy. Sweet are indifference and oblivion to the man who sits in the sanctuary of his family, surrounded by smiling faces, while the wintry blast blows without, and the snowflakes, swift and fine, beat against the panes of a double window. Do you hope to drag these favourites of the world from their apathy, by the simple expression of the *economic situation* and what should be its substitute in a well-organised society? Do you hope to shake them from their selfish repose, merely by cold analysis of what happens in a sphere to which they never penetrate? They will approve perhaps in theory your utilitarian doctrines; but do not ask them to promote them. Why should they? You speak in the name of *interests*. Is not the first of all interests enjoyment? And they do enjoy.

There is a great gulf between approving a thing and sacrificing yourself for it, a gulf which you with your methods cannot cross. And yet this is just the

problem.   Man is *thought* and *action*.   Your theories
may modify the former; they cannot create the latter.

We must therefore modify, reform, transform, the
whole man into a unity of life.   We must teach him
not *right*, but *duty*; awaken to better things his degenerate nature, his half-exhausted soul, his drooping
enthusiasm; we must give him the consciousness of
human worth and men's mission here below, and thereby
raise the strength to act which now is crushed by his
indifference.   And this is a work for principles, and
belief, and religious thought, and *faith*.

This was the work of Jesus.   He did not try to save a
dying world by criticism.   He did not speak of interests
to men whose souls were poisoned by the cult of
interests.   He preached, in God's holy name, certain
truths till then unknown; and these few truths, which
now after eighteen centuries we are striving to realise,
changed the face of the world.   One single spark of
faith achieved what all the sophisms of the philosophic
schools had never caught a glimpse of: a forward step
in the Education of the Human Race.

The problem of to-day—we shall never weary of
repeating—is, as in the days of Christ, an *educational
problem*.   But what is Education unless it rest upon
principles, and draw its being from a common faith, and
strive for its victory?

FAITH AND THE FUTURE

"Faith and the Future" was written in French at Bienne in 1835, at a time when Louis Philippe had thrown off the mask and frankly broken with the democratic movement to which he owed his throne. Its object was to hearten the popular party, dispirited with the failure of the revolution of 1830, and to urge them to push forward the revolutionary agitation. The parliamentary strategy of 1815-30, a policy of compromise and small reforms, had failed; it had only exposed the defects of the existing system, without suggesting a better substitute. The constitutional reformers had been defeated by their own doubts and fears; the democratic party must reproduce the enthusiasm, the unflinching adhesion to principle, of the Great Revolution. It must cut itself clear from conventions and prejudices, and boldly avow a republican policy. Not that the mere form of republican institutions had any magic in it. The world needed the republican spirit, the essence of which was the devotion of the individual to the common good, and which found its outward expression in the substitution of associated effort for individual enterprise. Men who had a great principle like this to assert could not be patient or silent; and in Italy and Poland and Germany, where the press was gagged, and public agitation led to the scaffold, there was no road but that of open conflict with the government. Not that Mazzini, as he was careful to explain in a later note, advocated feverish, ill-considered, insurrectionary movements; the education of the secret press and the secret society must precede revolution.

NOTE

The figures in parentheses on pages 150 onwards refer to notes too long to put at the foot of the text which will be found at the end of the essay, pages 184 to 194.

FAITH AND THE FUTURE

I

THE crusade is being organised. The monarchy arrays itself for battle. It has returned to the dictatorial habits of Louis XIV. and is preparing *coups d'état* with the arms of the sixteenth century.

In the midst of the great popular excitement of 1830 the monarchy was distraught for a moment, and thought its doom had come. In truth we, and we alone, saved it from its doom. We lost a marvellous opportunity. We forgot that the morrow of victory is much more perilous than its eve. Intoxicated with triumph and pride, we pitched our tents when we ought to have hastened on, and, like thoughtless children, we betook ourselves to play with the arms of those we had vanquished. Diplomacy lay well-nigh crushed under the popular barricades, and yet we welcomed it as a friend into our ranks ; we made its arts ours, and, raining notes and protocols, learned to ape our discomfited masters. Like the condottieri of old, we sent back free and armed the prisoners of battle. The monarchy was stretched low and at our mercy, and we, like medieval knights, we republicans, drew back two paces as though to give it an opportunity to remount. Coldly calculating, it took advantage of our chivalrous ardour to begin its work again, a work undertaken with a constancy and unity of conception that should make us blush at our discords and slackness.

While we were numbering our dead, they began silently to increase their ranks. While we were disputing among ourselves whether to march in the name of

'91 or of '93, of Robespierre or of Babœuf, they were
marching on, slowly, silently, caressing some, threatening
others, working their way underground when they thought
themselves not powerful enough to venture into the
light of day, avoiding obstacles they could not overcome.
Instead of snatching from the grave a shred or so of the
banner of the past, they clothed the whole past with
a semblance of life, and re-decked it with the colours
of the future. Anger, ambition, jealousy, everything
yielded to the one end of gaining Power. In the North
the form was given up to preserve the substance, and the
habits of despotism were renounced that the monarchy
of the usurper might fraternise with the monarchy of
divine right. In the South they knelt in the mire, and
suffered the insults of diplomacy, to obtain from it peace
and help. To-day the alliance is concluded, the equilibrium re-established between the old and the new
powers; and both alike weigh upon us. The enemies of
progress touch the apogee of power. Corruption has
conquered souls that fear could not reach; gold has
finished the work of the prisons. Consciences have been
bought and sold, genius prostituted, anarchy sown among
thinkers, crosses and pensions showered upon some,
proscriptions and terrors upon others; the bourgeoisie
has been seduced by trickery, suspicion sown broadcast,
espionage raised to a system. The monarchy in the pride
of its strength has cast the cloak aside, and to-day
impiously denies God, Progress, the People, Humanity.
With the constable[1] on one side and the executioner on the
other, it wipes out our right to free movement and to the
future; it destroys our memories and hopes, puts brute
force in the place of ideas, bids us to our knees as
it bade our fathers when they were serfs, when thought
was banned, intellect and conscience dumb, and silence
the law for all. And we, what shall we do? Shall we
give way to despair? Shall we renounce for a time our
battle-cry, frank, loyal, strenuous as our soul? Repeat
the fifteen years' comedy? Show that we are tamed?
Deceive the monarchy which we could, and would not,

[1] See Note, p. 134.

vanquish? Copy its methods, its habits, its tactics?
Lead it smilingly by tortuous ways, to the precipice's
edge, then suddenly unmask ourselves, stab it in the
back, and hurl it down the abyss?

Men who adopt and counsel such as the only policy
left to us, who preach patience as the sole remedy for
our ills, or who admit the necessity of the struggle but
leave the powers that be to begin it, such men do not,
I believe, understand the present state of affairs. They
change a call to create into a call to oppose. They
falsify the stamp of the age; they betray unconsciously
the cause they seek to further; they forget that the task
assigned to the nineteenth century is one whose very
essence it is to create, initiate, make new, one which
only free spontaneous action and a free and daring
conscience can complete.

It is not enough to drag a monarchy to the abyss:
we must be prepared to fill up that abyss, fill it up
for ever, and on it raise a lasting edifice. Monarchies
can be un-made and re-made in a day. The mighty
hand of Napoleon overturned half a score; but monarchy
still lives, and greeted his grave with a smile of triumph.
In 1830, a throne of eight centuries vanished under
three blows struck by the people; and yet we to-day
are proscribed by a monarchy which has risen from
its ruins. Let us never forget this.

What was called *the fifteen years' comedy* was played
in France wondrous well. The skilful and flawless
jesuitry of the actors might merit the envy of crowned
heads. What were the consequences?

The *fifteen years' comedy* killed the monarchy of the
elder branch of the Bourbons; but it killed at the
same time the frank, austere, revolutionary energy
which had placed France at the head of the nations
of Europe. While it doomed the powers that be to
sleepless dread, it doomed the advanced party in
France to a long rôle of dishonesty. For, through
it hypocrisy wormed itself into the souls of men,
calculation took the place of enthusiasm, the brain
superseded the heart, and theories of passive resistance

succeeded ito the genius that ever presses forward to things new. The masculine, vigorous national thought languished under a multitude of petty, bastard incomplete conceits, and apostasy entered the sphere of political life. That disloyal, treacherous war of subterfuges spread over French civilisation a stratum of corruption whose results last to this day : another such war would be fatal indeed. Here is matter for reflection. When the times are ripe for breaking from the present and advancing towards the future, all hesitation is fatal : it unnerves and dissolves. Rapid movement is the secret of all great victories. When the consequences of a principle are exhausted, and the edifice which has sheltered us for centuries threatens to fall, we should shake the dust from our feet and hasten elsewhere. Life is outside. Within, there is but the cold, benumbing air of the tomb, scepticism wandering among the ruins, egotism following in its track ; then, isolation and death.

And to-day the times *are* ripe. The consequences of the principle of *individualism* which dominated the past are exhausted. The monarchy has reached its second restoration and finds no more creative virtue in itself ; its life is but a wretched plagiarism. Show me, if you can, a single important act, a single sign of European life, that does not proceed from the *social* principle, which does not depend upon the *people*, the king of the future. The old world can only *resist* ; its remaining strength is but the strength of passive resistance. The aristocracies of to-day are but corpses, now and again galvanised into motion. Monarchy is the reflection, the shadow of a life that has passed away. Since 1814 the future calls to us. For twenty-two years the people, eager for a step forward, strain their ears for that cry. And would you travel once more over the old ground, fall back, begin again a task that is done, copy the past, and, because the monarchy is in its dotage, return to infancy ?

What do you hope for when you beg inspiration in the enemy's camp, and follow in its footsteps ? Whither

will you fare along the tortuous road of revolutionary
diplomacy over which you would drag the younger
generation ?   Beware ! the roads of mere *opposition* such
as yours lead only to monarchy.   There exists generally
an essential relation between the means and the end ;
and constitutional tactics can only result in constitutional
changes.   The fifteen years' opposition gave birth to
1830. Every analogous opposition will (unforeseen circumstances apart) give birth to similar results.   In 1830 the
people confined within the Charter the limits of the
attack, because it had used itself to confine in the same
bounds the limits of the defence.   It will be ever the
same.   If, in the old revolution, the French people angrily
answered the challenge of the allied monarchies of
Europe by beheading a king and raising the republican
banner, that challenge, we must never forget, was un-
provoked and a war to the death.   Of the members of
the royal family, some were in arms against France on
the frontier ; others were persistent conspirators against
her in Paris.   Without these causes the revolution would
never have reached so easily that state of things.   The
impulse given by the demands of the States-General
would not have passed beyond the movement of '91.
But monarchical Europe to-day wages no open war of
arms against the revolutions of a people thirty millions
strong : she offers them a traitor's hand, and the kiss of
Judas.   She does not challenge them to battle : she tries
to dishonour them.   Then she creates a solitude about
them ; surrounds them like scorpions with a circle of fire,
and in that circle they consume their own strength, and
since the life of revolutions consists in growth, they
perish.

But suppose it happen otherwise ; suppose the people,
outstripping the first impulse, wipe out a principle instead
of simply modifying it ; suppose they change a monarchical revolution into a republican one, and attain the
purpose you have at heart.   You will then have gained
the form, not the habits, customs, ideas, beliefs, of a
republic.   The people which moves not from faith, but
by simple reaction against the abuses of monarchy, will

preserve the antecedents, the traditions, the education of
the monarchy : you will have the form of a republic, but
the substance of a monarchy. Questions of *political*
organisation will overlay the true, the supreme question,
which is a *moral* and a *social* one.

Criticism will not regenerate the peoples. Criticism
is powerful to dissolve, not to create. Criticism is incapable of passing beyond the theory of the *individual*;
and the triumph of *individualism* can only engender a
revolution for protestantism and liberty. Far otherwise
is the republic. The republic, as I at least understand
it, means association, of which liberty is only an element,
a necessary antecedent. It means association, a new
philosophy of life, a divine Ideal that shall move the
world, the only means of regeneration vouchsafed to the
human race. Opposition is an instrument of mere
criticism. It kills ; it does not give life. And when it
declares a principle to be dead, it takes its seat upon the
dead body and stirs no further. Only a new Ideal can
thrust the corpse aside, and move forward in search of a
new life. For this reason the revolution of '89, a revolution essentially protestant in its character, ended by
enthroning criticism, by affirming the brotherhood of
individuals, by organising liberty. And by reason of this
the revolution of 1830—a revolution purely of opposition
—proved itself from the first incapable of translating into
action that *social* conception of which it had distant
glimpses. Opposition can only demonstrate the barren-
ness, the decadence, the exhaustion of a principle.
Beyond, for it, there is the void, whereon men build not.
A republic is not planted upon a demonstration *ad
absurdum*. Direct proof is indispensable. Authoritative
Truth alone can give us salvation.

II

Two things are essential to future progress : the manifestation of a principle, and its incarnation in deeds.
Apostles of a faith which aims at construction, we cannot advance save with banners unfurled, confronting the

hostile faith in deadly battle. Wait, they say. But for what? For opportunities? But what are opportunities save a special arrangement of the circumstances whose office it is to give birth to deeds? And whence can opportunities arise except from our own efforts? Do you want war? Whom will the combatants be drawn from? From those who are marching in full accord, peoples who have even now renewed a covenant of brotherhood, who have one end in view, one enemy, one fear? Will it be against peoples prostrate in the mire? War will never arise in Europe except by insurrection. Do you want *coups d'état*? Only a strenuous, obstinate struggle can make them inevitable. But how maintain the struggle? By conspiracy? The preachers of patience object, even as they object to insurrection. By the printing press? The governments kill it : you have everywhere laws which fetter it, censors who vex the writer, judges who condemn thought and shut it within prison walls. Can you surmount these obstacles? In France, perhaps. But take the case of a country absolutely without a Press ; without a Parliament or a Council where politics may be discussed; without literary journals ; without a national theatre ; without popular education; without foreign books. Suppose that country to suffer, suffer terribly, the upper and middle classes as well as the mass of its people, from poverty, from domestic and foreign oppression, from constant violation of the national principle, and the absence of all intellectual and industrial development. What is that country to do? Whence can arise that slow and gradual progress which you admire?

And yet that country does exist. Its name is Italy, Poland, and for some time, Germany. It embraces nearly two-thirds of Europe.

Look at Italy !

In her there is neither progress, nor any chance of progress, save by revolution. Tyranny has raised an impenetrable wall along her frontier. A triple army of spies, of customs officers, and of constabulary[1] holds

' See note to page 134.

nightly and daily vigil to prevent the circulation of thought.   Mutual instruction [1] is prescribed.   The universities are closed or enslaved.   The penalty of death hangs not only over those who print clandestinely, but over those who possess or read the forbidden book.

The introduction of independent foreign newspapers is forbidden.   Intelligence perishes in infancy for lack of nourishment.   Young men sell their faith for self-indulgence, or waste their strength in fits of barren cynicism.   They oscillate between Don Juan and Timon.   And privileged souls, souls afire for Right, who for an instant caught glimpses of the Future, when environment weighs heavy upon them, let their light go out, and perish, without an object, without a mission, like flowers unwatered or the Peri shorn of her wings.   Who, I ask again, shall give progress to this people ?   Who shall give it to Poland, who lies in equal case ?   Who shall give it to Germany, whose lot will soon be the same, when, in obedience to your counsels, her patriots have stayed the struggle which peoples indeed the prisons, but awakens, little by little, the masses ?   How may we introduce into those countries the undefined but sacred thought invoked by all, if we are influenced by personal calculations, and draw back in face of the danger, if we dare not with arms in our hands, like the smugglers of the Pyrenees, defend the contraband of the intellect ?

Insurrection : I see for those peoples no other possible counsel : insurrection as soon as circumstances allow : insurrection, strenuous, ubiquitous : the insurrection of the masses : the holy war of the oppressed : the republic to make republicans : the people in action to initiate progress.   Let the insurrection announce with its awful voice the decrees of God : let it clear and level the ground on which its own immortal structure shall be raised.   Let it, like the Nile, flood all the country that it is destined to make fertile.   We speak here especially for those who lie at the base of the European social system—for those who wander in

---

[1] *i.e.*—the Bell-Lancaster system of teaching.

darkness condemned to silence by a double tyranny, while others more privileged can walk illumined by the sun, and discern clearly the end of the common labour —for enslaved races who for long centuries have sought in vain the mission assigned to them by God—for Poland, for Hungary, for Italy, for Spain, a country of great destinies, to-day wasting its strength between two systems, each one the translation of a false principle— for Germany also, poor, sacred Germany, who awoke us all with Luther's manly voice, for whom to-day we can only show a sympathy so lukewarm as to show like indifference. We speak for all, because all are indispensable elements of the European commonweal that is to be—because above and beyond the special mission which each of us is called to fulfil on earth, there is a common mission which embraces all Humanity —because we fail to see that men have as yet duly realised how essential it is that the republican Party should be morally united by the apostolic power of the written word, and that it is the written word which determines the choice of the system round which all the forces of the progressive press of Europe must rally. We have men to-day, republican writers of merit, who maintain that there is no light to guide the people to a better land except it come from the hands of those who hold watch and guard to keep them in the slough in which they lie—others who are content to implore, almost as an alms, some fraction of liberty for the people—others who desire that European association should ripen under the sun of constitutional monarchy, who reject as dangerous any attempt at regeneration by means of a great religious principle, who protest against every bold movement of the people as inopportune and ineffectual, against every really creative belief displayed by the defenders of the people. And I protest against the false theory, which confounds the material expression of progress with progress itself, and redoubles, as it were, the burdens of the peoples, by condemning them to an *initiation* by degrees, parallel to the stages of suffering they have passed through.

No: those peoples will sink to the depths of hell in their fall; but if they rise, they will attain to heaven.

Nations are initiated into the worship of liberty by the sufferings of servitude. They have endured beyond words; when they rise, they will grow, beyond all imagination, to a giant's stature. Their grief was blessed. Every tear taught them a truth. Every year of martyrdom prepared them for an absolute redemption. They have drained the cup to the dregs. Nothing is left to them but to dash it to pieces.

What, then, is to be done?

(1) Preach! fight! act!

The republican Party must change neither attitude nor language. Every modification introduced, for dubious tactical reasons, into its conditions of life, would bring it from its high estate to a mere political party. Now, the republican Party is not a political party: it is an essentially religious party. It has its faith, its doctrine, its martyrs from Spartacus onwards; and it must have doctrine inviolable, authority infallible, the martyr's spirit and call to self-sacrifice. Forgetfulness of this duty, imitation of the monarchy or aristocracy, the substitution of negations for positive beliefs, have often wrecked it. The *Idea*, the religious thought, of which it is, even unconsciously, a manifestation on earth, has raised it to giant stature when all men said that it had gone for ever. We must not forget that political parties fall and die: religious parties never die, except when the victory is won, when their vital principle has attained its full development, and become identified with the progress of civilisation and of morals. Then, but not till then, in the heart of the people, or in the brain of some individual, powerful by virtue of genius and love, God plants a new thought, vaster and more fruitful than that which is passing away; the centre of faith advances a step, and only those who gather around it constitute the party of the future.

The republican Party need not fear for the final issue of its mission, or be discouraged for temporary defeats that do not affect the main body, and only concentrate

around it the combatants who, in the heat of battle, have
strayed too far away ; or fear because at every turn men
try to set up might for right, matter for spirit. The
danger is elsewhere.

Having regard to the essence of things, and without
reference to the passing hour or the men of our day, the
position of the republican Party is, by reason of the
recent persecutions, better than before. The law of 9th
of September,[1] which was to prove fatal to us, has given
representative monarchy its death-blow. It has settled
the eternal question between the citizen monarchy and
the dynastic opposition. It has discredited systems
which professed to reconcile the sovereignty of the
people and the irresponsibility of its deputies, continued
progress and the immobility of an hereditary power. It
has demonstrated the impotence of the *doctrinaire* and
destroyed political eclecticism. The period of transition,
which unnerved the combatants by deceptive hopes and
foolish terrors, is at an end. Slaves or victors : "To be
or not to be" : the question is now clearly stated in
these terms : we must choose between debasing our
nature and intelligence and become renegades to every
sacred idea, every powerful conception, or rising in open
war and appealing from the justice of kings to the justice
of peoples, to the *judgment of God*. The truce is broken
for ever. People and monarchy are to-day enemies,
enemies confessed and beyond recall. On one side
monarchy, its centuries of life in the past, its traditional
authority, its sicarii, its tax-gatherers, its constabulary [2] :
on the other, the people, its centuries in the future, its
instinct of new things, its immortal youth, its countless
hosts. The jousts are cleared for the two combatants.
The battle may begin at any moment.

III

"You are deceived, they tell us. "The peoples lack
faith. The masses lie torpid. So used are they to wear
chains that they have lost the habit of motion. You

have to do with helots, not with men. How will you drag them to battle, and keep them in the field? Many a time have we called them to arms ; *we* have raised the cry of 'people, liberty, vengeance ! ' and they lifted for a moment their drowsy heads, and then fell back into their old torpor. They saw the funeral procession of our martyrs pass by, knew not that their rights, their life, their salvation, were being buried with them. They follow riches, and fear condemns them to stand still. Enthusiasm is spent and cannot easily be rekindled. Yet, without the masses you are powerless to act ; you can face martyrdom, not gain the victory. Die if you think that one day a generation of avengers will spring from your blood, but do not involve in your fate those who lack alike your strength and hope. Martyrdom cannot be made the baptism of a whole Party. It is useless to waste in abortive attempts forces which one day may be effectively employed. Do not delude yourselves about the times. Be resigned and wait patiently."

The problem is a serious one. It involves the future of the Party.

The peoples lack faith. But what effects should we argue from this fact, and what are its causes ? Shall we affirm a false identity between faith and power ? shall we say that where faith is wanting the power to achieve does not exist ; that to-day the people are impotent from the very nature of things, that they have not suffered enough, that the times are not ripe, that the atonement— if indeed the peoples have aught to atone—is yet unaccomplished ?

To accept such opinions would be to accept a system of historical fatalism which the intelligence of the age has rejected. We should make cowardly obeisance to a fact, without any effort to explain it, and deny the innate potentialities of humanity. The existence of a fact does not prove its necessity : it can only govern the actions of those who press materialism to its extremes and renounce the study of causes to lie passive under their influence. Will you deny to a man power to walk because he stands

motionless before you ?   The actual condition of things
is no measure of the forces which are latent in the peoples.
Are the peoples essentially weak, or do they simply lack
faith, that faith which reveals itself in deeds and sets
forces in motion ? These are the true terms of the problem.
Yes ; the peoples lack faith ; not the individual faith,
which makes martyrs, but the common, *social* faith, which
gains victories ; the faith which awakens the multitudes ;
that faith in their destiny, in their mission, in the mission
of the Age, which illumines and rouses, prays and fights ;
which fearlessly advances along the paths of God and
Humanity, bearing in its right hand the people's sword,
in its heart the people's religion, in its soul the people's
future.   But this faith which was preached by Lamennais,
the high priest of the age, and which should be translated
by others in the terms of their own national life, will it
come to us from our sense of strength or from our
conscience ?   Is it an instinct of our real impotence that
has banished it from our lives, or is it opinions falsely
conceived, and prejudices that we can fight ?   Would not
one act of strenuous will suffice to restore the balance
between oppressor and oppressed ?   And if this be so,
are we working to evoke it ?   Are our tendencies, our
manifestations of the thought we would promote, sufficient
to achieve our purpose ?   Are we impelled by fate to lead
the movement, or are the masses who follow us responsible
for the present sleep of death ?
   Consider Italy. Misfortune, suffering, protests, individual sacrifice, have reached their extreme limit in
that land.   The cup is full.   Oppression, like the air, is
all-pervading : rebellion also.   Three separate States,
twenty cities, two millions of men revolt in a week,[1] overthrow their governments and declare themselves emancipated, and not a single protest was made, not a single
drop of blood was shed.   Insurrections follow in quick
succession.   Is force wanting to those twenty-five millions ?
Italy in revolution has strength enough to fight three
Austrias.   Do they lack the inspiration of traditions,
the religion of memories, a storied past ?   Nay, the people

G 224   [1] See Appendix, p. 285.

still bow before the holy relics of a greatness that was once. Do they lack a mission? Nay, Italy alone among the nations has twice given the gospel of Unity to Europe. Is courage wanting? Ask of the days of 1746, of 1799; of the memories of the *Grande Armée*; of the martyrs, thrice holy, who for fourteen years have died for an idea, silent and inglorious.

Consider Switzerland. Can any one deny true valour, the deep sense of independence, of those sons of the Alps? Five centuries of struggle, of intrigues, of civil and religious strife, have failed to soil their flag of 1308 with foreign oppression. And yet Switzerland—that Switzerland who defeated Austria in twenty battles, whose war-cry would suffice to raise Germany and Italy in insurrection, and who knows well how kings would pause ere they embarked on a European war that the peoples clamoured for, because they know that its last battle would be the Waterloo of Monarchy—yet Switzerland to-day, as the months come round, accepts dishonour and bows her head before each petty dispatch of an Austrian agent.

Remember 1813 and the German youth who deserted the lecture-rooms of the Universities to hasten to the battles of Independence; remember the thrill of excitement at the cry of Nationality, Liberty, a common Fatherland, which ran through Germany from one end to the other, and then tell me if the Deputies, Electors, public writers, and all the men of position who were content to lose themselves in the maze of constitutional opposition, if all these had rallied around the banner of Hambach,[1] whether that would not have sufficed to rouse the whole people.

Remember Grochow, Waver, Ostrolenska,[2] and then tell me to what straits Russia would have been driven, if Poland had wasted no precious time, begging help of the

---

[1] The *Constitutionsfest* of 1832 at Hambach—a great popular demonstration in favour of Constitutional Reform held near the old castle of that name. It was an echo of the French Revolution of July 1830, and was attended by thousands of people from all parts of South-western Germany.
[2] Battles during the Polish Insurrection of 1831. See Fyffe's *History of Modern Europe*, Vol. II, c. v.

diplomacy who had stabbed her for a hundred years; if her armies had at once shifted the active revolutionary movement to its natural centre beyond the Boug; if some great conception of a people's freedom had called to insurrection the races, whose true heart Bogdan Chmielnicki revealed in 1648; if, while enthusiasm was dictator, and terror paralysed the enemy, while the masses of Lithuania, of Galicia, of Ucrania, were quivering with hopes of liberty, the insurrection had flown from the Belvedere to Lithuania.

I state with profound conviction, that there probably does not exist a single people in Europe which is not able by faith, by self-sacrifice, and by the logic of revolution to break its chains in the face of monarchical Europe conspiring to work its doom—not a people that is not able through the holy creed of the Future and of Love, through the mighty watchward inscribed on its banner of insurrection, to start a crusade in Europe—no, not a people which has not had its chance since 1830.

But in Italy, in Germany, in Poland, in Switzerland, in France, everywhere, men, unfortunately influential, have perverted the orginal character of the revolution—ambitious and covetous men have seen in the uprising of a people only a chance to slake their own thirst of pelf or power—weak men who trembled at the difficulties of the undertaking, have, at the very onset, sacrificed the logical development of insurrection to their own fears. Everywhere false and deadly doctrines have turned revolutions from their goal. The theory of class rule has supplanted the people's theory of the emancipation of all by efforts of all. The national idea has been weakened or destroyed by the idea of foreign assistance. Nowhere did the promoters and directors of the insurrection cast into the scale of their country's destiny the sum-total of the forces that a strenuous and inspired will would have brought into play: nowhere have consciousness of a high mission, faith in its fulfilment, and a knowledge of the age and its dominant idea, guided the men who assumed the control of events, and made themselves responsible to humanity for their success.

They had before them a task for giants, and they grovelled on their bellies. They saw darkly the secret of the generations; they heard the cry of tribes of men eager to shake off the dust of their sepulchres, and, youthful or regenerate, confront a new life. It was their task to publish, without fear, on the housetops the gospel of the People and the Nations; and instead, they stammered halting words of royal concessions, of a charter, of compacts between right and might, justice and injustice. They tried, like old men whose natural force is spent, to prolong an artificial existence, and sought in the policy of the old régime the secret of its imperfect and fleeting life. They mingled life and death, liberty and servitude, privilege and equality, past and future. We were bound —though even on their dead bodies—to raise the flag of revolt so high that all nations might read on it a promise of victory. And they dragged it through the mire of royalty, overlaid it with protocols and nailed its motionless folds, like the sign of a bawdy house, on the doors of all the Foreign Legations: they believed in the promises of every minister, in the hopes held out by every Ambassador; in everything, except in the people and its omnipotence. ● We saw revolutionary leaders immersed in the study of the treaties of 1815, seeking therein, forsooth, the charter of Polish or Italian liberty; others more guilty, denied Humanity, and made selfishness their God, when they wrote on their banner a principle of *non-intervention* worthy of the Middle Ages; others, more guilty still, denied their brothers and their Fatherland, broke up national unity at the moment that they should have introduced its triumph; they uttered the impious words, "Men of Bologna, the cause of the Modenese is not our cause," even while the foreigner was advancing to their gates. They all forgot—in their zeal to give, as they said, a *legal* character to revolution—that every insurrection acquires legality from its aim, legitimacy from victory, means of defence from offence, pledges of success from expansion: they forgot that the charter of each nation's liberty is a clause in the Charter of Humanity, that they

alone deserve to conquer who are prepared to conquer
or to die for all.

And then—seeing the men who started the revolutions pale in front of their undertaking, retreat when
action became imperative, or take a devious and timid
path, without a goal, without a programme, without
hope except in foreign help, the people also were afraid
and paused, or rather perceived that the hour had not
yet come, and stopped short. With revolutions before
them betrayed in their inception, the masses abstained,
nascent enthusiasm was stifled, *faith* disappeared.

IV

Faith disappeared; but what have we done, what
are we doing, to raise it up again? Oh shame and woe
to us! Since that holy light of the nations vanished,
we have been wandering in the darkness, without a
bond, without a purpose, without unity of direction;
or have folded our arms upon our breasts like men
without hope. Some few lifted a long cry of anguish,
renounced all earthly progress, to croon a chant of
resignation, a death-bed prayer[1]; or they made themselves rebels against hope,[2] and with a bitter smile
proclaimed the advent of the powers of darkness : they
accepted scepticism, cynicism, faithlessness, as inevitable, irrevocable facts of human nature; and the
echo of their blasphemies translated itself in degraded
natures into corruption, and in untainted natures into
the suicide of despair.[3] Our literature of to-day
oscillates between these extremes. Others, suddenly
remembering the light which illumined their infancy,
dragged themselves back to the sanctuary whence it
issued, and laboured to rekindle it;[4] or were absorbed
in contemplation of self, and began to live in the *ego*,
and there forgetting or denying the world of phenomena,
never advanced beyond the study of the *individual*,

[1] *e.g.*—The German Romancists, and partly, Manzoni and Foscolo.
[2] *e.g.*—Byron.
[3] See Foscolo's *Jacopo Ortis*, a favourite book of Mazzini's.
[4] *e.g.*—Chateaubriand, Manzoni, and, in his early days, Victor Hugo.

And this is our philosophy. Others, finally, born for battle, spurred by a passion of self-sacrifice, which, under wise guidance, would have worked miracles, dominated by sublime but imperfect and ill-defined instincts, snatched a banner from their fathers' tombs, and rushed forward; but in the first few steps they parted. Each of them tore a shred from the flag and vaunted it as the flag of all the host. This is the history of our political life.

We ask pardon of the reader for our insistence on these complaints. They are our *delenda Carthago*. Mine is not the work of a writer: it is the stern and fearless mission of an apostle. This mission permits of no diplomacy. I am investigating the causes of a delay which seems to me to have its source outside the hostile forces. I seek a way of stating the problem in such terms as may permit us quickly to win back the power of making a new departure. Therefore I must be silent or speak the whole truth.

Now, it seems to me that the delay has two chief causes, both due to the Party wandering from its goal, both tending to substitute the worship of the past for the worship of the future.

The first of these causes has led us to mistake for a programme what was nothing more than a concluding chapter, a powerful summary, a formula which gave expression to the work of a whole age and its conquests. It has made us confound two distinct philosophies of life and two distinct ages, and reduce a mission of social regeneration to the narrow proportions of a work of development and deduction from old premisses. It has caused us to abandon the principle for its symbol, God for an idol; to stay the soul's flight towards a New Ideal, that fiery cross that is transmitted by the hand of God from one people to another; to degrade and smother the national spirit of the peoples, which is their life, their mission and the strength given for its achievement, the part assigned to them by God in the common task, in the development of thought one and manifold, which is the soul of our life on earth.

(2) The second cause has led us to confound the principle
with one of its manifestations, the eternal element of
every social organisation with one of its successive
developments, and to consider a mission as completed
which was only expanding and, in consequence, changing
its character.   Because of that error we broke up the
unity of the conception precisely when it required a wider
development; we travestied the function of the eighteenth
century ; we made a negation the starting-point of the
nineteenth, and abandoned religious thought when it
was more than ever necessary to revive and to extend
it till it embraced every element that is destined to be
transformed, and to gather together in one great social
conception all the truths that to-day lie unrelated and
apart.

V

The eighteenth century, which is too generally regarded
as a century of scepticism and negations, devoted entirely
to a task of criticism, had its faith, its mission, and
practical schemes to fulfil it.   It was a titanic, boundless
faith in human liberty and power.   Its mission was to
tabulate—if the expression be permissible—the *assets* of
the first Epoch of the European world : to epitomise and
reduce to a concrete formula that which eighteen centuries of Christianity had examined, developed, made a
fact : to constitute the *individual* as he was called to be,
free, active, sacred, inviolable : that was its mission.
And achieved it by the French Revolution, a translation
into political terms of the (3.) protestant revolution, a
deeply religious manifestation, whatever superficial
writers may think who judge the whole period by the
aberrations of a few individuals, secondary actors in the
drama.   The instrument employed to effect the revolution and to achieve its mission was *Right*.   Its power, its
mandate, the legitimacy of its actions, lay in a theory
of Rights : its supreme formula was a Declaration of
Rights.   What else, in fact, is *man*, the individual, save
Right ?   Does he not, within the ever-advancing boundaries of progress, represent the human *person* and the

element of individual freedom ? And the *aim* of the
eighteenth century was precisely to complete that *human*
evolution which was foreseen by the ancients, announced
by Christianity, and attained in part by protestantism.
Between the century and that aim stood a multitude of
obstacles ; fetters of all kinds on free spontaneity, on
the free devolopment of individual faculties ; warnings,
rules, and orders, that limited human action ; the
traditions of a force that was spent ; aristocracies which
seemed capable and strong ; religious forms that forbade
progress. It was necessary to overthrow them all, and
the century overthrew them. It fought a long and
terrible but victorious battle against every influence
that frittered human power into disconnected fragments,
that denied progress or stayed the flight of intellect.
Every great revolutionary thought needs an ideal for its
centre of action, its fulcrum. This ideal the century
found by *subjectively* centring itself in the individual ; and
it was the *ego*, the human conscience, the "I am"[1]
of Christ to the Powers of His day. Centred in that
conception, the Revolution, conscious of its own strength
and sovereignty by right of conquest, disdained to prove
to the world its origin, its roots in the past. First it
professed its faith. It cried like Fichte : "Liberty !
without Equality there is no Liberty ; all men are equal."
Then it proceeded to deny. It denied the dead past :
it denied feudalism, aristocracy, monarchy. It denied
the (4.) Catholic dogma, a dogma of absolute resignation,
that poisoned the springs of liberty and planted despotism
at the summit of its structure. Unnumbered wrecks
strewed the ground. But in the midst of them, amid
all those negations, a mighty Yea arose—the creature
of God ready to act, radiant with power and will—
the *ecce homo*, repeated after eighteen centuries of
suffering and strife, not by the voice of the martyr,
but on the altar raised by the revolution to victory
—Right, *individual* faith, rooted in the world for ever.

Is this all we seek ? Should man, endowed with
power to progress, idly repose like an emancipated slave

[1] John viii. 58.

content with his own solitary liberty ? Does nothing
remain, to fulfil his mission on the earth, but to carry
the principle to its logical conclusions, to translate them
into facts, and to defend the ground we have won, but
advance no further ?

Is the series of terms which make the great equation
closed because the human *unknown quantity* is known,
because one of the terms of progress, that which constitutes the *individual*, can be placed among quantities
that are *known* and defined ? Is the faculty of progress exhausted ? Is no movement possible but in a
circle ?

Because man, consecrated by thought to the kingdom
of the world, has broken through an outworn form of
religion that imprisoned his activity and denied him
independence, shall we never more possess a bond of
common brotherhood, or religion, or conception of
universal Providential law that all may take and believe ?

No, eternal God ! Thy word is not finished ; Thy
thought, the thought of the world, is not yet all revealed. It still creates, and will continue to create,
for long ages beyond all human calculation. The
ages that have run their course have only revealed to
us a few fragments. Our mission is not ended. We
scarcely know its origin ; we know nothing of its final
end : time and our discoveries do but extend its confines.
It ascends from century to century, towards destinies
unknown to us : it seeks its own law, of which we possess
but the first few lines. From initiative to initiative
through the series of Thy successive incarnations it
purifies and extends the formula of self-sacrifice : pursues
its own path : learns thy ever-widening law. Forms are
altered and dissolved. Religions die. The human spirit
leaves them behind, as the wayfarer leaves the fires that
warmed him in the night, and goes in search of other Suns,
But Religion remains. Thought is immortal ; it survives
all forms, and is born again from its own ashes. The idea
frees itself from the shrunken symbol, escapes from the
chrysalis which prisoned it, which criticism had eaten
through. It shines forth pure and bright, a new star

*G 224

in the firmament of Humanity. How many has faith
yet to add that the whole way of the future may be
illumined ? Who can say how many stars, thoughts
of the ages, have yet to rise in cloudless splendour
and shine in the firmament of mind, that man may
become a living epitome of the Word on the earth,
and may say to himself, " I have faith in myself ; my
destiny is accomplished " ?

This is the Law. One task succeeds to another ; one
ideal of life to another. And for us the one that pre-
cedes us directs our task and declares its method and
order. It includes all the terms that the earlier systems
have won, and adds the new one which becomes the end
and aim of all our efforts, the *unknown* quantity that we
have to solve. Criticism, too, has its work, but finds its
performance in the positive belief of the age. Criticism,
in fact, lives only a borrowed life ; it exists only in
phenomena ; it draws from other sources its purpose,
mission, standard. A part of every age, it is the banner
of none. The [1] thinker who divides Epochs into organic
and critical falsifies History. Every Epoch is essentially
synthetic and organic. The progressive evolution of
thought, of which our world is the visible manifestation,
takes place by continual expansion. The chain cannot
be broken. The diverse *aims* are bound together. The
cradle is linked to the tomb.

VI

Thus, scarcely had the French Revolution concluded
one Epoch, when the first rays of another appeared on
the horizon ; scarcely had the human *individual*, with
the charter of rights in his hand, proclaimed his triumph,
when human thought presented another charter, that of
principles. Scarcely was the *unknown* quantity of the so-
called Middle Ages solved, and the great purpose of the
(5.) Christian system attained, when another *unknown*
quantity asked solution of the present generation, another
aim called for its efforts. On every side men were ask-

' The St. Simonian.

ing : **What** is the end of liberty, or of equality, which in
its ultimate analysis is only the liberty of all ? The *free
man* is only an *active force* ready to work. In what
manner shall it work ? Capriciously ? In every direction
that presents itself? That is not *life*, rather a simple
sequence of acts, of phenomena, of symptoms of vitality,
without connection or relation, or continuity : its name is
anarchy. The liberty of one will inevitably clash with
the liberty of another ; we shall have continually shock
and counter-shock among individuals, waste of force and
useless dissipation of that productive faculty within
which should be held sacred. The liberty of all, without
a common law to direct it, leads to a war of all, the more
inexorably cruel, the more the individual combatants are
equally matched. And men imagined they had found
the remedy when they had disinterred from the foot of
the cross of Christ—that cross which dominates a whole
age in the history of the world—the phrase of *brotherhood*
which the Man-God when dying had left to the human
race : a sublime word unknown to the pagan world,
through which the Christian world had, often unconsciously, fought many a holy battle from the Crusades to
Lepanto. They wrote it on all their banners, and with
its sister watch-words, liberty and equality, it formed the
programme of the future. Then they tried to restrain
progress within the circle marked out by those three
points. But progress burst through the ring. Once
again the eternal " *cui bono* " appeared. We all in fact
demand an *aim*, a *human* aim : what else is existence
but an *end* with means calculated to attain it ? And
brotherhood does not include a common social ideal for
men on earth : it does not include even its necessity : it
has no essential necessary relation to the development of
a purpose, that shall bind together in harmony all our
faculties and powers. *Brotherhood* is certainly the base
of every society, the first condition of social progress, but
it is not progress itself. It makes progress possible, it
supplies it with a necessary constituent, but it does not
define it. The principle of brotherhood is compatible
with movement in a circle. And the human mind began

to understand that *brotherhood* — the necessary link between two principles of *liberty* and *equality*, that epitomise the *individualistic* philosophy—never passes beyond their limits, that its activity can only operate between individuals, that it easily assumes the name of *charity*, that though it can fix the starting-point whence Humanity shall reach the social Ideal, it can never be substituted for it.

The quest was pursued further. We saw darkly that the *end*, the function of existence, must also be the final goal of that progressive development which constitutes existence itself ; that hence in order to make straight and swift for this *end*, it was necessary to know exactly the nature of such progression and bring our actions into harmony with it. *To understand the Law and to regulate our work in accordance with it*, is the true way to state the problem. Now the law of the individual can only be discovered in the *species*. The mission of the individual can only be learnt and defined from an elevation which commands the whole field. Hence to know even the law of the individual it is necessary to ascend. Only from a conception of Humanity can we deduce the secret, the standard, the law of life for *man*. Hence the necessity for the co-operation of all, for harmony in our labours, in a word, for *association*, in order that the work of all (6.) may be accomplished ; hence also the need for a thorough change in the organisation of the revolutionary Party, in theories of government, in the study of philosophy, politics, and economics, all of which have been till now inspired by the sole principle of liberty. The horizon has changed. The sacred word *Humanity*, uttered with new significance, has discovered to the eye of Genius a new world, which hitherto had been no more than a presentiment ; a new Age has begun.

Do we need a book to prove it? Do we need time for the principle to develop in order to demonstrate that such is really the present intellectual movement, that the century is labouring in search of its own philosophy of life? Have we not seen, for a period of nearly twenty years, all the schools of philosophy occupying themselves, even when they stray back to the past, in the search after a great *unknown*? Is not this confessed almost despite themselves by those who would gain most by diverting men from the end? We see to-day a Catholicism that attempts to reconcile Gregory VII. with Luther, the papacy with the free and independent human soul. We have a retrograde and hypocritical party, that gropes dubiously among theories of government, and a stammering mystic kind of jesuitism, which sacrilegiously mutters the name of *social* party. And daily we hear the word *Humanity* on the lips of materialists, [1] who cannot understand its worth, and who betray every moment their natural affinities to the individualism of the Empire. Whether as a heartfelt belief, or homage given perforce, the new Age has won its rights over nearly all intellects. Some of the perfervid apostles of progress were not long since complaining that the hostile camp had pirated our words without even understanding their significance; it was a puerile complaint. It is just in this very accord, instinctive and unwilling as it is, that we find a potent mark of the Word of our Age, HUMANITY.

Now, every Age has its own peculiar faith. Every system includes the conception of an *ideal* and a mission. And every mission has its own instrument, its own forces, its own lever. Any attempt to translate into facts the mission of one Age with the machinery of another, can only end in an indefinite series of abortive efforts. Defeated by the utter want of proportion between the means and the end, such attempts might produce martyrs, but never lead to victory.

And this is the point we have reached. All our hearts and intellects have the presentiment of a great Age; and yet we would give it, for the ensign of its faith, mere criticism and the negations with which the eighteenth century was forced to surround its new conquest of liberty. We mutter by God's inspiration the sublime words, regeneration, progress, a new mission, the future;

---

[1] St. Simonians

and yet, when we try to realise the programme they
contain, we obstinately use the weapons of a mission
that is dead. We invoke a *social* world, a vast harmonious
organisation of the forces which are seething confusedly
in this vast workshop we call earth ; and to call that new
world into life, to lay the foundations of a peaceful
organisation, we hark back to old habits of rebellion,
that waste our strength within the circle of *individualism*.
We raise the cry of " the future ! " with the wrecks of old
systems all about us. Though our chains are lengthened,
we are prisoners still, and we brag of our liberty because
we are free to move round the post to which our chains
are fastened.

And because of this, faith slumbers in the hearts of
the peoples : because of this not even the blood of a
whole nation can revive it.

VII

Faith requires a purpose that shall embrace the
whole of *life*, that shall concentrate all its manifestations and direct its diverse modes, or subordinate them
to the controlling activity of a single one : it requires
a fervid, unshaken belief that that purpose shall be
attained ; the profound conviction of a mission and
the obligation to fulfil it ; finally, the consciousness of
a supreme power that guards the believer's progress to
his goal. These are the indispensable elements : and
where any one is wanting, we may have a sect, a school,
a political party ; not a faith, nor an hourly self-sacrifice
for the sake of a high religious ideal.

But we have no definite religious ideal, or deep
conviction of the duty implied in a mission, or the
consciousness of a supreme and protecting authority.
Our apostolate to-day is an opposition of criticism.
We fight by appealing to selfish interests, and our
weapon is a theory of rights. We are all, sublime
presentiments notwithstanding, children of rebellion.
We move, like renegades, without God, without Law,
without a banner which shall beckon to the future.

The old *aim* has disappeared : the new one, which, for an instant we dimly saw, is annulled by the doctrine of rights, that alone directs our labours. For us the *individual* is at once *end* and *means*. We use the essentially religious phrase, *Humanity,* and banish religion from all our works. We look only at the political side of things. We talk of harmonising human faculties, and neglect the most obvious and active element of human nature. We are bold enough not to shrink from the dream of a material European unity, and yet we thoughtlessly break up its moral unity by ignoring the fundamental conditions of all association —uniformity of belief and of religious sanction. In the midst of such contradictions we attempt, forsooth, to make a new world.

Nor do I exaggerate. I know the exceptions and admire them. But the Party, speaking generally, is such as I describe it. Its presentiments, its aspirations, belong to the new Age : the characteristics of its organisation and the means it proposes to adopt, belong to the old. The Party has long divined the mission entrusted to it, but without understanding its character or the machinery adapted to its fulfilment. Hence it is powerless to succeed, and will be, until the day come, when it shall understand that the cry " God wills it " is the eternal cry of every movement which has, like ours, self-sacrifice for its foundation, the peoples for its instrument, Humanity for its end.

What ! You complain that faith is dead or dying ! you lament that souls are scorched with the breath of egotism—and yet you mock at belief, and proclaim in your pages that religion no longer exists ; that its day is past, and the religious future of the peoples for ever closed ! You marvel that the masses advance but slowly along the path of self-sacrifice and association, and in the meantime you lay down as your principle a theory of *individualism* that has only a negative value ; a theory that results not in association, but in loose concourses of human atoms, and which in ultimate analysis is only egotism draped in the mantle of philosophical formulas.

Your purpose should be a work of regeneration, of moral reform—for without this any political organisation is barren—and you delude yourselves with expectations of success while you banish from your work the religious idea.

Politics deal with men *where* and *as* they are : they define their tendencies and regulate their actions in accordance with them. It is only religious thought that can transfigure both.

Religious thought is the breath of life of Humanity : at once its life and soul, its spirit and its outward sign. Humanity exists only in the consciousness of its own origin, and the presentiment of its own destinies. It reveals itself only when it concentrates its forces on some point between the two. Now this is precisely the function of the religious idea. That idea establishes a belief in the common origin of all ; it places before us, as an article of belief, a common future ; it concentrates all the active faculties round a central point, from which they move on unceasingly in the direction of that future ; it directs all the forces latent in the human soul to its attainment. It comprehends life in all its aspects ; in its every manifestation, however minute ; it breathes good wishes over the cradle and the tomb ; supplies, in philosophic language, the higher and most general formula of a given Epoch of civilisation, the simplest and most comprehensive expression of its *knowledge*, the common principle which governs the whole, and controls all its successive evolutions. That idea is, for the individual, the symbol of the relation that exists between him and the Age to which he belongs, the revelation of his function, and standard of conduct ; the flag that makes him able to fulfil his mission. That idea elevates and purifies the individual ; dries up the springs of egotism, by changing and removing outside himself the centre of activity. It creates for man that theory of *duty* which is the mother of self-sacrifice, which ever was, and ever will be, the inspirer of great and noble things ; a sublime theory, that draws man near to God, borrows from the divine nature a spark of

omnipotence, crosses at one leap all obstacles, makes
the martyr's scaffold a ladder to victory, and is as
superior to the narrow, imperfect theory of rights as the
law is superior to one of its corollaries. (7.)

Right is the faith of the individual : Duty is the
common, collective faith. Right can only organise
resistance; destroy, not found. Duty builds up and
associates ; it springs from a general law, whereas Right
has its origin only in individual will. Hence nothing
prevents attacks on rights : every injured individual may
rebel against them ; and force alone is the supreme
arbiter between the antagonists. This, in fact, was the
reply that societies founded upon *rights* often made to
their enemies. Now societies that make *duty* their basis
would not be driven to use force ; once admit the
principle of duty, and the possibility of strife has gone,
the individual is made subordinate to the common aim,
and thus duty cuts at the very root of the evil for which
right has only palliatives. Moreover, the doctrine of
rights does not include progress as a necessary element :
it admits it merely as a simple fact. The exercise of
rights being necessarily optional, progress is abandoned
to the caprice of a liberty without rule or purpose. And
Right kills self-sacrifice, and banishes martyrdom from
the world. In every theory of individual rights, material
interests alone dominate and martyrdom becomes absurd :
what interests can exist beyond the tomb ? But for all
that, martyrdom is often the baptism of a world, the
solemn initiation of progress. Every doctrine that does
not rest on progress as an essential law of its being is
inferior to the ideal and to the needs of the Age. And
yet, the doctrine of *rights* even to-day reigns sovereign
among us ; it rules that republican party which announces
itself as the advanced party in Europe : and yet—for it
matters little if our lips instinctively utter the words,
duty, self-sacrifice, mission—the liberty of the republicans
is merely a theory of resistance : their religion, if indeed
they mention it, only expresses the relation between God
and the *individual* : the political order they invoke and
honour by the name of *social* is only a series of prohibitions

promoted into laws, which ensure to each the power of
pursuing his *own* aim, his *own* interests, his *own* tendencies : their definition of Law does not go beyond the
expression of the general will : their formula of association
is the *Society of Rights* : their creed does not pass beyond
the limits laid down nearly half a century ago in a
Declaration of Rights, by a man who was himself the
incarnation of the struggle : their theories of Authority
are theories of *mistrust* : their organic problem—an old
remnant of a patched-up constitutionalism—is reduced to
finding a point around which *individualism* and *association*,
liberty and general law, may oscillate for ever in barren
antagonism : their people is often a caste—the most
numerous, it is true, and the most useful—in open
rebellion against other castes in order to enjoy in its
turn the rights that God intends for all : their republic
is the, turbulent, intolerant democracy of Athens (8.) :
their war-cry is a cry of vengeance : their symbol,
Spartacus.

Now, this is the eighteenth century once more, its
philosophy, its theory of mankind, its materialistic polity,
its analysis, its protestant criticism, its sovereignty of the
individual, its rejection of an old religious formula, its
mistrust of all authority, its spirit of strife and emancipation.   It is the French Revolution over again ; the
past with some new glimpses of the future ; servitude to
old things surrounded by the prestige of youth.

VIII

The past is fatal to us.   The French Revolution, I
state with conviction, is crushing us.   It weighs almost
like an incubus upon our heart and impedes its action.
We are dazzled by the splendour of its gigantic struggles,
fascinated by its victorious glance, and so remain to-day
still prostrate before it.   We expect everything, both in
men and things, from its programme ; we attempt to copy
Robespierre and St. Just, and search in the records of the
Clubs of 1792 or 1793 names for the *sections* of 1833 or
1834.   Now, while we are aping our fathers we forget

that our fathers aped no one, and were great because of this.   Their inspirations flowed from contemporary sources, from the needs of the masses, from the nature of their environment.   And precisely because the instrument they employed was adapted to the purpose they had in view, they worked miracles.   Why do we not act as they did?   Why, while studying and respecting tradition, should we not move onward?   We ought to worship the greatness of our fathers, and seek in their tombs a pledge of the future, not the future itself.   The future is before us, and God, the father of all revelations and all ages, alone can point out the infinite way.

Up, then! and let us be great in our turn.   For this, it is necessary to understand our mission in its fulness. We stand to-day between two ages, between the grave of one world and the cradle of another, between the last boundary of the *individualistic* philosophy and the threshold of HUMANITY.   With eyes fixed on the future, we must break the last links of the chain which holds us in bondage to the past, and with deliberate stages move on.   We have freed ourselves from the abuses of the old world : we must now free ourselves from its glories.   The task of the eighteenth century is accomplished.   Our fathers repose tranquil and proud in their tombs.   They sleep, like warriors after battle, wrapped in their flag. Fear not that you will grieve them.   The red banner of the blood of Christ which Luther handed on to the Convention,[1] to be planted on the slain in twenty battles of the peoples, is a trophy sacred to us all.   None will dare to touch it.   But let us advance in the name of God.   We will return hereafter to lay at its foot, there where our fathers lie, some of the laurels that our own hands have won.   To-day we have to found the polity of the nineteenth century, to climb through *philosophy* to *faith* ; to define and organise association, proclaim HUMANITY, initiate the new Age.   The old Age can attain its actual fulfilment only in the baptism of the new.

These things are perhaps not new.   I know this and

[1] The French National Convention of 1793.

confess it gladly. My voice is but one among many that preach nearly the same ideas, and proclaim *association* as the fundamental principle that must henceforth direct our political work. Many powerful intellects have condemned the cold doctrine of *rights* wherever they have found it alone and disconnected, condemned it as the last formula of *individualism*, to-day degenerating into sheer materialism : many schools, some extinct, some still active, invoke *duty* as an anchor of salvation for a society tormented by fruitless desires. Why, then, do I insist on protesting against their want of fore-sight ? What does it matter if the end preached be the centre of a new programme, or only the development of the old ; if men whose cry, like ours, is *forward !* persist in confounding *association* with *fraternity*, or HUMANITY —the compendium of all human faculties organised to one end—with more liberty and equality for all ? Why proclaim a new Age, and so involve ourselves in all the difficulties of a fresh task ?

Is, then, our contest one of names alone ?

I think not.

It is important to proclaim a new Age : to affirm that all we preach to-day on earth is verily a new pro-gramme ; and, for this reason, that it is bound to be henceforth universally recognised.

We desire not only to *think*, but to *act*. We desire not only the freeing of one people, and of others through it, but the freeing of all the peoples through their own efforts. Now, conscience alone frees the peoples. They will act only when they recognise a new ideal whose attainment demands the exertions of all, the equality of all, and a new departure. Without such recognition, there is no hope of faith, of self-sacrifice, of enthusiasm mighty to work. The peoples who lie crushed by the burden of the earlier movement will lightly surrender the accomplishment of the new one to the nation that has taken the responsibility, and therewith the glory. They will be content to follow from afar, and ask no more. And if through causes unknown to them that people shall halt on the way, they will halt with it.

And then we shall have silence, inaction, suspended life. This is the spectacle that, while I write, the whole of Europe presents.

The ideal of a new Age, which includes a new end to be attained, gives the initiative to the future, and kindles the universal conscience into life. By it we learn to start afresh and not to copy; we work out our own mission, not execute another's; we put Europe in the stead of France. We furnish a potent element to feed revolutionary activity. By proclaiming a new Age we proclaim the existence of a new philosophy of life, a general conception destined to embrace all the terms of earlier philosophies with yet one more; and, working from that new term, we co-ordinate all the historical series, all the facts that are grouped around it, all the manifestations of life, all the aspects of the human problem, all the branches of human knowledge. We give a second, a new impulse to the labour of the intellect. We proclaim the need of a new encyclopedia, which shall summarise all the progress we have made, and in itself be one step forward more. We place outside controversy all the aims which formed the purpose of past revolutions, the liberty, the equality, the fraternity of men and of peoples; we put them in the list of undisputed truths. We part for ever from the exclusively *individualist* Age, and with greater reason, from that *individualism* which is the materialism of that age. We block the roads to the past.

And finally, by that affirmation we reject every doctrine of eclecticism and transition, every imperfect and issueless phrase that states a problem without attempting to solve it. We part from every school that tries to reconcile life and death, and to reform the world by an extinct philosophy. We bind God Himself surety for the sacred doctrine of the people, and its sovereignty. We place, in the very stamp of the age, a new title to universal suffrage. We raise politics to a philosophical conception. We establish an apostolate of Humanity, by vindicating that common right of nations which should be the symbol of our creed. We consecrate those spontaneous, sudden, collective movements of the peoples, whose work it is to proclaim the new Ideal of life, and translate it into action. We lay the corner-stone of a Humanitarian Faith, to which the republican Party must rise, if it still wish to conquer. Therefore it is that every Age has its baptism of faith ; ours still lacks it, and we can, if nothing more, prepare the way, and make ourselves its heralds.

IX

Ours is therefore no idle contest of words. The triumph or the failure of the cause we uphold depends upon the road which the Party takes.

We fell as a political party : we must rise again as a religious party.

The religious element is universal and immortal : it binds men together in a universal brotherhood. Every great revolution is marked with its imprint, and reveals it in its origin and aim. Heralds of a new world, we must found a moral unity, the Catholicism of Humanity. And we move encouraged by the holy promise of Jesus : we seek the new Gospel, of which He left us, ere He died, the immortal hope, and of which the Christian Gospel is the germ, as *man* is the germ of HUMANITY. On the soil fertilised by fifty generations of martyrs, we hail with Lessing that immensity of future which finds its fulcrum in the Fatherland, and its goal in Humanity. Then shall the peoples make a common covenant, and define in brotherly compact each one's mission in the future, the office which devolves on each in the general association, which owns one Law, one God for all. It is for us to hasten the moment when the Revolu-tion, the tocsin of the peoples, shall call together a new Convention, that shall be a true Council of the faithful. Therefore our war must needs be a holy crusade. Let God shine on our banner, as on our destinies. Raise we on the old world's wreck an altar where the people may burn the incense of reconciliation. And know we all at least what answer to make to Him who would ask of us : Whence come ye ? In whose name do ye preach ?

Often have I heard such questions. Often has it been said of our little band of apostles : " The republicans have no philosophic basis, no indisputable principle, as the fountain of their creed." The accusers, it is true, were men who think they have a philosophy because some among their followers have made a collection of philosophies, a religion because they have priests, a political doctrine because they have soldiers and grapeshot. None the less the charge was taken up by men of good faith, who could not fail to note in our ranks a visible lack of unity or of a harmonious philosophy ; an absence of religious belief that could not be easily reconciled with the social and essentially religious *end* that republicanism now and again proclaims.

Now, we are able to reply : We come in the name of God and of HUMANITY.

We believe in one God, author of all that exists, the living absolute Thought, of which our world is a ray and the Universe an incarnation.

We believe in one Law, general and immutable, that constitutes our mode of existence, that embraces every series of possible phenomena, and exercises a continuous influence upon the universe, and on all it contains, both in its physical and in its moral aspect.

Since every *law* requires an *end* to be attained, we believe in the progressive development in all existing things, of faculties and forces—which are faculties in motion—towards that unknown *end*, without which law would be useless and existence unintelligible.

And since every *law* is interpreted and verified in its own *subject*, we believe in HUMANITY, a collective and continuous Being, in which is epitomised the whole ascending series of organic creations, and in which, as the sole interpreter of the law, is most fully manifested God's thought on earth.

We believe, that inasmuch as harmony between the *subject* and the *law* is the condition of all normal existence, the manifest and immediate end of all our labours is to effect the greater completion and security of that harmony, through the fuller discovery of the *law* and its realisation in its *subject*.

We believe in ASSOCIATION—which is but the *active* belief in one God, in one Law, in one End—as the only means possessed by us to *realise* Truth, as the method of progress, as the only existing road to perfection, so that the higher the scale of human progress the more embracing may be its corresponding formula of association won for men, and applied to their life.

We believe therefore in the HOLY ALLIANCE OF THE PEOPLES as the broadest formula of association possible in our age—in the *liberty* and *equality* of the peoples, without which association has no true life—in *Nationality*, which is the conscience of the peoples, which assigns to them their share of work in the association, their office in HUMANITY, and hence constitutes their mission on earth, their *individuality*; for without Nationality neither liberty nor equality is possible—and we believe in the holy *Fatherland*, that is, the cradle of nationality, the altar and patrimony of the individuals that compose each people.

And since the LAW is one, since it governs equally the two aspects, internal and external, of the *life* of every being, the two modes of self and relativity, of the subjective and the objective that appertain to every existence, we believe for each people and its component individuals the same that we believe for HUMANITY and *its* component peoples. As we believe in the association of peoples, so we believe in association between the individuals who compose each nation, and in it as the sole means of their progress, the principle destined to govern all their institutions, and the pledge of concord in their labours. As we believe in the liberty and equality of the peoples, so we believe in liberty and equality among the men of each Country, in the inviolability of the *ego*, which is the conscience of individuals, and assigns to them their share of work in the secondary association, an office in the Nation, a special mission of citizenship in the sphere of the Fatherland. And as we believe in HUMANITY, the sole interpreter of God's Law, so we believe for every State, in the PEOPLE, the sole master, the sole sovereign, the sole interpreter of the Law of Humanity which rules the mission of each Nation : in the People one and indivisible, that knows neither caste nor privilege, save that of Genius and of Virtue, neither proletariat nor aristocracy of land or money, but only faculties and active forces consecrated, for the good of all, to the administration of the surface of the globe, our common heritage :—in the people free and independent, with an organisation that shall harmonise individual faculties and social thought ; the people living by its own labour and the fruits thereof, pursuing in concord the greatest possible good of all, yet respecting the rights of the individual :—in the people made one family, with one faith, one tradition, one thought of love, and advancing to the ever fuller accomplishment of its mission :—in the people, progressive, consecrated to an apostolate of *duties*, never forgetful of a truth once won, never slacking its efforts because of that victory, reverent to the message of the generations, but resolved to use the present as a bridge betwixt past and future, worshipping revelation, not the revealers, able, little by little, to approach the soluton of its destiny here on earth.

God and His Law, HUMANITY and its work of interpretation, progress, association, liberty, equality, the doctrine of the PEOPLE, which is the vital principle of the republican Party, all meet on the common ground of our creed. (9.) We reject no conquest of the past. Before us spreads a future where meet in close embrace the two eternal principles of every organisation, the individual and Humanity, liberty and association; where one philosophy, a genuine expression of religion, shall embrace in equal balance, every revelation of progress, every holy idea which by providential design has been successively transmitted to us.

" When before Young Europe's dawn all the altars of the old world have fallen, two altars shall be raised upon this soil that the divine Word has made fruitful : and the finger of the herald-people shall inscribe upon one, *Fatherland*, and upon the other, *Humanity*.

" Like sons of the same mother, like brothers who will not be parted, the people shall gather around those two altars, and offer sacrifice in peace and love.   And the incense of the sacrifice shall ascend to heaven in two columns that shall draw near each other as they mount, until they are confounded in one point, which is God.

" And so often as they move asunder whilst they rise, fratricide shall be on earth, and mothers shall weep on earth, and angels in heaven." [1]

Now, suppose these things repeated in Europe, not as an expression of the individual, but as the expression, the Word, the Conscience of the republican Party, of the whole party of progress—suppose the religious principle to shine again on our path and unify our labours— suppose God and Humanity conjoined in our popular symbolism, as phenomenon and idea, thought and form ; think ye not that our word would not kindle the doubt-tossed multitudes who pray, and wait, and hope, because no crusader's cry, no religious cry, sounds in their ears ? Do you believe that between our HOLY ALLIANCE and the *accursed compact*, between the apostles of progressive free movement, and the stagnant sophists of old Europe, they would discern on which side stands God, his Love, his Truth ?   And where God is there is the people also. The people's philosophy is its faith.

And when faith shows not only on your lips, but in your hearts ; when your deeds answer to your words, and virtue hallows your lives as liberty hallows your minds ; when as a band of brothers, believers in one flag, you appear before men as they who seek the good ; when the people say of you, *they are a living faith*,—think ye the people will be slow to answer to your call ?   Think ye that the guerdon desired of all, of saving power to all, which falls to them who shall herald the way to Europe, think ye that that will not be gathered, aye and quickly ?

Great thoughts make great peoples.   Let your life be the epitome of one great organic thought.   Widen the

[1] *The Faith of Young Europe* (unpublished).

peoples' horizon. Free their conscience from the materialism that weighs it down. Point them to a vast mission. Baptize them once again. Anger at wrong done to material interests can only bring forth revolts ; principles alone effect revolutions. Go back to first principles and the people will follow you.

The question which agitates the world is a religious question. Criticism and anarchy of belief have ex- tinguished faith in the hearts of the peoples. A philo- sophy that constructs, and unity of belief, will revive it.

Then—but not till then—will return that active energy which grows with difficulties, but now collapses at each trifling disappointment. Then will cease that state of isolation and mistrust which wearies us, which multiplies parties, obstructs association, makes of each individual a separate rallying point, which makes us camps enough but no armies to tenant them, which parts the poets to one side, the men of prose and calculation to the other, divides yet further the men of action, and further still the high speculative intellects. Then we shall lose from our ranks those who dishonour us, the clan of unclean hearts and canting tongues, whose inconsistency of language and performance suggests doubt concerning our symbol, who prate of virtue, of self-sacrifice, of charity, while vice is in their hearts, shame on their foreheads, and selfishness in their souls ; who nail their immorality on our banner, and hide themselves in the day of battle, to reappear when danger is past that they may gather the spoils of the vanquished and stain our triumph by robbing it of its fruits. Then will disappear, one by one, the prejudices and the influence of those nameless, feeble men, who blame our war-cry because themselves lack courage, who beg at an ambassador's gate a dole of hope for their country, who drag the exile's sacred name in the mire of cabinet intrigues, who dream of salvation for the nations from the chicanery of diplomatists ; men who ape in their conspiracies the rusty tricks of the police, who mock at enthusiasm, deny the power of inspiration and self-sacrifice, call martyrdom quixotic, and try to regenerate the peoples by statistics.

Then will vanish the thousand inconsistencies that make
the party inferior to its mission ; patriots' lips lisping
foreigner almost as a reproach—what a blasphemy on the
cross of Christ from men who call themselves Christians,
republicans, and brothers—the guilty hesitation that robs
so many of our friends of strength to confess their
belief, that frightens them at every charge made from
the enemy's camp, that makes apostles of truth appear
as erring and guilty men ; that fascination of old names
which, by supplanting principles, has ruined so many
revolutions, and sacrificed fresh ideas to the petty traditions of the past ; the illogical, inconsistent spirit that
denies the oneness of mankind, that demands unlimited
liberty for some and absolute intolerance for others,
preaches political freedom and refuses literary freedom,
which shakes the social edifice to its foundations, and
petrifies religion. Then we shall see no more the angry
polemic that feeds on hatred, which snarls at every
reminder, which neglects principles for personalities,
which betrays in every sentence its jealous national
exclusiveness, and wastes its strength in unimportant
petty scuffles ; and lastly, we shall lose the frivolity, the
inconstancy of opinions, the forgetfulness of the martyrs
who are our saints, of the great men who are our priests,
of the great actions which are our prayer. *Faith*, which
is intellect, will, love, will blot out all those vices, and
end the discords of a society without a church, without
a head, that invokes a new world, but forgets to ask its
secret from God. And then, made fruitful by the breath
of God and of holy beliefs, poetry, now exiled from a
world that is a prey to anarchy, will blossom yet again ;
poetry, the flower of the angels, that martyrs' blood and
mothers' tears have fed, that oft will grow amid ruins,
but is ever coloured by a rising Sun. It speaks to us in
prophetic tones of Humanity, European in substance,
national in form. It will teach the Fatherland of the
fatherlands to the nations still divided ; it will translate
into Art the religious, social philosophy ; it will surround
with its own beautiful light, *woman*, who though a fallen
angel, is ever nearer to heaven than we. It will hasten

her redemption, restoring to her the mission of inspira
tion, of pity, and of prayer, which Christianity divinely
symbolised in Mary. It will sing the joys of martyrdom,
the immortality of the vanquished, the tears that expiate,
the sufferings that purify, the memories and the hopes,
the traditions of one world interwoven in the cradle of
another. It will murmur words of holy consolation to
those children of sorrow born before their time, those
fated and puissant souls who, like Byron, have no con-
fidants on earth, and whom the world of to-day strives
to rob even of God. And it will teach the young the
greatness of self-sacrifice, the virtue of constancy and
silence, how to be alone and yet despair not, how to
endure without a cry an existence of torments half
understood, unknown, long years of delusions and
bitterness and wounds, all without a complaint ; it will
teach a belief in future things, an hourly travail to promote it, without a hope in this life of seeing its victory.

Are these illusions ? Do I presume too much when I
ask of faith such prodigies in a century still corrupted by
scepticism, among men who are slaves of *self*, who love
little, and quickly forget, who are troubled in soul, and
heed only the calculations of egotism, and the sensations
of the hour ?

No ; I do not presume too much. It is necessary
that this come to pass, aye, and it will come. I have
faith in God, in the potency of truth, and in the *spirit*
of the age. I feel in the depths of my heart that we
cannot stay as we are. The principle which was the
soul of the old world is exhausted. It is for us to open
the way to the new principle, and even should we perish
in the attempt we will lead the way.

X

The times were wrapped in shadow. Heaven was
a void. The peoples wandered, pricked by strange fears,
or paused in torpid, puzzled wonderment. Whole nations
disappeared ; others just raised their heads as though to
see them die. A hollow sound as of dissolution was

heard in the world. All creation, earth and sky,
trembled. Man seemed in hideous case. Placed between two Infinites, he knew neither; he knew not past
nor future. All belief was dead : dead the belief in the
Gods, dead the belief in the public. Society was not;
nought but a Power that drowned in blood, or ate itself
away in deeds of shame and sin ; a senate, poor parody
of the majesty that had been, which voted gold and
statutes to the tyrant; pretorians who despised the one
and slew the other ; informers, sophists, and a slavish
and obsequious multitude. There were no principles of
saving virtue : there existed but the calculation of
antagonistic interests. The Fatherland was exhausted.
The solemn voice of Brutus from the tomb had told the
world that Virtue was but a name. And the good
withdrew from that world, to keep their souls and
intellects from stain. Nerva starved himself to death.
Thraseas made libation of his own blood to Jove the
Liberator. The soul had disappeared : the senses alone
reigned. The people asked for bread and circus games.
Philosophy had become scepticism, epicureanism, or
mere sophistries and words. Poetry was satire. From
time to time man stood appalled at his own solitude,
and drew back from the wilderness. Then voices of fear
were heard at night by the wayside. Then the citizens,
almost frenzied with dread, clasped the bare, cold statutes
of the Gods that once they worshipped, and prayed of
them a spark of moral life, a ray of faith, even some
illusion ; but they went away unheard, with despair in
their hearts and blasphemy on their lips. Such were
those times, so like our own.

But yet, that was not the death-agony of the world;
it was but the end of one phase of the world's evolution.
A great epoch was exhausted, passing away to leave the
road clear for another, whose first notes were already
ringing in the north, and that awaited only its *initiator*
to declare itself. He came. His was the soul most full
of love, most virtuous and holy, most inspired by God
and the future, that men have ever hailed on this earth:
it was JESUS. He bent over the decaying world, and

murmured in its ear a word of faith. To that obscene
thing which retained nought but the aspect and notions
of a man, he uttered words unknown up to that day :
love, self-sacrifice, celestial origin. The dead arose; a
new life thrilled through that obscene thing which
philosophy had tried in vain to bring to life. From it
came forth the Christian world, the world of liberty and
equality. *Man* was made manifest, the image and fore-
shadowing of God. Jesus died. As Lamennais has
said, he asked of men to save them only a cross to
die on. But ere he died, he announced to the people
the *good news.* To those who asked him whence he had
it, he answered : From God the Father; and from the
cross twice he called on Him. But from that cross his
victory began, and still endures.

Have faith, then, O ye that suffer for the noble cause,
apostles of a Truth that even to-day the world ignores, ye
soldiers of the holy battles which the world condemns
and calls rebellious. To-morrow, perhaps, that world,
to-day incredulous or careless, will bow with fervour
before you. To-morrow, victory will crown your
crusading banner. Onward in faith, and fear not. That
which Christ did Humanity can do. Believe, and you
will conquer. Believe, and the peoples will end by
following you. Believe, and act. Action is the Word
of God : passive thought is but its shadow. Those who
sunder Thought and Action dismember God, and deny
the eternal Unity of things. Thrust them from your
ranks ; for whoso is not ready to testify to his faith with
his blood is no believer.

From your cross of misfortune and persecution
announce the whole faith of the Age ; but few days
will pass ere it receive its consecration of faith. Let
your lips not utter the cry of hate, nor the conspirator's
hollow phrase, but the tranquil, solemn word of the
days that are to come. From our cross of poverty and
proscription, we, the men of exile, who represent in our
heart and faith the races of the enslaved, the millions
doomed to silence, we will reply to you, and say to our
brothers : *the alliance is made.* Hurl at your persecutors

the legend GOD AND HUMANITY. For yet a little time
they may rebel and strive against it and stammer
blasphemy. But the masses will worship it.

There was a day in the sixteenth century, in Italy, in
Rome, when men called *inquisitors*, who pretended to
have science and authority from God, were gathered
together to decree the immobility of the Earth. Before
them stood a prisoner. Genius illumined his face. He
had outstripped his times and his fellow-men, and
revealed the secret of a world.

He was Galileo.

He shook his bald and venerable head. The soul
of that sublime old man rose in rebellion against the
senseless violence of men, who would have forced him
to deny the truth that God had taught him. But long
oppression had tamed his former energy. Frightened
by the threats of those monks, he was at the point of
yielding. He raised his hand to swear, even he, the
immobility of the Earth. But as he raised his hand, he
lifted his weary eyes to the sky which he had scanned
during long nights, to read in it a line of universal law;
they caught a ray of that sun which he knew to be fixed
in the centre of the revolving spheres. Remorse pricked
his heart, and a cry in his own despite escaped from the
depths of his soul: STILL IT MOVES!

Three centuries have passed away. Inquisitors, inquisition, the senseless propositions that force dictated,
all have disappeared. But still the Earth moves on, its
motion proved beyond a doubt, and still the words of
Galileo soar over the generations of Mankind. Lift thy
countenance to the sun of God, thou child of Humanity,
and read that legend in the heavens: *it moves*. Faith
and action. The future is ours.

NOTES TO FAITH AND THE FUTURE

(1.) Act, I say; but, by making this principle of
Action a standard of conduct, I do not mean action at
any price, feverish, disorganised, unreflecting action. I

mean Action as a principle, a programme, a banner, as
that which ought to be the tendency and avowed end of
all our strivings. The rest is a question of time, with
which it is futile now to concern ourselves. It is sufficient
for us that a temporary necessity be not elevated to a
permanent theory; that the peoples be not deluded
into substituting for revolutionary *activity* an indefinite,
uncertain, peacefully progressive force of events; that we
no longer persist in handing over the great illumining
power of the revolutionary philosophy, to a spasmodic,
coldly critical work of constituted *opposition*. We reject
the systematic want of movement, the silence that broods,
the dissimulation that betrays; we invoke the frank, loyal
preaching of our doctrine. Ours is the cry of Ajax. We
want to fight in the open day illumined by the light of
heaven. Is this childish impatience? No: it is the
complement of our doctrine, the baptism of our faith.
The principle of action that we inscribe on our banner is
closely bound up with our belief in a new Age. How
shall we initiate it save by the people and by Action, the
Word of the people? Without this principle of Action,
which we take as the standard of our efforts, we should
only produce a purely reactionary movement, and hence
an imperfect, superficial, material change of things.

(2.) My ideas on the French Revolution, considered as
the last word of the expiring Age rather than the first
word of the age which the nineteenth century initiates,
are already indicated in an article "On the Revolutionary
Initiative" published in the *Revue Républicaine* of 1835,
and I intend to develop my argument further when the
opportunity offers.[1] I shall then perhaps be permitted
to prove that, in subjecting the past to a new test, I am
seeking, in the historical evolution of the stages of
progress, data for a new social *aim*; a new European
philosophy that shall shift the new departure from a *single*
predominant people, in order to communicate to *all* that
activity which is now lacking; that I am not following
nebulous German metaphysics; but only desire that thought
may be translated into *fact*, that the vicious circle in

[1] See "Thoughts on the French Revolution," p. 251.

which our activity is confined may be broken, and a
decisive battle forced between the two principles that are
now struggling for mastery in Europe.

It was said, in the preamble to my article in the *Revue*:
"Ought we to forget facts in order to improvise, by
merely wishing it, a Revolutionary force where it does
not really exist? Can we blot out the past? Can we
leave out of our calculations the Revolutions of Modena
and Bologna?"

Theoretically, the position in which we are placed by
our religious and philosophical belief leaves us untouched
by any argument deduced from those facts. We are near
to one of those periods of regeneration which, by introducing a new element into the great terrestrial scheme of
life, generates new forces and shifts the central point of
all questions. We hail the dawn of a new age. The
Revolution of which we have a presentiment will embrace
a large part of Humanity. Now, every new purpose calls
into action new forces latent in the peoples. But, putting
aside the main question, why do our critics forget that in
Italy the *people*—the only true Revolutionary force—has
never entered the lists ; that our insurrections never went
outside the circle of a military or bourgeois caste ; that
the masses were never called upon to share in the undertaking? Why do they forget that the insurrection never
assumed an avowed *Italian* character? Why argue from
the *monarchical* risings of 1821 to the prejudice of the
republican insurrection for which we are striving? How
possibly calculate the results of a principle by studying
the consequences of a contrary principle? Between us
republicans of "Young Italy" and those who laboured
before us, between those who desire to move the masses
with the cry of "God and the People" and the inconsistent, timid men who forget God and fear the People,
a great gulf is fixed.

"The risings of Modena and Bologna failed because
France did not support them." True. How is it
possible for an insurrection not to fail when betrayed by
the very principle upon which its life was based? Now,
this principle on which the leaders of the Italian

Insurrection took their stand was the principle of *non-intervention*. And blind faith in *non-intervention* prevented them from taking the steps that self-preservation demanded in order to work out their salvation. The masses were repulsed, the young discouraged, every force that had a germ of life ignored ; they omitted to procure arms, they denied the idea of Nationality, they confined the area of the insurrection within the limits of a single province. Are these *permanent* causes of weakness ? From then till now every Italian who has not perverted his national sentiment in the conventions of the Parisian *juste milieu* will reply that if our forces are still sterile, if even to-day we number so many martyrs and so few fighters, we owe it mainly to the doctrine that the initiative of the European struggle devolves upon France, and that when she will not stir no one must attempt to move. It is urgent, therefore, to combat this doctrine preached among us by those very men who, from their resources in means and influence, should be first to take action. It is a doctrine that destroys the conscience and future of the peoples, a doctrine which the French republicans ought to join with us in fighting. I do not therefore blame France. I only ask the republican Press to introduce the new tendencies and language that correspond to the new mission. But I deservedly blame the men who, living in the midst of oppressed peoples, increase the difficulties of the work of emancipation by the insincere belief that marks worse than lukewarm convictions ; I blame those who boast themselves the apostles of a humanitarian philosophy, and yet, with their theory of a single revealer and their rejection of the continuity of progress, sink by stress of logic to the rejection of the doctrine of the intelligence and sovereignty of the people, only to evoke some vague revival of the Papacy ; I blame the men who declare Humanity to be impossible until France be hailed Queen of the universe. (See *Histoire Parlementaire de la Révolution Française—Christ et le Peuple, par A. Siguier.*) And this is not an isolated thought of one individual ; it is the doctrine of a whole school. Now, we protest against the doctrine of that

school, against its national egotism, its tendencies to
trespass on others' rights.   Brothers of all who desire the
Association of the equal and free, we feel a special affection
for that people which for fifty years has fought for the
emancipation of the nations, and translated into the
sphere of politics the grand results of the Christian
Age.

(3.) It is an error to base our estimate of the work of
moral freedom achieved by the Reformation upon the
accident of a protest against the Diet of Spires, from
which the term *protestantism* originated.   Protestantism
was not, as the neo-Christians affirm, a negation, a work
of criticism in relation to the age.   It was a positive
Christian product, a solemn manifestation of the *individual*
—which is the *aim* of Christianity.   It protested, doubtless, but only against the Papacy, which by desiring what
it was unable to perform, and attempting to establish a
social unity with an individualistic instrument, was
necessarily fated to degenerate into tyranny and thus
place itself outside that Christian philosophy of life
which, before it had attained its complete development,
said to man, "Be free."   It is not therefore a protest
against the philosophy of its age, but in *favour* of the
philosophy which the Papacy, impotent to realise a
sublime instinct of the future, destroyed instead of developing.

(4.) No one can reasonably charge us with ignoring
the catholic spirit that presides over the destinies of
modern civilisation.   Everybody knows the meaning
generally given to the word *catholicism.*   If *catholicism*
were only synonymous with universal, we might recall
the fact that every religion by its nature tends to become *catholic,* and notably so the philosophy that writes
Humanity at the head of its articles of faith.

(5.) I anticipate the objection : "Success is a de-
lusion : slavery, inequality, remain everywhere.   The
struggle was scarcely begun by the French Revolution.
The *individual* still dominates every question ; and while
you talk of a new age, unanswered prayers are raised on
every side imploring that the social ideal declared by you

to be exhausted, may even now be attained and translated into fact."

We must not confound the discovery of an element of progress with its realisation and triumph, the *ideal* evolution of the thought of an age with its *material* application, the conquest with its practical consequences. The positive application of a given principle to the different parts of the political, economic, and civil organism cannot successfully begin except its moral development in men's minds be completed. That development constitutes the work of an Age. Scarcely is it completed when some power—an individual or a people—proclaims its results and hands its formula to the nations. Then a new Age has already begun, in which, while men's minds are working at the newly revealed principle, the gradual completion is effected of the principle of the dead or dying Age. The thought of one Age is only realised when the mind is already fixed upon the ideal of the new Age. Were this otherwise, the chain that connects the Ages would be broken, and what is termed a lapse of continuity would take place.

Now I affirm, that if on the one hand the *material* application of the two principles, liberty and equality, that constituted the doctrine of the individual, be not effected—nor will it be effected until a people has marked the new principle as the *end* and *aim* of the common task—yet, on the other hand, their development is *morally* accomplished. I maintain that the *unknown* factor of the Middle Ages can now be placed in the category of *known* quantities, that what was hypothesis is now an axiom ; that the theory has become an admitted, recognised law. Who denies liberty or equality ? Who doubts the Right ? The most illiberal king speaks in the name of that liberty he abhors in his heart. If we may believe him, he is protecting the liberties and rights of his subjects against the anarchy of factions. The question is decided in the sphere of principles : the only difference of opinion relates to its application. We dispute, not about the law, but about its interpretation.

The *individual* is now no longer the *end* of our labours. He, even he, indeed, will be seen to be sacred when the *social* law is proclaimed, and we are bound to bring our duties and rights into harmony with it; while the worship of *individuality* has given place to an ignoble *individualism*, to egotism, to a nameless immorality.

(6.) Association, say some, is no new principle: it cannot therefore, as the objective of the forces of mankind, constitute a new system or induce its necessity. Association is nothing but a method, a means for realising liberty and equality. It belongs to the old system, and we see no necessity for a new one.

Association, I admit, in its more general signification, is no more than the *method of progress*, the means by which it is gradually achieved. To every step forward there corresponds a new degree of force, a new expansion of association. And in this sense, so far as we are concerned, association began with the progress that is coeval with the origin of our planet. Its work appeared in every dead philosophy, most of all in that which men wish to see dominant to-day.

Nevertheless, though association has always exercised an influence upon us, it has been without our knowledge. Men were unconsciously under its influence. Thus it was with progress, with the law of gravitation, with all great physical and moral truths. They were at work before they were revealed.

But is there not a difference between an undiscovered law and one that is proclaimed, recognised, accepted— a difference sufficient to change the starting-point of intellectual labour? The law, when defined, imposes a *duty* on us of ruling our actions in accordance with it. The fulfilment of the law becomes an *end* for all our efforts, and the study of every thinker is how to derive the greatest possible results from it. Minds no longer risk going astray and osing precious time in researches whose object has been already obtained. Forces are increased a hundredfold by concentration: they work in a determined direction. Formerly the instinct of law only produced a right—and a right that was nearly always contested.

The great historical ages date, not from the birth of a law, a truth, a principle, but from their promulgation. Were this not so, it would be absurd to speak of distinct ages or philosophies. Truth is one and eternal : *thought*, the germ of the world in God, contains it all.

Equality existed in principle long before Jesus, and the world was unconsciously tending towards it. Why, then, recognise the Christian age ?

The earth did not wait for the revelations of Copernicus or Galileo, or the formulas of Newton, to describe its orbit round the sun. Why, then, do we recognise the two distinct astronomical Ages of the Ptolemaic and Newtonian systems ? And, coming nearer to the present day, did not the theories of the English economists, and those, too quickly forgotten, of the St. Simonians, mark out two radically different periods of economic science ? Yet the only difference between them is the substitution of the principle of association for that of liberty.

Now, we believe the time has arrived for the principle of *association* to be solemnly and universally proclaimed. and become the centre of all study, theoretical and practical, which aims at the progressive organisation of human societies, to shine at the head of our constitutions, our codes of law, the articles of our faith. And furthermore, I maintain that the promulgation of a principle which marks out an entirely new direction for our studies is sufficient to constitute, or at least to indicate, a new Age, if nothing more.

And, moreover, our motto is not *Association* merely : it implies the association of Europe, and by its means of Humanity in all its faculties and forces, with the necessary conditions of Liberty, Equality, and Fraternity, for the purpose of achieving a common *end*, namely, the discovery and progressive application of its law of life.

(7.) Right is obviously a secondary idea, a deduction which forgets the principle it sprang from, a mere consequence which has been inflated to an absolute and independent doctrine. Every right exists in virtue of a law, the law of Being, the law that defines the nature of the subject treated. Where is this law? I do not know. Its discovery is the *aim* of the present Age, but the certainty of its existence is enough to make us substitute the idea of *duty* for that of *right*.

(8.) The word *democracy*, although when endowed with historical precision it may express vigorously enough the ideal of a world, at least of the ancient world, is, like all the political phrases of antiquity, unequal to the conception of the future Age which we republicans are called to initiate. The expression *social government* would be preferable as indicating the conception of *association*, which is the life of the Age. The word democracy was inspired by an idea of rebellion, sacred indeed, but still rebellion. Now, every such conception is evidently imperfect and inferior to the idea of Unity which will be the doctrine of the future. There is a note of strife in the word democracy : it is the cry of Spartacus, the expression of a people in its first attempt to rise. "Social government," "Social institutions," represent a people organising itself after victory. The extinction of *aristocracy* will efface the name *democracy*.

(9.) We are not expounding a doctrine, but a series of bases for belief, disjointed and merely stated, but nevertheless sufficient to indicate the nature of our religious and philosophical conceptions. Our political beliefs are only consequences more or less direct and evident. It is easy to understand how the mere fact of preaching a new age, and a new philosophy of life, separates us from all who believe themselves to be carrying on the old principle, and entrust a new development only to those nations who are guardians of the highest expression of progress yet attained to. The principle that a new system of philosophy must include all the elements of the preceding philosophies besides its own, is the formal rejection of every theory that *destroys* and does not *harmonise* ; of every political school which only asks to substitute one class for another, one social element for another ; of every exclusive

system which, like that of Babœuf, destroys liberty for
the sake of a chimerical, deceptive equality, which
eliminates the most sublime moral factor, that of the
ego, and renders all progress impossible ; or which, like
the *American* School, centres itself in the *individual*,
solves every political problem in the sense of liberty
alone, smothers the principle of association under the
omnipotence of the *ego*, condemns progress to the
irregularities of a fitful, intermittent movement which
defies calculation, plants distrust in the civil organisation, dismembers social unity in an independent dualism
of the temporal and spiritual powers, and introduces
materialism, individualism, egotism, and contradiction
into the minds of men through the doctrine of the
atheism of the law and the sovereignty of rights and
interests.   Our conception of Humanity as the sole
interpreter of the Law of God separates us from every
School that divides progress into two distinct Ages,
confines it almost by force within one single defined
philosophy or religion, or which imprisons the traditions
of Humanity in the theory of one sole revealer, or
which breaks the continuity of our labours by the
theory of a constant supernatural intervention, by the
theory of a series of complete dispensations without
relation to each other, by a chain of social formulas
all revealed, all sundered by a void between.   Our
principle of the People, which is simply the application of the doctrine of Humanity to every nation,
is the direct and sufficient cause of the principle of
universal suffrage, which is the manifestation of the
people, and of the exclusion of all authority that is
not delegated by the people, or is exercised by one
caste or individual.   The principle of association, considered as the sole method of progress, involves unlimited liberty for all associations for secondary or
special objects not in conflict with the moral law.
The principle of moral unity, without which association
is impossible, implies the duty of a general elementary
education to expound the programme of such association
to all who will be partners in it.   Lastly, the principle

that declares the individual sacred and inviolable, carries with it not only the absolute liberty of the press, the abolition of the death penalty, and of every other punishment, that, instead of developing, improving, and perfecting the individual, tends to suppress and limit him, but also a whole theory of work considered as a manifestation of the individual and the representation of his *worth*.

THE PATRIOTS AND THE CLERGY

The Essay on "The Patriots and the Clergy" is an appeal to the liberals and the clergy to show mutual tolerance. There had been a good deal of the ultramontane propagandism, which culminated ten years later in the Sonderbund. The liberals, on their side, had been disposed to put it down with a high hand. Mazzini believed that there were many among the Catholic clergy whose real sympathies were with reform, and he appeals to them to carry out the democratic teaching of the Gospel. The sceptical and stunted ideas of the liberals were largely responsible for their alienation. A bigger national policy and mutual forbearance would, he hoped, range many of the priests on the side of progress.

The lasting interest of the Essay lies in Mazzini's exposition of his views as to the relations of Church and State. In advocating the independence of the two, he was, as he recognised, at variance with his ideal. Brought up in a Catholic country, he had a Catholic's craving for unity of belief. Fusing as he did in his mind religion and politics, the conception of a "Free Church in a Free State" was repugnant to him. Sooner or later, he had no doubt, Church and State would be identified, and till then there could be no true social unity. But at present such an identification could only work harm. The Church taught doctrines that intelligence could not accept. The men who ruled the State were too limited in their ideals to be entrusted with spiritual authority: the future social unity lay outside their comprehension, and their only logical position was to apply the principle of liberty all round. Hence, all religious propagandism, so long as it respected the liberty of others, should be treated as a matter of opinion, and the Government must hold its hands off. Possibly, had Mazzini's advice been followed, the Civil War of the Sonderbund might have been avoided : it is probable though that the ultramontane party was too aggressive, and the question too much complicated with that of cantonal rights, to have made it possible for the Government to leave matters alone.

Incidentally the Essay touches a good deal on contemporary Swiss politics.

They had a dull outlook at the time. The different cantons were connected by the loosest of bonds ; the Diet was a mere "ghost of authority," and meekly obedient to orders from Paris or Vienna. Many of the cantons were governed by narrow oligarchies ; the reforming movement which had followed the French Revolution of 1830 had been checked. The Great Councils of the cantons debated with closed doors. Customs' lines checked trade, privileged guilds fettered industry, there was no common money or common standard of weights and measures, public offices were openly sold, Jesuits had been admitted into the Catholic cantons. There were three political parties : the Conservatives, anxious to preserve the old cantonal autonomy ; the party of Union, aiming at a single centralised Government and the practical abolition of the canton ; and the Federalists, who wished to combine a strong Federal Government with a large degree of local independence. Mazzini threw in his lot with the latter ; he held unity to be the ideally best policy for Switzerland, but thought that the canton was too deeply rooted in the history of the country to be abolished. He exerted himself to persuade the Unionists to combine with the Federalists. Federalism, he thought, would lift Swiss politics into a purer air. Switzerland was in a critical condition : the absence of a strong Government laid her at the mercy of Austria and France ; timidity and compromise predominated in all her political actions ; the narrow cantonal life threatened to smother her in "a mud-death." Publicity of deliberation, a constituent assembly to determine the question of Federalism, greater independence towards foreign powers, was his programme. Thirteen years later the constitution of 1848 realised his wishes except on the latter point, and it is worthy of note that Druey, one of the two framers of the constitution, was his personal friend

THE PATRIOTS AND THE CLERGY

I

October 7, 1835.

"THERE is no power on earth that surpasses or equals that of the Clergy, when they are imbued with the genius of a nation, and guide it faithfully in its natural progress according to the laws that direct the procession of its life. But if, by error or from interest, they set them-selves in opposition to those eternal laws, if they attempt to hold the people in a state which it knows to be not good, and so block the roads to the Future, they lose thereby the power they had. Their words excite mis-trust, they are involved in the hate born of the evil they have tried to perpetuate, and the people regard them as the enemy. Once they lived by the love the People gave them for their own trust in it ; now faith and love have vanished, their living force is spent, and voices of scorn and cursing are the only obsequies that follow their dishonoured bier.

"Ireland and Poland have given, and still give, us the example of a clergy strong in its union with the People whose rights they have ever defended. But where the priesthood ranges itself with despotism against the People, what is its fate ? Will the Anglican clergy save a de-crepit aristocracy rejected by the nation ? Will the Spanish monks perchance place the legitimate Don Carlos on the throne of Philip the Second ? Will they restore the system under which Spain has suffered so much and fallen so low ? Yet, is there another country where the influence characteristic of their organisation was more widely diffused ?   But yesterday men spoke of *Monkish Spain* ; to-morrow, probably they will seek in vain from one end of the peninsula to the other a single remnant of those who but a short time since were so powerful."

He who recently wrote these grave and true words is a Christian and republican priest,[1] who spent half his life combating the movement towards freedom of those Peoples whom God is urging to an unknown end.   One day, perhaps while reading the Gospel over again with all the faith of which a man is capable, he perceived that he had erred ; he reconsidered his position, and, like a man of high intellect and pure conscience, he confessed his error.   Then, after having at Rome looked his idol in the face, he returned a sad and disillusioned man, and placed himself at the head of the crusade which the men of progress in all countries have proclaimed in Christ's name for the People's cause.

We, on our side, have long felt the need of expressing something similar, to that portion of the Swiss clergy, which is reactionary at heart and takes its orders from Rome and Vienna alike ; which fights, without rest and apparently with some definite purpose, against that national progress which leads our people to new conquests of science and liberty and equality.

Between the dark plots of one party and the growing irritation of the other, our feeble voice will not perhaps be listened to to-day.   Our words will pass by like so many others, barren and unheeded ; none the less, we are forced to utter them, if only to discharge a duty to our conscience.   In the party which we are apt perhaps too much in Voltairian fashion to prejudice under the name of the *clerical party*, there are men of good faith ; men who are not perverse but only misled ; devout souls, whose sincerity and zeal only serve the machinations of those who libel the patriots and liberalism, who paint the former as the enemies of all religion, and insult the latter by giving it the characteristics of anarchy.   To those we offer sincere words of peace and fraternity ; because, although they have turned to reactionary ways, they

' Lamennais

represent in the Church what we are accustomed to
respect wherever it shows itself—*faith* and religious feeling. The others, conspirators and reactionaries by system,
only represent class interests and greed and lust of
power. For those we only feel contempt.

We must leave on one side all that touches the present time : we attach no importance to intrigues of the
moment or petty local encroachments ; they were easily
foreseen. The *coups d'état* that have lately taken place
in France could not fail to find a certain correspondence
among us. Rome, Paris, St. Petersburg, Vienna, and
Berlin, all form an alliance of homogeneous elements,
so many links in a chain, so many fires that radiate in
unison their sinister flashes, now singly, now together ;
and just at the present moment we see their united
flare. The word of command was passed round that
the whole chain should move. Hence there is no need
to wonder at all those petty plots that are being hatched
and unhatched in the night, and will perish in the night,
unless they win a fictitious importance. We are bound
to say that, if considered in a merely political light, the
question does not seem to us worthy of serious attention ;
nor do the acrid polemics started on the subject by
some cantonal newspapers deserve it. So far as we
are concerned, we recognise in politics neither clerical
party, nor catholic party, nor romanist party. From
our point of view there are only two great parties : the
progressive and the *reactionary*. They are composed of
individuals of every order, of every rite, of every sect.
But neither order, nor rite, nor sect should save the
factious from punishment. Governments have the right
to control and repress any individual interest which
disturbs the social order, or arbitrarily overrides or
excepts itself from the public law (which is the bond
and seal of association for all the inhabitants of a
country), and thus revolts *de facto* against the common
weal. But, outside the circle within which this legitimate authority may be exercised, there is not, and
cannot be, especially in the existing state of things, any
rule save full and perfect liberty ; liberty for every

citizen and every opinion, it matters not whether they be reactionary or progressive; liberty for all actions that have naturally the sanction and support of the public law.   In the present state of theories and facts, every question of religious worship and organisation is a question of the public law and liberty.   So long as the actions and pretensions of a sect, or of any religious association, do not exceed the limits of its own constitution, or do not touch the civil order of society, you have no right to interfere.   The intervention of Government can only be applied at the present day to actions that directly violate existing laws.   The rest belongs to the sphere of ideas, and is a question of belief.   Reform belief, spread the light, meet fanatical newspapers with other newspapers.   Do not thwart the work of the patriots, do not obstruct their progress with unjust suspicions, or a disgraceful and cowardly compliance with the demands of foreign courts, or an obvious disposition to stagnate in the *status quo*.   Defend the free press instead of being frightened by it, and have no other fears.   Allow the Pope to select at his pleasure bishops who are foolish, and ignorant, and out of touch with the times: what can they do other than hasten the downfall of the papal power?   Let the Jesuits and others of the factious make expensive journeys, hold their conferences, write their wretched articles, their contemptible and inept pamphlets: suffer them to go their ways.   Persecution would only exalt them by giving them an excuse to pose as victims; it would invest them with an importance that neither their writings, nor their meetings, nor the intrigues in which they exhaust themselves could ever win for their sect.   The old Catholicism is dying : let it struggle even in its death-throes.   Its death-blow will come from some idea that shines with the light of truth, not from the hammer of restrictive laws.   All the regulations and curbs you may invent will not be worth one single school of thought.

Therefore, as far as the political question is concerned, we agree with the opinion expressed by Troxler at the time of the Baden Conference, an opinion supported afterwards, if our memory serves us rightly, by a daily paper that gave effective assistance to the cause of progress in Geneva: we mean the "*Europe Centrale.*" There is a conception which must one day (we, at least, have no doubt) harmonise, or rather identify the two Powers of Church and State ; but until this is clear and definite in the mind and conscience of the Nations, until political thought rises to the height and sacredness of a religious idea, and true social unity is established, till then ecclesiastical and political authority should be exercised freely, and, so far as possible, independently of each other on distinct lines. Their respective activities must not clash, and hence they must not interfere with each other. Each has the right to associate itself with whomever it pleases ; to receive inspirations from any source it likes ; to pay those whom it chooses and accepts as the interpreters of its religion and the rulers of its conscience. So long as ecclesiastical bodies do not overstep the limits of the religious sphere in which they move, it is within their power to do whatever they please, and propagate their beliefs by speech or writing in the way that seems good to them. We do not fear the influence of political or religious prejudices where we are allowed a free hand and a fair field to confute them. We do fear—if for nothing else, for the example of a dangerous precedent—the intervention of Government where it is not absolutely required by the force of circumstances. We wish to concede the smallest possible amount of power to the present Governments, just because we have no faith in them. Nor do we expect from their efforts any fruit of national progress, because we suspect that, while they accentuate certain questions under the colour of religion, their only purpose is to distract public attention from national questions. In 1830 the conquest of Algeria was designed to conceal from the French—a brilliant and chivalrous people— the odious nature of the projected decrees. And now, in our case, it is perhaps not too daring to presume, that the ostentatious energy displayed against the foolish encroachments of the *ultramontane* clergy has been merely used to defend the want of energy in dealing with political encroachments much more pernicious. We desire to substitute for governmental influence quite another weapon. We should wish to see the activity necessary to progress transferred from that influence to a national Centre. We should like to find the breach less often filled by the Authority of the law, and more often by the men of progress, not excluding those members of the Christian priesthood who are equally inspired by the love of fatherland and liberty. The latter should place themselves as apostles of truth and light between the people, who have strayed through lack of education, and the leaders of agitations. They should apply the activity and constancy that evil-minded priests give to the cause of Satan and his powers of darkness, to the defence of Christ's heritage—that is to say, equality and the improvement of the greatest number.

With these premisses we purpose ascending to the social question, and, from the Pisgah of a religious conception and of the future destinies of the People—or rather of the Peoples—to address, with faith in our own rectitude, with our hand on our heart, the following words to the erring members of the clergy.

II

October 10, 1835.

In the name of Christ, whither are you hastening? In the name of Him who walked with the People and whom the mighty put to death, why walk you with the mighty? Why do you abandon the People's cause? Why do you stand aloof from those who hold His banner on high and seek to translate into facts the teachings of Christ?

Christ said : " Love God first, and love ye one another with brotherly affection."

And He also said : " He who would be first among you let him be the servant of all."

In those words is comprehended the whole essence of Christianity. Unity of faith, mutual love, human brotherhood, activity in good works, the doctrine of self-sacrifice, the affirmation of the doctrine of equality, the abolition of all aristocracy, the perfecting of the individual, and liberty, without which neither love nor perfection can exist—all this is summed in those two precepts.

If we inscribe on our banner the words : *Liberty, Equality, Humanity*, we become the heralds of a Christian faith. We seek the unity of belief that Christ promised for all Peoples, for all the earth. We are neither Catholics nor Protestants : the true doctrine of Christ has made Christians only.

If we cry to the Masses : " God and the People ! There is only one master in heaven, God : one master on the earth, the People ; the whole People associated in an active belief, fruitful in peace and love, in order to advance under the eye of God to the knowledge and interpretation of his universal law," we take upon ourselves the office of Christ's apostles. Christ came for all ; He spoke to all and for all. He did not have one teaching for some, another for others. He spoke from the Mount in the same language to all who crowded around Him. He hurled His anathema against the Scribes and Pharisees, who were the men of caste, the privileged classes of His time. Before His coming there were, in the opinion of the world, two natures of men—the nature of the master and the nature of the slave. He destroyed this fallacy. He proclaimed the unity of human nature by teaching the unity of its origin. He burst the chains of servitude. He raised up the People and died for it.

And if we follow out His teachings to their consequences, if we try to apply them to civil society, if we protest with all our might against every opposition, every inequality, every violation of His Holy Word, we incarnate in our very selves the moral teaching of Christ. We are labouring for His faith, for the salvation and organisation of the Church of Humanity, which is the *congregation of the believers in that faith.* Since man was made in the image of God, we are labouring that human society may be fashioned, so far as possible, in the image of the divine society, of that celestial country where all are equal, where the same love and the same happiness exist for all. We seek to learn the ways of God upon the earth because we know that this earth was given to us as the workshop of our labour ; because only by fulfilling His task upon it, does man become worthy to ascend to heaven ; because we know we are to be judged by our works in this world, by the help we have given to the poor, by the consolation we have shown to the afflicted. We may not lock ourselves up in barren and selfish prayer for our own souls, while the cry of the poor and oppressed smites our ears, nor turn away our faces from our neighbour, and be content with our own spiritual progress, while all around us is falling to wreck ; while the country that God has given us is in danger of a dis-honourable death from the despotic influence of the foreigner, and the germs of anarchy that vitiate its institutions ; while those who should be first to expel the evils that threaten us allow themselves to drift on in fatuous security, and prostitute the house of God to foreign insolence and that base trickery that goes by the name of *diplomacy*. The law of God has not two measures. It is *the* law for heaven as for earth. We cannot wish that our immortal spirit should deny on earth the gift of liberty, which is the source of Good and Evil in human actions, and whose exercise constitutes in the eyes of God the virtuous and the wicked man. We cannot wish that the brow that was made to lift itself to heaven should bend in the dust before any man, whoever he may be, nor suffer that soul which aspires to eternal Truth to grovel in the mire, ignorant of its rights, its power, and its noble origin. We cannot call ourselves Christians, and permit men, instead of *loving one another like brothers*, to be selfish, hostile, divided, city from city, canton from canton, nation from nation. We therefore preach Association as the means of general perfectibility ; liberty, equality, human dignity, enfranchisement from all servitude ; the progress of all institutions ; the sacredness of every land from the invader ; the honour and well-

being of every People; an alliance of all nations; the
destruction by free speech of all prejudices. We preach
the doctrine of the *Fatherland*, the abode and temple of
our race; the doctrine of *Humanity* that Christ announced,
the ambit and bond of fellowship of all countries, who
shall be free and independent, but sisters in one faith,
one love, one Gospel. And when we preach these things,
we are ready, if needs be, to seal them with our blood, to
die as Christ died for their realisation and the salvation
of all men.

Now, these ideas germinated at the foot of the
cross of Christ—of the Christ you serve. For eighteen
hundred years they have been permeating the world,
now under one, now under another form; to-day they
are applied to politics, a short time since to the movement of the intellect. Their virtue destroyed feudalism,
abolished in nearly every country the aristocracy of
blood, and is about to deal it the last blow in feudal
England. The princes of Europe leagued themselves
against these ideas; the forces of all the privileged
classes were often gathered to oppose them; but in the
end every one of their attempts failed. Those ideas
seemed to fall vanquished; you would have said they
were banished for ever from the world; yet they reappeared. They were drowned in blood, and they
reappeared. In one age they were condemned to the
fires of the Inquisition, in another to the gallows
of kings; and they reappeared more potent, more
ubiquitous, more threatening than ever. They in-
vaded the armies assembled to destroy them, the
tribunals called to condemn them, and even the
remnants of those very aristocracies that had been
wounded to death by them. They marched to a
national crusade in Poland under the banner of the
mother of Christ. In the name of the cross of Christ
they gave back Greece to Europe. They move the
world, advancing between victory and martyrdom.
And do you call movements like these the work of
a sect? In this potency of new life that is agitating
the whole of society, can you see nothing but the

underground work of a few conspirators? In this ever-increasing sound of Peoples rising in their might, of multitudes who desire to found a better future, of oppressed races that demand their place in the light of the sun, do you see nothing but the effect of an obscure word thrown at a venture to the crowd, by a few factious men?

Men of the clergy, clear your minds of cant! There is in this an influence more serious and potent than the vain conceit of a writer, or some rebels' plot. The stake is the whole destiny of the civilised world, ordered and impressed by the finger of God on the heart of the generations. It sweeps you also along with it in its advance. It involves a law of continual progress of which we are the conscious or unconscious agents, and without which there would be neither life, nor progress, nor religion. If you oppose it, you are fighting against Christ, against God, and against Humanity—God's interpreter on earth.

Now, do you realise the effect of this impotent strife of yours? Do you see the fruit of your exertions among the Peoples whom you wish to fetter?

It is the fruit of scepticism, of doubt, of negation. It is the fruit of anarchy in belief, and all the immorality that has its roots therein. Its offspring are violent reactions, excesses of civil anger, the fires of Bristol, or of the Spanish convents. It dissociates religion from the great humanitarian movement. It dishonours the priest and the altar. It destroys the temple. It has ruined the people, and will ruin, if you persevere long in your reactionary path, the Christian faith and its future.

III

October 14, 1835.

We addressed a few words to the authorities to this effect :—Interfere as little as possible in religious questions. Allow them to develop freely in the field of ideas; do not be frightened by a few impotent, secret agitators, who have no definite purpose, and

The Patriots and the Clergy 207

Do not be irritated by the vagaries of the factious
Catholic press, because the universal contempt will
set them at their value. The future *unity* of the
human family—*social unity*—is beyond your comprehension, belonging as you all do, body and soul, to
the old school and the old age. Your sole principle
is *liberty*, nothing more. At least be consistent, and
desire liberty in all things, liberty for all, for religious
society as for political society. Watch over and punish
acts that directly touch public order, the liberty and
safety of the citizens. Punish them from whatever
quarter they proceed, but do not claim attributes
outside your functions, or make yourselves dictators
in matters that do not concern you. Be not over-
zealous to *prevent*, since that is not your province.
The public law is sufficient to *repress*.

And we said to the factious priests, to the priests
who sell Christ a second time to the aristocracy and
the Princes of the earth:—Beware! You are few in
number, and fallen from your high estate; fallen
because of the countless faults of your leaders; because
they have deserted the People's cause for that of their
masters, the cause of the poor for that of the idle
rich. You are fallen, because you have wedded religion
to material things, because you have made of public
worship an empty ceremony, and divided the sons of
God, cursing some and blessing others, while Christ
came to preach and pray and die for all. What is your
object? The world moves; progress is its law; the
patriots are the faithful, the apostles of that law. Would
you try to stop the world, or infringe the law that God
has given it, or strive against his apostles? That is
not in your power. Your opposition may indeed awaken
tremendous reactions, increase the germs of discord
which already exist, foment irreligion and scepticism,
discredit Christianity as you have discredited Catholicism. Is this your will? So be it: but think upon
it, and remember that the flames of the Spanish convents are but a reflection from the fires on which the

Spanish monks a century ago burned the victims of their intolerance and greed.

To-day we are forced to speak to you—priests, patriots, men in authority, protestants and catholics. The few words we are about to say are directed to you all.

The reaction is fatal to us ; each of us in this wretched age absorbs some of its venom. There is a spirit of hatred abroad that corrupts our best thoughts with mutual hostility and mistrust. We talk of peace and have curses on our lips ; we speak of liberty and fatherland in a tyrant's accents. We struggle without purpose for the mere love of strife. This is the source of that opposition of detail, which exhausts its strength on minute points when it does not descend to personalities, makes a great ado about petty applications of principles, and then neglects the most important aspects of the principles themselves. This is the origin of that cantonal, parochial, sectarian spirit that predominates in all great national and humanitarian conceptions, in all the questions on which depends in the last resort the peaceful and orderly adjustment of our destinies.

And if we turn our attention to religion, we find yet worse.

We are forced to steer between Scylla and Charybdis : the intolerance of the priests, and the intolerance of the patriots. On either side we find a spirit of pure reaction and destruction. The former, out of hatred to Voltaire and Rousseau—who nevertheless were as great believers as any of them—would wish to abolish the printing-press, destroy books, close schools, enthrone ignorance, do violence to conscience. To listen to their pious eloquence you would imagine them inquisitors in full function. The latter, because they happened to en-counter bigots and fanatics, because they saw despotism disguising itself under the cloak of religion, and the teaching of Christ corrupted in the hands of Popes, deny religion, faith, and even religious philosophy. They become materialists, sceptics, or, what is worse, indifferent. They ignore the great services that strong beliefs have rendered to the cause of Humanity. They ignore how much there is that is noble and sublime and potent in faith in a great religious principle. They forget that religion is immortal, that it is born with the world, and " will endure as long as the world shall endure," [1]— and that materialistic theories lead directly to the principle of individual interest, and hence to egotism and all its attendant evils.

Yet, above all these petty contests of diocesan elections, of examinations, of jurisdiction, there exists something immeasurably greater, holier, more vital for the Church, and conscience, and faith. Above all the ecclesiastical diatribes, the futile demands of the particular absurdities of which the so-called religious question is composed, there is something whose essence is independent from, and alien to, all these squabbles ; something immeasurably more important for our future, for our social condition, for the growth of our Country.

We mean THE RELIGIOUS SENTIMENT.

The religious sentiment is the divine fount of all religions, of all beliefs that have God for their beginning and Humanity for their end, and which are animated by the *spirit*, without which every belief is passive and barren, every religion no more than a sect, every faith but a tradition, a habit, and outward profession.

It is the religious sentiment which hallows the thoughts and actions of Man, that ennobles the human creature in his own eyes, and gives him the consciousness of a mission to fulfil. It gives him the sense that God has not cast him at a venture upon this earth of trial, but that his existence is a function of universal life and harmony, a link in the great chain of beings, a necessary point in the line that connects Man with God and our earth with His universe : it is that which makes all his life a scene of self-sacrifice and charity.

The religious sentiment is brotherhood, and association, and love. From it flow strength and constancy in the struggle for these great principles, indifference to danger, noble resignation in persecution and misfortune.

[1] " Durerà quanto il mondo lontana."—Dante, *Inf.* II. 60.

Such is the religious sentiment, by means of which alone you can advance along the path of progress; for materialism—be assured—however you may desire to consider it, will verily give nothing but the consciousness of your own individuality, the certainty of a few Rights, the power to use them or not at will, or the habit of seeking your own material success even at the cost of your brother's weal, wherever society does not rebel and allow it with impunity. But you will never draw from materialism, either capacity for progress, or the virtue of self-sacrifice and martyrdom.

Now, this religious sentiment is the foundation and bond of all social fellowship, the only pledge of security for the continuous and pacific progress of every people that desires to be a nation, since it unites the souls of men in one purpose, and refers to a *superior law* what rival theories make the result of *chance* and the moment's ebb and flow, thus placing under God's own tutelage the Rights, and happiness, and independence, and improvement of the Peoples. How is it, then, we ask, that this religious sentiment is wrecked, and whither will it sink?

Where sink all good and great sentiments of the human soul, when it has no guide save a narrow, contentious, ambitious conception; where all religions sink when they forget the principle of love and brotherhood that launched them on their way; where all societies sink when they substitute mere opposition for zeal in good works, mistrust for unity, interests for duty. The religious sentiment is declining day by day, is perishing amid petty contests, amid the irritation born of barren party strife, under the evil influence of an odious and reactionary policy. Wherefore some among you—who are prone to confound ideas with those who bring them into disrepute, and institutions with those who profess to represent them—speak evil of religion because it is administered by false priests, of sacred things because they are profaned by men, of beliefs because the blind and ambitious have falsely interpreted them. Others, conversely, deny progress because it was in some degree misunderstood, and condemn the patriots because they sometimes met in their ranks rogues and hypocrites. They deny holy Liberty, Equality, the People, Association, Humanity, because the long series of sacred and high-principled struggles was interrupted by the sad days of '93, when the People of France, goaded to excess, attacked by all monarchical Europe on one side, and domestic conspiracy on the other, swept along in a terrible and unprecedented flood of reaction and vengeance, that will never be repeated, because the circumstances that produced it can never be repeated anywhere.

This is our position to-day; and when perchance from one or the other of the two parties, some one comes forth to join us, seeking to free Truth from the bands of discord that swaddle it, we distrust him as a hypocrite with some secret, ulterior purpose, and we brand his quiet, honest conduct as mere strategy.

This is the attitude of the clergy towards the patriots, and this, too often, is the attitude of the patriots towards a part of the clergy, who perhaps need only to understand and believe in us in order to join our ranks.

Now, if the clergy were to rally to us, or rather to the holy belief that we preach concerning the words of Christ, would the scepticism they deplore be so general and hostile? If they ceased to struggle against the light of intelligence, and the movement that springs from it, would they be defeated and routed by it, and should we be divided from them? We fight against scepticism equally with them, and if we are not allowed a speedy conquest, the fault is theirs, who make Christ's law and God's progress the monopoly of a caste, who rob the masses of their heritage of common rights, and their fair share of the blessings that God has given to His creatures. The clergy have the destinies of the Church in their own hands: they will wreck it where they persist in the narrow and reactionary path that they have followed so long.

And if the patriots, the men of progress, would not,

from excess of irritation, confound faith with its ministers, religion with the priest; if they were not too disposed to exceed the bounds of moderation in the great movement that urges us on; if they did not believe it their duty, through some feeling of mistaken dignity, to free themselves at the same time from the religious principles which alone can prepare the future; if they did not forget so often how our fathers, when preparing themselves for the battles of liberty, knelt before God, how they rose up stronger after prayer, and conquered in the fight, while we, though so proud and presumptuous before God, drag the national flag in the mud and let our country cringe to an ambassador; if the patriots acted otherwise, think you that all the clergy would oppose us? Think you not that honest and devoted men, who have erred in good faith, would part themselves from the majority, often greedy and radically immoral, and join us? And would you fear the predominance of what is called the *clerical party* anywhere, where the people found in you religion, the true religion, that shows itself in good works, that loves and consoles, and consecrates itself to the brethren?

IV

October 17, 1835.

Rise to principles—to universals. Do not scorn truth because men have obscured it. Strive rather to free it from the errors which envelop it, and the prejudices which corrupt it. Do not dash to pieces what has always been the instrument of great deeds because some fanatic has misconceived its omnipotent action. We are on the threshold of a great Age, the *Age of the Peoples*. Learn to understand the vast, sublime, religious meaning of these words. Rise to the height of your mission as men and citizens. The co-operation of all can alone achieve the work of all. Seek such co-operation in all possible ways with that sincerity of soul that wills the good. There must be no revenge, no premeditated hostility, no blind invectives against a whole order of persons. All

general invectives are unjust. Grieve for those who stray
from the right path, but do not persecute them. Do not
embitter your resentment with useless recrimination.
The past is nothing. Open your minds to our words :
we begin a new work. Let the angel of peace and
concord spread his wings over your young flag, and let
the spirit of love proceed, not only from your lips, but
from your hearts. Trust in God, in the goodness of
your cause, and in the power of Truth. Be faithful, and
you will conquer.

To the priests we say : Do not forget that all great
revolutions are fulfilled by virtue of a law ordained of
God to guide the motion of human affairs, and recognise
that what is seething around you to-day is a great revolution, not a mere revolt. Its development is at work in
the hearts of every People. In spite of every obstacle,
it has been gaining ground for the last fifty years, and
everything militates in its favour—its persistent and
cosmopolitan character, its audacity, its eloquence, its
self-sacrifice, its martyr's crown. To stand apart and
fight against it is to fight against God's will, and to part
oneself from Humanity, the interpreter and executor of
His commands ; it is to stand aside from God and the
movement of Humanity ; it is self-destruction. Remember that every *social* revolution must be either *with*
you or *against* you, and that if you ally religion to resistance you wreck religion without profiting your cause.
Remember that the Church—THE CONGREGATION OF
THE FAITHFUL—when it is not an instrument of progress
becomes a corpse ; that it was instituted to hallow, to
harmonise, to unite, not to impede and divide the elements of life given by God to man ; that your mission is
to bless and not to curse. Remember that Christ Himself announced the NEW AGE, in which the *spirit* would
come and reveal to us in *pure truth* what He could only
signify to us in Parables[1] ; and that, according to St.
Paul, we are destined here below, not to organise a

---

[1] "The Spirit of Truth . . . the Comforter . . . no more in proverbs
but plainly . . . will teach you all the Truth."—John xiv. 16, 17, 26, 30 ;
xv. 26 ; xvi. 7, 13, 25.

stationary City, but to seek and to attain to the *holy City of progress and of the future.*[1]

And to the patriots we say : Remember that our doctrine is the doctrine of liberty and association ; that we fight for all ; that our office is to unite and not to divide ; that it is our duty to attack intolerance in whatever place and form it shows itself, and not to substitute a new intolerance for the old one.   Remember that it is not given to you to found your authority, save upon a general, immutable, eternal principle ; that this principle is *the Law of Progress* ; that every law has its legislator ; and that if you forget this you wander in the void, you lose your rallying point, and leave your doctrines and their triumph to chance.   Remember that religion is a want, a necessity of the People ; that all changes of form that have been in the world have never succeeded in extinguishing the religious sentiment ; and that if you neglect this element of human nature, you condemn yourself to a task that cannot be completed because it has no organic vitality, you divide man and the world into two parts, you rob your labour of a fruitful source of activity, you deny that moral unity which is the end and aim of every great revolution, and the necessary condition of its permanency.   And remember that every *social* revolution is essentially *religious* ; that every Age has its *belief* ; that without unity of faith Association is impossible ; that to preach Humanity, Fatherland, the People—those great formulas of Association which dominate our Age from on high—while you deny or neglect the *religious sentiment,* is to misconceive the significance of those words, to will the end without the means, the work without the necessary instruments.

These are our beliefs, and they give our rule of action. We ask those who have been educated in the habit of mistrust, which is only too certainly the fruit of party passion, and who might doubt a single instant our full and entire good faith, to watch carefully our acts and words ; and where they find us in one single instance in

---

[1] " For here we have no *abiding* city, but we seek after the city *which is to come.*"—Epistle to the Hebrews xiii. 14.

contradiction with ourselves, let them point it out : from that day forth we will be silent.

We patriots, we men of a new Age, whose souls look for a religious future for all Humanity, we are bound to lift its banner boldly on high.   We cherish in our hearts the vision of a *faith*—not of a *school*—of progress and successive improvement for the Peoples, and in particular for our Country, which the Peoples will salute and acknowledge as the land which has kept in trust for them the germ of republicanism ; we cherish the vision of a thorough and sincere agreement among all who believe in Country and Humanity ; the vision of a union of all societies in one great association, strong by its activity, by its devotion, by its conscious rectitude and one sacred belief for all—societies that to-day have no flag, no principles, and therefore die of stagnation almost before they are born, and never fulfil their national mission ; the vision of a periodical Press animated by brotherly sympathies, pressing to the same battles under the same flag, intent to achieve its task without bitterness, and spite, and jealousy, intent to gather to itself the great Voice of the Nation, intent to fulfil one and the same mission, because it is convinced that national progress advances more rapidly when a People realises and incarnates *one single principle*, than when it wages a losing fight for a thousand petty details that even in the mass would give no result, precisely because they do not centre round one great constructive principle, set as the keystone of the nation's structure.   We cherish the hope that patriots will arise, with deep convictions and vast ideas, spurred onwards, not by threats of aristocratic restorations, nor rumours of foreign wars, but because it is a duty to advance along the road which our country's welfare marks out ; because it is the office of a virtuous man to contribute to the happiness of his fellows and the perfecting of the nation's institutions, and because the man who has *a faith* is bound to witness to it every hour of the day.   We look forward to a generation of Swiss who will feel that they are free by their fathers' heritage and by their own right, who will hold their heads high alike before enemies and friends, who with a free and fearless soul will do what their own well-being demands and conscience bids, who will not bow their national pride before any man, who will put their trust only in God, and in their own powers, and in the might of the fraternity of nations—a true fraternity, not of vain words,—an unresting activity,—a republican morality,—a sincere faith, free from hypocrisy, and intolerance, and prejudice.

And why should we exclude Christ's priests from this movement of general consecration that we have foreseen, in which, by virtue of its own intrinsic nature and its goal, all classes, all orders, all sections of religious belief, all men of good faith, will be gathered together ?   Or rather, why should not the priest of Christ take his place there of right because of his faith ?   And why should not his blessing descend on the banner of the new crusade, on the ardent souls of the young, in whom lies the future of our Country ?

We know that many will remain cold and impassible to these words, these hopes, the enthusiasm that dictates this language.   The *reactionary patriots* will smile with an air of scorn ; men whose hearts are perverted or sealed by materialistic philosophy, will shrug their shoulders.   Let them go their ways.   But we know, too, that among those priests of Christ who stand aloof because of false opinions concerning us, among men whose hearts are sound, but who are mere tools and counters in the hands of an immoral Power for ever incapable of inspiring a faith that it has lost, there will perchance be found some few who, when they hear these words that come from our conscience and our heart, will be moved to reflect upon the part they are made to play, and the true import of the jesuitical schemes in which they have tried to entangle them ; to feel that faith, true faith, is elsewhere ; *that where the spirit of God is, there is liberty* [1] ; and that we, the friends of liberty, are men who are true to God.

And we are comforted by the thought, that among

[1] St. Paul.

our readers, in some corner of our Switzerland, in the
recesses of our mountains, or maybe on some shore of
our blue and tranquil lakes, will be found perchance the
white and virgin soil of some virtuous youth that will
draw its inspiration from our faith, some mother who
loves in all holiness, and who will receive our words, and
gently whisper them in her children's ears.

And this is enough to recompense our labours.

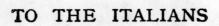

TO THE ITALIANS

TO THE ITALIANS

The Programme of the " Roma del Popolo "[1] (1871)

THE first number of our publication appears on the ninth of February. It bears in front the title, LA ROMA DEL POPOLO; at foot, the names of men who, whatever may be their intellectual worth, have never, despite delusions and baits of worldly success, despite suffering, exile, imprisonment, denied the ideal of their hearts. It should not, therefore, be necessary to lay a *programme* before our readers. Everybody knows who we are. Our programme, the Republican Unity of Italy, dates back more than a third of a century. We have been silent concerning it at times when the people had strayed in opposite directions, and it needed experience and disillusion to confirm its truth; we have never abdicated it. And to-day, more than ever convinced by the experience of the last ten years, we raise again in Rome the flag we planted there forty years ago. Our publication is the cry of the Italian conscience, to uphold that formula of the national life which historical tradition and the instincts of our people have pointed out, to condemn all that spirit of conventionality or falsehood that betrays it with a kiss, or deliberately denies it.

The ninth of February recalls a period, short but splendid in glory and promise, when, in the face of a policy of egotism and fear that obtained through Europe, and while the monarchy was betraying the honour and future of Italy on the fields of Lombardy, at Milan and Novara, Rome lifted her head in solemn protest from the

[1] Rome of the People.

grave, and sealed her protest with the blood of her noblest sons; when she showed by the concord of her citizens of every order, what time she drove the papacy to dishonoured flight, and met four hostile nations in manly fight, how much virtue of love and endurance the ancient republican faith could one day rouse in Italian hearts.   A long probation in the school of political jesuitism, and servile patience, has worked since then to extinguish the memory of those days in shameful oblivion. But in Rome great memories have ever been the germs of new life ; and if Romans have not changed their nature, the memories of 1849 will flower again more quickly and more effectively than some imagine.   Do you not see how the monarchy, that was impelled to Rome by our agitation, by talk of the *Republic* at Paris, how it shrank timidly in apprehension from the need of planting itself there permanently, how it strove for a delay of months, as if it trembled at these memories, and the shades of the generous souls that left them to your city as a sacred legacy to be fulfilled ?

The title that we have chosen betokens the mission of Rome in the world, and the historical evolution that calls upon her to spread for the third time among the nations a gospel of civilisation, a gospel of that moral unity which has vanished for the present in the slow death-agony of the ancient faith.   "This Unity all pray for "—I wrote as long ago as 1844—"can come, Italians, whatever men may do, from your country alone, and you can only write it on the flag, which is destined to shine on high above those two milliary columns, that mark the course of thirty centuries and more in the world's life—the Capitol and the Vatican.   ROME OF THE CÆSARS gave the Unity of civilisation that force imposed on Europe.   ROME OF THE POPES gave a Unity of civilisation that Authority imposed on a great part of the human race.   ROME OF THE PEOPLE will give, when you Italians are nobler than you are now, a Unity of civilisation accepted by the free consent of the nations for Humanity."   And this faith, that sustained our life through bitterest trials, is still ours. The materialists who misgovern us see in Rome no more than a fraction of Italian earth, peopled by a certain number of inhabitants capable of paying taxes and furnishing armed levies : we look on Rome as the sanctuary of the Nation, the Sacred City of Italy, the Historic Centre, whence by providential mission came Italy's message to Men, the message that makes for unity, and our *initiative* in the world. A few months ago they doubted the necessity of having Rome as a metropolis, and published in their newspapers the foolish and wicked phrase, that *Rome belonged to the Romans.* To us, Rome did, and does belong, to Italy, as Italy to Rome. Country and metropolis form, like human organism and brain, a whole, an indivisible unity. From Rome must come, must permeate Humanity, that message that the common thought of all Italy has shaped, the message that two earlier worlds have baptized and consecrated. Without a common faith, without conception of an *ideal* that shall bind the nations together, and show to each its special function for the common good, without unity of standard for its whole moral, political, economic life, the world to-day is at the mercy of caprice, of dynastic and popular ambition and egotism. The *initiative,* which France has lost since 1815 lives no longer, visible and accepted, in any people. England deliberately abdicated it when she introduced, under the name of *non-intervention,* a policy of local *interests.* Germany threatens to sterilise all her vast power of *thought,* by surrendering the *action* that should be collective, and the formation of her unity, to a military monarchy hostile to liberty. The Slav populations, who have so great a part in the future reserved for them, dismembered and without centre of national life, still hesitate between the rule of a Czar fatal to them all, and the old difficulty of local antagonisms. And, faced by such a void, we—who are ready to hail and applaud the *initiative* wherever it may arise—we cherish as the ideal of our heart the sacred hope that it may arise on the ruins of the Papacy and of every similar lie, from the third Rome, from the ROME OF THE PEOPLE. Reborn at the cradle of an Age, Italy and Rome are called to inaugurate it, if only they know their destinies, and the moral force they have behind them.

Unity at home, and a new development of civilisation abroad—these two terms include the whole programme of our publication.

But all great questions resolve themselves into a question of *method*; the question, how can they pass from the sphere of *ideas* into the sphere of *facts*? Can we hope to conquer, and translate into action, the two-fold *end* I have spoken of, with the institutions by which we are governed? Is the instrument that we can use to-day equal to our purpose?

Deliberately, but resolutely, and with firm conviction, we answer: *No!*

We will not spin again the long and painful story whose pages are marked with the names of Villafranca, Nice, Venice begged as an alms from the foreigner, Aspromonte, Mentona, Custoza, Lissa. Fatal and pregnant with inevitable consequences as these pages are, Prussia teaches us how even a monarchy might, if it so willed, escape them and fight alone, and, trusting to the national energy, win its own battles. We will not mention, in condemnation of the monarchy, the financial ruin passed on from ministry to ministry, aggravated by an economy of petty expedients, met ineffectively by immoral taxes that are a source of inequality and misery to the present generation, or by onerous loans that alienate and dry up future sources of wealth. Sully, Colbert, Turgot, and others honest and capable as they, were the ministers of monarchies; and, though men like them were few and far between, and they were nearly all made powerless for good by a crowd of courtiers that always dog the throne, they nevertheless afford ûs glimpses of a possible selection of men better than the feeble blunderers of to-day. We will not found a theoretical attack on the habits of corruption now prevalent in high places, on the subjection of the law to the perennial caprice of individual administrators, on the continual violation of the liberty of the Press and the right of Association, on the absolute contempt for public opinion, on the hundred infringements of its *duty* by every Department, which are brought to light month by month and reported by every organ of the independent daily press. Some might point to us, as a distant hope, the example of the English monarchy, tolerant of every liberty, abhorrent of absolute rule, and following, though at a distance and imperfectly, the movement of public opinion. And though the conditions of life in England are, as we shall point out in this and subsequent numbers, radically different from our own, though it may seem strange and indecorous, that a people who have a better path before them, should be content with the vain hope that its rulers may, some day, choose this one example out of all others to follow, still, we will respect even that one example, and be silent concerning crimes and vices that others might think are confined to a single period. Our attack on the ruling form of government has a higher source.

When a people has in the course of centuries defined its own mission, and revealed, conquered, incarnated in itself the *principle* that forms the essence of its life ; if it is ruled by the form of government that has presided over the long historical development of this *principle* ; then that people has a vista of *reforms* before it, which multiply the practical applications of this vital *principle*, or slowly eliminate the defects inseparable from every system of social polity. Such form of government can, on condition that it preserve intact liberty of *thought* and of the *individual*, continue to direct, if only in appearance, that slow movement of secondary manifestations. But when the necessity of things, and of the times, demands the manifestation of a new principle ; when it is a question of defining a new mission, which, with its new or regenerated people devotes itself to the European task ; when everything points to the revelation of a new conception of *national* or *international* life ; then there inevitably begins a period of *revolution*. *Reforms* inspired by theories of the past become dangerous. The form of government that ruled and represented, well or ill, the old form of life and the formulas of the old doomed system, is incapable to direct the sudden, spontaneous movement, and becomes an obstacle to the attainment of the *ideal*. No form of government has represented, or can represent in the world, *two* different principles. New things ; new forms of Government : new forms of government ; new men.

The Europe of to-day is, on the whole, we believe, in this second stage, seeking, like the Israelites in the desert, a promised land still unknown,—seeking a new *principle*, a new order of things, since the old one is exhausted.   He who watches Europe under the light of the great historical tradition, at once recurs to the memory of those times that eighteen centuries ago announced the slow breaking-up of Paganism, and the inevitable rise of Christianity.   The absence of an *initiative* of any general and harmonious civilisation in the world, the moral anarchy that is its consequence— the wars promoted by the interests of dynasties or some few individuals—the neutrality founded on the indiffer- ence of egotism—the treaties of peace based on foolish theories of an *equilibrium* which is impossible so long as it takes into count material facts only—the question of nationality, which to-day is dominant over all others, and, as eighteen centuries ago, points to a new European birth—the emancipation of the working classes which has become, as in those times was the emancipation of the *slave*, the universal subject of a powerful agita- tion—the awakening of the Slav races, as in those days of the Teutonic races, to a life that now is assured them —the materialism—the exaggerated rejection of old beliefs—the aspirations after new beliefs dawning everywhere—the insensate attempts at an impossible reconciliation between the old and the new—every- thing points to the near advent of an order of things, founded on *principles* radically different from those that preceded the development of the present Age that now is visibly exhausted.   A new conception of Life, and of the divine Law that governs it, throbs in every manifestation of the two faculties of *thought* and *action*. that make up the unity of human nature. Monarchy can neither strangle it nor make it its handmaid.

Monarchy had its day and mission. It came to fight and destroy *feudalism*, which was a system of territorial dismemberment, that hindered all possibility of unity in countries destined to form *nations*. Fronted by a *principle* of privilege based on mere force and conquest, the *king*, himself head of the feudal aristocracy, came to wear out and suppress its power, in the name of another *principle* of privilege, analogous to the first, but founded on divine authority, and consecrated by the then recognised interpreter of a living faith. This mission is the *justification* of Monarchy in history.

To-day, the *feudal* organisation has disappeared for ever, and with it the function that gave life to the monarchical idea. A new conception, based on the Divine Law of PROGRESS, takes the place of the conception that was based on the doctrines of the Fall and the *Atonement*, and hence perishes the Papacy, the authority that ordained the *monarch* for his function.

The world is seeking, not the *material* solidarity which is now assured, and which is only the outward form of the nations, but the vivifying spirit that shall guide their life towards its end ; the *moral* unity that can only be based on the *association* of men and nations equal and free. Monarchy, based upon the doctrine of inequality, on the *privilege* of an individual or of a family, can never give that unity. The flag that leads towards that destined future means PROGRESS, and dynastic interests means *stagnation*. Now that its *end* is reached and its doctrine rejected, the monarchy, like the Papacy, lacks some foundation and potency of life. Throughout Europe monarchy either *follows* or *resists* the impulse that comes from elsewhere : nowhere it *initiates* or leads. Constitutional compromise, concessions that contain within themselves their own condemnation, attempt an impossible equilibrium between two powers *de facto*, that lean on the past, and a third power *de jure*, that moves with irresistible and swifter step towards its future. This can only end in the rejection of *progress*, and the necessity of violent and periodical revolutions.

We shall often have to speak of this condition of things in Europe. But if we look at Italy, our position becomes clearer, and is much strengthened by the history of the past and present.

Monarchy has no traditions in Italy. It has never been a source of national life. The captains who, strong by means of corruption and mercenary pretorian troops, degraded ancient Roman Italy from the glories and titanic energy of the Republic to the Empire, only hastened the work of dissolution that had already set in, extinguished all power of conception and will, and opened the way to the invaders of the North. In the second life of Italy and Rome, Monarchy had no mission, not even that which we mentioned as fulfilled by it in every other country. *Feudalism* was destroyed by our republican Communes. When, after a long period that gave the world a new civilisation, our slow death-agony began, under the solvent agency of the Papacy, amidst the materialism that swept over us, the civil wars, and the abuse of riches and power, then principalities arose under the auspices of successful *condottieri*, men whom the factious imprudently took as their leaders, or the nephews or bastards of ambitious Popes; all of them supported by the foreigner, who wished to divide us that he might tyrannise over us; all vassals of France, or Austria, or Spain, sometimes servants of all three in turn. The sad pages of the history of our princes have no virtue or greatness to recall.

They naturally sought aggrandisement at the expense of their neighbouring rivals, more by intrigue or matrimonial and mercenary alliances than by open war. Not one was thrilled by a great Italian ideal, a vast ambition of a Nation founded by its own strength. Monarchy neither did, nor attempted, anything for the Unity or Liberty of the Country. It lived inglorious, satisfied to exist even at the cost of dishonour, a persecutor of thought in the domain of religious and political belief, a corrupting influence in the field of Letters. When

France arose to epitomise an age, to solemnly proclaim the *Rights* of the *individual*, our princes at first
threatened, without prowess to perform, then fled. When
they returned, not by their own efforts, but through the
arms of others, they punished the peoples for having
witnessed their flight. In Turin, Modena, Naples,
Rome, every aspiration after a free Country and national
unity, even when offered as a new jewel for their crown,
was inexorably proscribed, stifled in blood by the bullet
and the gallows. Journalists may be bought, records
suppressed or kept closed to investigation, men may
be cowards and forget their mission and their power,
but that page of history can never be blotted out.
Italy has no debt of gratitude, or aught else, to
princes.

One day, three-and-twenty years ago, the *idea*,
triumphant as ever over every persecution, rose, with
potency of life and holy daring, from the grave where
the princes thought to have buried it for ever. The
people of Italy, in their own name, and without the
intervention of regular troops, won battles of giants.
They might, they should have gathered for themselves
the fruits of their own victories ; but, intoxicated by
their independence of the foreigner, and only half-awake
to the consciousness of liberty, they brought them to
the feet of the Monarchy. Then was the time, had
the Monarchy possessed a single spark of Genius or
Love, to transform itself, receive the nation's baptism,
and initiate itself to destinies till then ignored or
betrayed. The Monarchy did not rise to the occasion. It entered the lists, late, hesitating, reluctant.
It was, by its own confession, decided solely by the
fear of republican movements. It could not fight, it
would not conquer ; it feared the deluded and applaud-
ing people more than the enemy, and embraced the
opportunity of the first reverse to descend to dishonourable treaties and withdraw from the war. Then Venice
and Rome alone, unable to do more, saved, under the
republican flag, the honour of the nation and its hopes
for the future.

Ten years later, when passions again were hot, and
destinies were ripe, the only statesman of the Italian
Monarchy, a man without creative genius, but endowed
with the ability to use others' talents, saw that it was
necessary to advance or perish. He drove the monarchy
along paths it loved not, lest others should seize upon
them. And, nevertheless, even he was unable to overcome the fatal destiny of the monarchical idea he
served. Unwilling to avail himself of the popular forces
of Italy, and anxious to secure an ally against them in
the future, he cringed, and bought with shameful compacts an alliance with the despot who had slaughtered
Rome at the feet of the Pope. He condemned the
national flag to be subject to the beck and call, the
errors, the crooked schemings of Imperial France.
Though Garibaldi proved soon afterwards that he could
win unaided what our ally had so suddenly abandoned,
the Monarchy accepted as the ally's gracious gift, those
fields of Lombardy that our people and our army had
dyed with their own blood, and then stopped halfway to
move no farther unless constrained. Men, who to serve
the royalist party look at the consequences, not the
causes of facts, may say to-day what they please; but
History and the Italian conscience will one day say
that the popular element desired unity when the
Monarchy was dreaming of royalist alliances with
Bourbon, Pope, and Austria,—that the scheme, which
the royalist intriguers favoured, of a Buonapartist kingdom
in the centre of Italy was defeated by the efforts of us
all, by the popular plebiscites,—that the emancipation
of the South of Italy was won by volunteers and the
populace,—that the invasion of the provinces subject
to the Pope was an inevitable necessity created by the
preparations for our powerful expeditions from Tuscany
and Genoa, and by the clear intentions of Garibaldi,—
that Venetia was another gift,—that, but for the terror
excited by the bands of Calabria and of the Centre, by
the risings at Piacenza and Pavia, by the movements
which were feared at other places, and by the sudden
inauguration of the Republic at Paris, the Monarchy

would not be in Rome to-day. No, we repeat, Italy has no debt of gratitude, or aught else, to princes.

A Government—and it is singular that we who are christened *utopians* must remind the "practical" men of this—is not an organisation that is invented or established *a priori*, copied from England or some other country, and arbitrarily thrust upon a nation without relation to its traditions, its inherent tendencies, its common beliefs—in a word, its *collective* conscience. A Government, to be legitimate and effective, must grow out of the whole of these conditions, as a branch, or rather as the fruit, grows from a tree.

The form of government must, if it is not to be injurious or useless, represent the sum-total of the integral elements of the country, must represent the *thought* that is its soul, the consciousness of the *ideal* to which the millions of men who are grouped within its natural boundaries strive instinctively. The function of government is to purify that thought from every foreign element, to show the method best calculated to reach the *ideal*, and initiate the progressive stages that lead to it. On these conditions—but on these conditions only—we are the friends of government, and part from the theories of reaction and systematic *mistrust*, that, at the present day, dominate a great part of our camp. Those theories are the natural fruit of the wretched Governments that nearly everywhere rest on caste, or family interests in opposition to the interests of the people; they are legitimate arms of defence against recurring dangers. But, if they became a doctrine applicable to every set of circumstances in the future, they would falsify every conception of government, and the antagonism they would create between government and governed would be a source of never-ending war, destructive of all progress.

In the ideal that Europe is seeking, and will realise, the Government will be the *mind* of a Nation, the people its *arm*, and the educated and free individual its prophet of *future progress*. The first will point out the path that leads to the *ideal* which at present is the only

thing that makes a Nation. The second will direct
the forces of the country towards it. The third will
protest in the name of a new and further ideal, against
intolerance, and every tendency to deny the possibility
of unlimited progress. [1]

Meanwhile the Monarchy, a stranger to the National
idea, without historical antecedents, without roots connected with the tree of Italian life, necessarily misconceives the meaning of events and the needs of the time.
In a new event of European importance that is destined
to initiate an Age, it saw nothing more than a question of
dynasty, the sequel of a small continuous movement of
aggregation to the territory of a royal house. It annexed,
like new links to an old chain, the peoples who rose and
embraced in the prophetic heart-beats of a third life, and
repeated, " the moment has arrived to become a Nation."
This Nation, which brings to Humanity a potential force
of incalculable strength, whose every fraction has written
a luminous page in the history of the world, this living
Being, the product of thirty centuries of labour, it would
not even allow to question its own mind concerning the
law of its own life. It was imprisoned, so to speak, in
the royal interpretation of a form of government which
represented the bygone life of a small population, [2] Italian
true, and dear to us, but parted from us while it had that
form. And we are now the only people who have risen
to a unity of collective existence without a NATIONAL
CONTRACT, which the best of the nation have deliberated
on, and the consent of the majority has made authoritative.

In an event which shows that the political doctrine of
Nationality, and a new European birth are the meaning
of the universal agitation, it merely sees the addition of a
new member to old Europe, to the old Diplomacy, to the
doctrines of ancient treaties. It allied Italy with despotic
Governments, with all the compromises that try to main-

[1] Almost every line of this essay would require an expansion that
cannot be given here ; but the reader will understand that this is a
programme on which the successive numbers of the publication will
be a commentary.
[2] Piedmont.

tain the impossible *status quo*. In the dualism between
us and the Papacy, from which, with the latter's fall, our
religious mission in the world was to be initiated, it only
saw the means of acquiring a patch of territory, and
narrowed the solution of an immense and fateful problem,
to a bastard compromise between soul and body, between
the moral and material, between Truth and Falsehood.
To develop and direct the Italian conception of Unity,
it chose, and chooses, men who never believed in it, the
advocates of federalism, the men who at one time persecuted its apostles.

The sense that they have no bond of intelligence and
love with the Nation, forces the Government to dread
popular progress, and adopt a policy of *resistance*. Its
rule is, never to give way to public opinion, except when
it threatens to break out irresistibly in open conflict.

This is the fundamental basis of our attack. The rest,
the perversion of the army from its primitive and only
mission, *the safeguarding of the national soil and honour*,
to become an instrument of repression within the country,
the creation of an army of useless officials, to acquire an
undue influence in the provinces, the repudiation of local
liberties, the absence of an international policy, the ruin
of the finances, a system of unjust and excessive taxation,
are only a series of consequences which logically derive
from that first irrevocable set of circumstances.

Those who deny this in the face of History and the
most recent events, delude themselves. Those who, in
the Chamber or outside, attempt to guide Italy to its *ideal*
without first removing this source of all our difficulties,
deceive themselves and the country. They are laying
up for themselves—and we deplore it—discredit and
isolation. They are laying up for the country yet more
prolonged and violent crises, the more violent the more
Italy stands in an exceptional position,—the position of
a Nation in process of formation, for which, like a child,
any deviation from the standard that educates to high
and noble things may have a peculiarly and terribly fatal
result.

To us the question is wholly a moral one. A form of

government either leads to good or corrupts. A form
of government that is based on lies, or that has no life,
and therefore cannot infuse it, condemns the country—
whether consciously or unconsciously is immaterial—to
a career of errors and crimes, or else by breaking up the
moral unity of the Nation, and condemning it to a war
of its own members that fetters its movements, ends by
making it sceptical and egotistic, and drugging it to
sleep. And sleep for a people of ancient growth, strong in
the education of the centuries, and recognised by the other
peoples as having largely fulfilled its mission, for such a
people sleep is more or less dishonourable, but not
deadly. But sleep, or long delay, is at once dishonourable and deadly to a people like ours, that is rising to
become a Nation, and must therefore of necessity grow,
and yet cannot without a power to direct its forces to one
end, a people that is pondering the road it has to follow,
the road which will determine the acceptance or refusal
of brotherhood with other Nations.

To one who sees in a Nation something more than an
aggregation of individuals born to produce and consume
corn, the foundations of its life are, fraternity of faith,
consciousness of a common *ideal*, and the association of
all faculties to work in harmony and with success towards
that ideal. You cannot make it believe that life and
growth are possible in a never-ending dualism between
its government and itself; that the temple of its worship
can have *privilege* written on its *summit* and *equality* on
its base ; or that it can live, a useless member of the
European family, abdicating every duty, every office,
every mission for the good of others, concentrating all its
activity on the petty interests of the individuals that
compose it, without debasing its moral sense, its intelligence, the exercise of its faculties, or compassing its own
destruction in loss of confidence, and apathy, and doubt.
And we see the symptoms of this growing only too fast.
The Italy of to-day is no longer the Italy of 1860. The
masses, cheated of the vast hopes they entertained at one
time of the benefits of Unity, are fast losing the national
political sense, and lending an eager ear to the fatal

whisperings of a federalist school that was dumb ten years ago. The middle class is becoming—as its abstention from the elections proves—more and more indifferent to the exercise of its political rights. The Chamber, part of it blindly subservient to government influence, part of it tied by the narrow formula which the Deputies swear, though they know it to be false and hurtful, has parted with its initiative, and is every day losing the importance that should belong to it. A feeling of torpor, the feeling of a man who sees no remedy for recurring dangers, infects men's minds with scepticism, and entices them from the public arena to the exclusive care of their own private concerns. What between the examples given in high places, and the logical consequences of the spread of materialism, which is partly the result of the Government's false tactics towards a dying religion, morality is losing its hold on the public mind. This is how Nations die, not how they are born.

It is high time to leave a policy of expedients, of opportunism, of entanglements and crooked ways, of parliamentary hypocrisy, concealment, and compromise, that characterises the languid life of worn-out nations, and return to the virgin, loyal, simple, logical policy that derives directly from a moral standard, that is the consequence of a ruling *principle* that has always inaugurated the young life of peoples that are called to high destinies.

The first condition of this life is the solemn declaration, made with the unanimous and free consent of our greatest in wisdom and virtue, that Italy, feeling the times to be ripe, rises with one spontaneous impulse, in the name of the Duty and Right inherent in a people, to constitute itself a Nation of free and equal brothers, and demand that rank which by right belongs to it among the Nations that are already formed. The next condition is the declaration of the body of religious, moral, and political *principles* in which the Italian people believes at the present day, of the common ideal to which it is striving, of the *special* mission that distinguishes it from other peoples and to which it intends to consecrate itself

for its own benefit and for the benefit of Humanity. And
the final condition is to determine the methods to be
employed, and the men to whom the country should
delegate the function of developing the national conception of life, and the application of its practical consequences to the manifold branches of social activity.

Without this, a *country* may exist, stumbling along from
insurrection to insurrection, from revolution to revolution;
but there cannot exist a NATION.

And these three conditions can only be fulfilled by a
NATIONAL CONTRACT, dictated in Rome by a constituent
assembly elected by direct or indirect [1] suffrage, and by
all the citizens that Italy contains.

The National Contract is the inauguration, the baptism
of the nation. It is the *initiative* that determines the
normal life, the successive and peaceful development of
the forces and faculties of the country. Without that
initiative, which gives life to the exercise of the vote,
and directs it to the common *ideal* under the guidance
of a *principle* and a *moral* doctrine, even popular suffrage
is at the mercy of arbitrary influence, or the passions of
the day, or the false suggestions of ambitious agitators.
Plebiscites taken under circumstances like these, the
perverted and unenlightened expression of mere brute
numbers, have, within the space of a few years, led, and
will lead again, to a republic, a limited monarchy, and
the despotism of a Bonaparte. Until a people is educated
to uniformity and brotherhood, the initiative determines
in every place and time the character of the solemn acts
to which the masses are called.

Every one knows what is the form of government that
we believe to be the logical deduction from the principles
in which we believe, and from the national Italian
tradition : we define it as *the development and application
of a Nation's ideal, duly entrusted by the chosen of the
Country to men of recognised capacity and proven virtue.*
We hope to show in our publication how it is only by
adopting this formula of government that Italy can

[1] The writer prefers an indirect suffrage in two removes; but this is a
question to be discussed in one of the ensuing numbers.

escape an indefinite series of more or less fatal crises, and fulfil her destinies, great, prosperous, educated to virtue. Quite recently it was said to us by partisans of the government : " Write and discuss with us. Every way of public propaganda is open to you. Why is that not enough ? We have a right to combat conspiracies and attempts at insurrection ; but we will all respect the peaceful and philosophical expression of ideas." We reply once again to the invitation, and write. We have often attempted it, but the Government did not keep faith with its interpreters, and answered our statements, even when they only repeated the pages of History, by sequestrating our property, and prosecuting us, without any one protesting against its action.

Nevertheless, we make another attempt, if only to see whether the Government can ever learn wisdom, or if the men who gave this invitation will join us to protect liberty of thought. Our publication is frankly Republican, but it will not call to arms, or teach the people to rise, or provoke rebellions.

When Italians are once convinced they will act for themselves. We, who are ever ready to follow them by any means, or any paths that may lead, without crime, to the *ideal*, will use the present to meet the errors and prejudices which are constantly turning many minds from the idea that is the basis of our mission. When we undertake to discuss in theory the present and future condition of Italy, Italians will be able to gauge from the attitude of the Government towards us the measure of its conscientiousness and moral strength.

And we will, above all, meet the errors that proceed from our own camp, and degrade, and warp, or lessen the purity of our Ideal. Many of the accusations that come from the opposite camp do not merit any lengthy refutation. Those who even now speak of anarchy and feebleness as inseparable from republican institutions, we can meet with the miracles of progress and power recently performed by the United States, and the steady peace which reigns by the side of liberty in the valleys

of Switzerland. Those who are not ashamed to cast
in our teeth their childish suspicions of popular tyranny,
or terrorism, or spoliation, we can answer with the
names of Venice and Rome, and all that we have done
or written during the last forty years. But the materialism that shatters the unity of human nature, and while
it supplies us with an object, suppresses all the noble
impulses, all the sacred beliefs that stimulate us to fulfil
it,—the false philosophies that lead, consciously or unconsciously, to the worship of accomplished *facts*, and
success, and Force,—the schools of politics and of
economics that select a single instance from among the
manifold integral terms of the social problem, and deduce
from it the solution of all secondary problems,—the
blind, servile copying of the old French Revolution,
still rooted only too deeply in most of our hearts, that
fetters us with theoretical formulas of *individual rights*
which are but the summary expression of a dead age
which we have abandoned for the *initiative* of the future
age,—the excessive tendency to mete out the same blame,
the same suspicion, so often unjust, to many who, like
us, love the Fatherland, but are intellectually at fault
as to method, that we mete to the few selfish schemers
who, through thirst of lucre and power, consciously
defile and betray the National Italian Revolution,—the
narrow-mindedness that anathematises a grand and fruitful past out of hatred to a poor and feeble *present*, that
falsifies History, that tries to deprive us of our glories,
and denies the tradition which is the very life of Humanity,—all these deserve, and we will give them, an
attentive and thorough examination. It is these and
other errors brought to our Democracy from foreign
schools of thought that have made the Italian intellect
stray from the right path.

It is time to call it back from barren criticism to the
National School, with its constructive methods, its tendencies to correlate and harmonise ; from a materialism
that presumes to understand, explain, determine motion
while it destroys the motive power, to the old ever-
present doctrine of the Spirit that harmonises motion

and motor. As far as our powers permit we will try to accomplish this.

Only on this condition can our National Revolution be achieved. Blind revolts lead only to victories of a day. Simple negations can overthrow an old worn-out edifice; they never lay the foundations of a new one; they never win a people to organised and effective action, or build the Temple of the Nation.

Our party is faithful to the ideal of our country's Traditions, but ready to harmonise them with the Traditions of Humanity and the inspirations of conscience; it is tolerant and moral, and it must therefore now confute, without attacking or misconstruing motives. We need not fear that we are forging weapons for the enemy, if we declare the religions of the world to be successive expressions of a series of ages that have educated the human race; if we recognise the religious faculty as eternal in the human soul, eternal, too, the bond between heaven and earth. We can admire in Gregory VII. the gigantic energy of will, the sublime moral effort that could not be realised with the instrument that Christianity could lend, and, at the same time, in the name of the progress we have made, declare the Papacy to be for ever dead. We can recognise the Mission which Aristocracy and Monarchy had for other peoples in the past, and yet proclaim, for all of us, the duty and the right to outstrip those worn-out forms. We may, without denying the reverence due to Authority— for that is the real object of all our efforts—claim the task of attacking every Authority that is not based on two conditions—the free and enlightened consent of the governed, and the power of directing the national life and making it fruitful.

We believe in God.

In a providential Law given by Him to life.

In a Law, not of the *Atonement*, not of the *Fall*, and *Redemption* by the *grace* of past or present mediators between God and *man*, but of PROGRESS, unlimited Progress, founded on, and measured by, our works.

In the *Unity* of Life, misunderstood, as we believe, by the Philosophy of the last two centuries.

In the *Unity* of the Law through both the manifestations of Life, *collective* and *individual.*

In the immortality of the *Ego*, which is nothing but the application of the Law of PROGRESS, revealed beyond doubt now and for ever by Historical Tradition, by Science, by the aspirations of the soul, to the Life that is manifested in the individual.

In Liberty, by which alone exists responsibility, the consciousness and price of *progress.*

In the successive and increasing *association* of all human faculties and powers, as the sole normal means of *progress*, at once collective and individual.

In the *Unity* of the human race, and in the moral *equality* of all the children of God, without distinction of sex, colour, or condition, to be forfeited by *crime* alone.

And hence we believe in the holy, inexorable, dominating idea of DUTY, the sole standard of Life. *Duty* that embraces in each one, according to the sphere in which he moves and the means that he possesses, Family, Fatherland, Humanity. Family the altar of the Fatherland ; Fatherland the sanctuary of Humanity ; Humanity a part of the Universe, and a temple built to God, who created the Universe, that it might draw near to Him. *Duty*, that bids us promote the progress of others that our own may be effected, and of ourselves that it may profit that of others. *Duty*, without which no *right* exists, that creates the virtue of self-sacrifice, in truth the only pure virtue, holy and mighty in power, the noblest jewel that crowns and hallows the human soul.

And finally, we believe, not in the doctrines of the present day, but in a great religious manifestation founded upon these principles, that sooner or later will arise from the initiative of a people of freemen and believers—perhaps from Rome if Rome knows her mission —and which, while it includes that chapter of Truth that former religions won, will reveal yet another chapter, and will open the road to future progress, destroying in their germ all privilege and intolerance of caste.

We have wished to express our principles briefly, that all who wish to help us may know what are the conditions of fellowship on which we will gratefully accept their help and counsel. From these derive all the rules that we prefix to questions of the intellect, and politics, and economics. We believe that to make politics an *art*, and sever them from morality, as the royal statesmen and diplomatists desire, is a sin before God and destructive to the peoples. The *end* of politics is the application of the moral Law to the civil constitution of a Nation in its double activity, domestic and foreign. The *end* of economics is the application of the same Law to the organisation of Labour in its double aspect, production and distribution. All that *makes* for that *end* is Good and must be promoted; all that contradicts it or gives it no help must be opposed till it succumb. People and Government must proceed united, like thought and action in individuals, towards the accomplishment of that mission. And what is true for one Nation is true as between Nations. Nations are the individuals of Humanity. The internal national organisation is the instrument with which the Nation accomplishes its mission in the world. Nationalities are sacred, and providentially constituted to represent, within Humanity, the division or distribution of labour for the advantage of the peoples, as the division and distribution of labour within the limits of the state should be organised for the greatest benefit of all the citizens. If they do not look to that *end* they are useless and fall. If they persist in evil, which is egotism, they perish : nor do they rise again unless they make Atonement and return to Good.

But to staunch the two sources of our worst wounds, —the dissension between the Government and the governed, and the selfishness that dominates individuals,—we must constitute a Government that represents the mind, the tendencies, the duties of the Nation, and we must determine the National ideal, the origin and standard of our duties. The former is a problem of form to be solved, in any practical way, by the initiative of the whole country ; the latter must be solved by the delegates of the nation, who shall make a NATIONAL CONTRACT, and found a system of national and compulsory Public Education, which the Contract shall determine.

For both, the preliminary and essential question is to recognise and proclaim where the Sovereignty resides.

Two Schools, both foreign, both founded on that dismemberment of the unity of human nature to which we have drawn attention, now hold the field, and solve in their several ways the philosophico-religious, political, and economic questions that are exciting interest in Europe.

The first places sovereignty in the *individual*, in the *Ego*. With no conception of Law, and hence none of collective duty, it finds, wherever it turns, a partial, temporary expression of life, the doctrine of *Rights* supreme, inviolable ; it bases all organisation on this latter doctrine. The spontaneous action of the individual, whether it leads to a power that is only *de facto*, or whether it instinctively reaches a standard of justice and truth, always bears, in its eyes, the mark of a *Sovereignty*. According to the disciples of this school, self-interest, or if that be insufficient, the action of the preponderant force, is sufficient to prevent the inevitable conflicts among all these petty local *sovereignties* from degenerating into civil war. This School leads, in Religion, to *protestantism* with the more timid, who stop halfway ; to *materialism* with those whose logic is more thorough. In politics it leads to *federalism*, to the almost absolute independence of local interests, to absolute liberty of education, to systematic distrust of all governmental control, and in international life to *non-intervention*. In economics it leads to *unlimited* competition, to the recognition of every acquired right without considering whether it is fatal to the progress of the majority, to the unrestricted doctrine of *laisser faire*. It accepts liberty alone among human faculties as the basis of civil society. The State is regarded as merely an aggregation of *individuals*, without any common *ideal* except the satisfaction of personal *interests*; the Nation as an aggregation of Communes, all sovereign and arbiters of their own development; and Government as a necessary evil, to be limited as much as possible, and confined to the exercise of a coercive force in cases of mutual robbery or slaughter.

The other School is opposed to the first on every point. It places sovereignty exclusively in the *collective* will, in the "*We*," and inevitably concentrates it slowly in the hands of a few, if not of a single man. The State is everything: the individual practically nothing. The social ideal is absolutely binding, and must be accepted by him. The Nation absorbs all independent local life in a strong centralised government. The ideal that directs the Nation is supposed, theoretically, to be founded on the *good*; practically it is neither confirmed, nor elaborated, nor modified by the intervention of the free examination or consent of the citizens. According to their system, the best are, and ought to be, called to apply it, but not by the people; they, the majority at least, have no part in the choice of the few who are already declared to be the most capable of the nation. *Association* is predetermined and ordained; but by authority and on a uniform and fixed plan. The instruments of Labour and of Production are one by one handed over to the State. The conditions of distribution are decided by authority. This school leads, in religion, to *Catholicism* with the timid; to *Pantheism* with the strong-minded. In politics it leads to despotism, whether of one, or a few, or many, is immaterial. In economics it leads to the search—the probably fruitless search—for a limited degree of material prosperity, at the cost of all possibility of progress or of increased production, at the cost of every stimulus to the growth of activity, the inventiveness, the initiative of the individuals. Just as Liberty is everything to the former School, so is Authority to this.

We reject those two Schools, which, under whatever name they appear, only continue the *dualism* of the

doctrine which we declare dead.   The republican form
of government, as we understand it, places the centre of
movement in a higher sphere, in which the two much-
abused terms, Liberty and Authority, shall not conflict,
but harmonise with one another.

The problem that is agitating the world is not the rejection of authority; for without authority, moral anarchy, and
therefore sooner or later material anarchy, are inevitable.
It is the rejection of all lifeless authority which is founded
on the mere fact of its existence in the past, or on
privileges of birth, riches, or aught else, and maintained
without the free discussion and assent of the citizens, and
closed to all progress in the future.   It is not the rejection of liberty, whose absence makes tyranny inevitable.
It is the restoration of the idea contained in that word
to its true meaning—*the power to choose, according to our
tendencies, capacity, and circumstances, the means to be
employed to reach the end.*   It is the rejection of that
liberty which is an *end* to itself, and which abandons
society and the mission of humanity to the caprice of
the impulses and passions of individuals.   *Authority* and
Liberty, conceived as we state them, are equally sacred to
us, and should be reconciled in every question awaiting
settlement.   *All things in Liberty and for Association;*
this is the republican formula.   Liberty and Association,
Conscience and Tradition, Individual and Nation, the
" *I* " and the " *We* " are inseparable elements of human
nature, all of them essential to its orderly development.
Only in order to co-ordinate them and direct them
to a purpose, some point of union is required which
is *superior* to all.   Hence practical necessity leads us
inevitably back to the high principles that we enunciated in theory in an earlier part of our work.

Sovereignty exists neither in the "*I*" nor the " *We* " ;
it exists in God, the source of Life ; in the PROGRESS
that defines life ; in the Moral Law that defines Duty.

In other terms, Sovereignty is in the IDEAL.

We are all called to do its work.

The knowledge of the *ideal* is given to us—so far as
it is understood by the age in which we live—by

our intelligence when it is inspired by the love of Good, and proceeds from the Tradition of Humanity to question its own *conscience*, and reconciles these two sole criteria of Truth.

But the knowledge of the *ideal* needs an *interpreter* who may forthwith indicate the means that may best attain to it, and direct its application to the various branches of activity. And as this *interpreter* must embrace within itself the "*I*" and the "*We*," Authority and Liberty, State and Individual; and as, moreover, it must be *progressive*, it cannot be a man or any order of men selected by chance, or by the prerogative of a privilege unprogressive by its very nature, or birth, or riches, or aught else. Given the principles contained in the contract of faith and brotherhood, this interpreter can only be the People, the Nation.

God and the People: these are the only two terms that survive the analysis of the elements which the Schools have given as the foundation of the social communion. Rome knows by what paths of self-sacrifice, civil virtue, and glory, the banner that bore these two solemn words inscribed upon it, awakened in 1849 the love of Italy for her.

And here for the present we may stop. The Italian Mission is therefore :—

The Unity of the Nation, in its *material* aspect, by the reconquest of the Trentino, of Istria and of Nice; in its *moral* aspect, by National Education, accompanied by the free and protected Instruction of every heterodox doctrine.

Unity of defence, or the *Nation armed*.

Unity of the Contract and every Institution that represents the civil, political, and economic progress of all Italians.

Steady activity of the legislative power; and the administration of the institutions that concern the national progress, to be entrusted, not to the executive power, but to Commissions by delegation from the legislative.

Communal liberty to be decreed so far as regards the special progress of the various localities.

Suppression of all offices intended at the present day to represent an undue influence of the Government over the different local districts.

Division of powers to be a consequence, not of an illogical distribution of *sovereignty*, but of the different functions of government.

A smaller number of State employees and a more equal payment for their services.

Abolition of political oaths.

Universal Suffrage as the beginning of political education.

Legislation tending to advance the intellectual and economical progress of those classes that need it most; and the nation to encourage industrial, agricultural, and labour associations, founded on certain general conditions, and of proven morality and capacity.

Special attention to be given to the uncultivated lands of Italy, to the vast unhealthy zones, to neglected communal property, and to the creation on them of a new class of small proprietors.

A general system of taxation so as to free life—that is, the necessaries of life—from all burdens, and so as to fall proportionately on superfluities, and avoid excessive expenses of collection.

Abolition of all impediments to the free circulation of produce within and without the country.

An economic system based on the saving of all useless expenditure and on the progressive increase of production.

Recognition of every debt contracted by the Nation in the past.

Simplification of the transfer of land.

Abolition of monopolies.

Responsibility of every public servant.

International policy to be governed by the moral *principle* that rules the Nation.

Alliances to be based on uniformity of tendencies and objects.

Especial favour to be shown to every movement that may fraternise Italy with the elements of future or growing Nationalities, with the Greek, Roumanian, or Slav populations, who are destined to solve the problem of Eastern Europe.

These, with many others, are but the consequences of the great *principles* we have enunciated, and will be developed in our Publication; and, if the Italians will help us with their effective assistance, a more popular explanation will be given in a paper which we will add, dedicated specially to the Working Classes.

THOUGHTS ON THE
FRENCH REVOLUTION OF 1789

THOUGHTS ON THE
FRENCH REVOLUTION of 1789

No. XI. of the " Roma del Popolo"

In 1835, when the French republican party was singularly powerful in its secret and public organisation, in men of strong intelligence, of generous daring and a civic courage till then too little known among us; when an insurrection seemed imminent and success seemed probable, and the eyes of all Europe were turned with anxiety and confidence to France, I wrote in a French Review [1]:—

"The *initiative* is lost in Europe, and while each of us ought to be working to recover it, we persist in trying to persuade the peoples that it still lives, active and potent.

"Since 1814 there has been a void in Europe, and, instead of labouring to fill it up, we deny the fact.

"From 1814 onwards, there has been no people to take the initiative, and yet we persist in saying the French people has the power.

. . . . . .

"*The French Revolution must be considered, not as a programme, but as a summary*: *not as the initiative of a new age, but as the last formula of an expiring age.*

. . . . . .

"The progress of the peoples depends to-day upon their capacity to emancipate themselves from France.

"The progress of France depends upon its power to emancipate itself from the eighteenth century and the old Revolution."

---

[1] "On the Revolutionary Initiative," in the *Revue Républicaine.*

The present article is a commentary on those words.

I write it because I see even to this day, more vivid and potent than I had believed, the inordinate prestige possessed by France and the memories of its great Revolution over the minds of our young men; a prestige that delayed our reawakening for long years, and still delays its completion or threatens to pervert its direction. The events of the past thirty-six years have confirmed in unmistakable language the truth of that statement. France still, as always, is self-deluded, believes herself to be the leader of European progress, and has from that time forth, almost of necessity, been moving in a circle, from monarchy to republicanism, from republicanism to despotism, and now she seems to be beginning the same revolution once again.   Equally incapable of repose or normal motion; never able, whether under monarchy or republic, at home or abroad, to take one of those upward steps that open out a new horizon to Nations already organised, or point an easier way for peoples wandering in search of a life as yet denied them. Nevertheless, the idea of France, mistress of the destinies of Europe and hastening to unfold them for the good of all, ploughs to-day like lightning through the soul of the young Italian generation, even as, when I faced the first battles and sorrows of life, it dominated the soul of the generation that is now dead or in lethargic old age. In each convulsive movement of France's great fall our people dream that the *initiative* is reborn.   Any thought that takes shape for few days in Paris, even when it proves the dissolution of the old power which was based upon unity and the prevailing anarchy, finds among us thoughtless and indiscriminating applause.   And at every fresh disillusioning, Italian lips utter, or Italian faces show, the cowardly thought : *how should we attempt what France attempted and failed to do?*   What! are we condemned to crawl for ever behind *man-king* or *people-king?*   Is Italy doomed to be the satellite of a greater planet ?   Cannot its population of twenty-five millions do for the new Age what twenty-five millions of French did for the Age that is passing away ?

Italy does not lack force, but the consciousness of the
force that she has within herself; she lacks *collective*
virtue; the trust of each city in its neighbour city, of each
individual in his brother; the trust of all in the latent
life that throbs in the tradition of a people that once
was great and is fated to be great again, the life that
makes a nation.　And among the many causes of this
mistrust—catholicism, materialism, our long servitude,
the contradiction between the *end* of our movement
and the *means adopted* to reach it—not the least
is the false conception universally prevalent of the
characteristics and historic value of the Revolution in
France.　Just as a new faith is only revealed when the
majority agree in boldly declaring the exhaustion and
extinction of the old one, just as a people surrounded
by enemies only finds salvation in its own strength when
it despairs of others' help, so a Nation can only move
resolutely onward along the road that leads to prosperity
and greatness when it is convinced that others will not
advance for it.　The initiative force which it fancies is
elsewhere, and which perhaps is hidden in its own breast,
cannot reveal itself, for no one thinks of evoking it.

And another evil consequence results from the belief
that the French Revolution has ushered in a new age,
—the blind tendency to imitate its actions, copy its
formulas, expend all our active strength in following
out the consequences or its ruling ideas, without advancing to the discovery or the confirmation of new
ones.　The three terms *liberty*, *equality*, *fraternity*, mark
out the circle within which all our social philosophy
revolves; it forgets that *association* is the mother-idea
of our Age, an idea unknown to the official inspirations
of the Revolution.　A bad and immoral definition of
life, *the search after happiness*, filched from the catechism
of Volney and the French republican constitutions,
rules with slight disguise the whole of our moral
philosophy, and cannot help instilling the poison of
Egotism into the veins of a society that nevertheless
is said to believe in the Law of Common Progress.　A
baseless speculation, without possible sanction, except

in the brute *force* of individual *rights*, which was
the one formula of every Assembly that controlled the
Revolution, summarises the whole of our political
science. We mutter the sacred words, DUTY and SELF-
SACRIFICE, but leave their interpretation to the caprice
of good instincts, and thus inadvertently admit all the
aristocracies of *rights*, won just for themselves by one
or another class. The theory that popular *sovereignty*
should be exercised, not as the interpretation of a
supreme moral Law which has been indicated by a
declaration of principles, and diffused by a uniform
National Education, but as the brutal despotism of
figures, which one day leads to republican liberty, and
on the morrow to the unlimited power of a usurper
and tyrant,—the doctrine of the impossible divorce of
Church and State, both, to-day, phantasms and lies,
but which nevertheless are destined sooner or later to
represent the harmony between *principle* and their
application,—the debased conceptions of *authority*, with
which Democracy wages war solely because the authority
of to-day is a lifeless corpse, though in the ultimate
analysis authority is the end and aim of all our efforts,—
the insane admiration for a period of *terrorism* which
some have taken for energy, but which was only fear
and which prepared France for the Empire, and even
now makes a number of unthinking enemies of Republican Institutions,—these and other fatal errors all
derive from that initial error that makes us forget our
own tradition and its message, and fetters us to the
tradition that the French Revolution was the *beginning* of
the present age, whilst we are all, consciously or unconsciously, apostles and heralds of an Age that is about
to dawn. In the meantime, the few bad men who are
opposed to us, and the many credulous men who accept
their charges without examination, take advantage of
that error to prophesy from the Republic, as we understand it, the same consequences as the deeds that stain,
only too deeply, the glories of the French Revolution.

The statement that I shall attempt to prove in my
article would, if true, ultimately change in part the

direction of the most important science called the
philosophy of History, which we define as the *perception* of the great Tradition of Humanity. To-day,
thanks to the avowed materialists who do not understand it, and the materialists disguised as Hegelians
who misunderstand it, that perception risks being lost.
And National tradition, which is so large a part of
that of Humanity, is forgotten. The writers and
ministers of the monarchical party have converted it
into a miserable *machiavelism* that dates precisely from
the time when the princely vassals of Charles V. and
Clement VII. interrupted that tradition. Perhaps, imperfect and weak as my work must inevitably be, it
may arouse some few to revive it among the young
who have warm hearts and austere genius. In any
case it will not be out of place if, in the absolute
lack of historical works on the French Revolution
among us, at least one Italian should recall us to the
need of considering that great event without either
blind servility or culpable antagonism, and starting from
a standpoint different from that taken by the French and
other earlier writers.

I

No. XII. of the " Roma del Popolo"

In a book nobly conceived and boldly written, my
friend Edgar Quinet asks himself in tones of grief[1] why
the political results secured by the Revolution are so
much inferior to the force, the gigantic energy, expended
in its course. How is it that even now we are obliged to
fight for the rights that it proclaimed more than eighty
years ago ; obliged to fight for that Liberty for whose
sake nearly two millions of men sacrificed their lives?
And he answers that it is because, instead of looking the
religious problem in the face, which is the basis of every
Society in process of formation, instead of resolutely
parting from Catholicism and attacking it as Christianity

[1] *La Révolution*, Vol. II. Book V c. v. 1865.

attacked Paganism, the Revolution hesitated, uncertain,
vacillating, before the problem, and timidly, hypocritic-
ally, condescended to a compromise with Catholicism.
All the other causes to which he refers in the course
of his work are, in his view, secondary and inferior.

But why did that cause exist? Why, in a generation
who were very giants in strength of will, did their daring
fail them here? A Revolution is never complete, says
the writer, except on condition of embracing and following
a new belief, or the rejection and open severance from an
old one.[1] Why did the Revolution effect neither the one
nor the other?

Quinet does not try to solve this question so indispensable to the right understanding of the mission, the
value, the historical significance of the Revolution. He
too, like all French writers, was tempted away by the
idea that the *initiative* belongs to France. He, in the
sphere of thought, succumbed to the timidity and
uncertainty for which he reproved the Revolutionists in
the sphere of action. He wanders in the dim domain of
an irrational, illogical despair. He sets to the fault of
individuals what belongs to the necessity of things, to
the laws that govern events; at times he misunderstands
the rôle of the revolutionary leaders, at times he contradicts himself[2]; he leaves the reader at the end of
a long, and in many aspects, splendid work, in the same
darkness that he undertook to dispel, still doubtful of the
road to be followed in the future.

The answer to that last question is this :—

The Revolution was unable, in spite of all its daring,
to accomplish the impossible. The Revolution was
directly descended from Christianity. The inspiration
that ruled its actions never passed beyond the limits of
Christian principles. Its work was to apply to mundane

---

[1] Book V. c. i.
[2] "The idea that predominates to-day, and *it is the true one*—the separation of Church and State—was very far from the minds of men in 1789"
(Book V. c. i.) ; and further on : " It was reserved for our times to fancy
that the human soul has nothing to do with political action, that the same
man might be forced in one direction in religion, in another in politics, and
that so radical a destruction of the human conscience might be effected
without injury " (Book V. c. vii.).

affairs, to political life, the fundamental ideas that
Christianity had pointed to the world as belonging to the
spiritual order of things, to be only verified by man in
heaven.

Christianity is the Religion of the *individual*. The
collective and *progressive* life of Humanity, and of its
component nations, is unknown to its dogmas or its
moral doctrines. Christianity consecrated the two
aspects, internal and external, of *individuality*; it knew
nothing of *association*, which we know now to be the only
method of Progress. It regarded men as *brothers*, because
they were the sons of one God; but the *ideal* was a
personal, and not a *collective* one; and *each individual*
had indicated to him the way to attain the *ideal*, without
learning that it was needful for this very end to unite
the capabilities and powers of *all*. To save oneself,
not *through* the world, or by working with the world, but
in spite of the world—that was the supreme formula of
Christianity.

The Revolution, being a result of the Christian teaching,
could neither rebel against it nor free itself from it. The
Revolution tried to introduce into political matters the
liberty, equality, fraternity of men. Its theory of *rights*
gave the political formula of the *individual*; it did not
go beyond that. It did not found a *new* Society; it
prepared the old one for liberty and equality. Liberty—
even when it is given to *all*, and called Equality—*cannot*
found a new Society; Association alone can do that.
Liberty is no more than an element of social life. It
provides the materials: it does not breathe into them the
breath of life.

The Revolution, being the daughter of Christianity,
did not cross its boundary, did not pass beyond its
primitive inspiration. It might, if the Latin nations
had not ingrained opposite tendencies, have adopted
the protestant doctrine, and freed itself from Catholicism;
but it could never escape from Christian forms.[1]

[1] In Quinet's book the question never goes beyond the terms of the
acceptation or rejection of Catholicism, which is only one of the forms of
Christianity; and it might be said that for the new age he only sees the
necessity of a *Christian* transformation. Book XIII. c. vi.

*K 224

The Revolution, therefore—save for those presentiments of the future that permeate every great Revolution—was not the *beginning* but the compendium, the *conclusion* of an age—a practical summary of the conquests of the past, not a *programme* of future conquests.

All the actions, the vacillation, the apparent contradictions, the conquests, the vagaries of the Revolution, and its descent to the Empire, find an easy explanation from this point of view. And if I am, as I believe, right, the Christian Age is concluded ; France's mission to *initiate* is completed. We have another conception of Life, and travel in search of a new earth and a new heaven. And the first People who shall arise in the name of that conception, with the faith that says, *I can*, and the energy that says, *I will*, and cry to the other peoples, "I am fighting for you all, follow me," this People will give its name to an Age

II

Among the French historians of the Revolution,—putting aside the first simple narrators who were more or less judicious in the choice of facts, more or less able to recall them, and at whose head are Thiers and Mignet,—putting aside among the more recent, Louis Blanc, who excels in many merits of clear and elegant style, in his thorough study of documents, and intellectual grip of several social questions, but who is warped by his blind partisanship for the men of the mountain, and destitute of the philosophico-religious sense,[1]—

---

[1] Louis Blanc in his work starts from a distinction between *three great principles*, that, *separately*, he says, *dominate the world and history*—namely, *authority, individualism*, and *fraternity*; and this is one of those arrogant, rash formulas that get repeated without examination, fascinate our young men, and falsify the sober, stern character of the Italian genius. In the meantime, to prove how much he misconceives the philosophic value of those three words, he begins by defining *authority* as the principle *that entrusts the life of nations to blindly accepted beliefs, to a superstitious respect for tradition, to inequality, and that employs force as a means of Government.* Such authority is, I will not call it Christian, but Catholic. Authority is a general and ruling principle, freely accepted as the basis of a society. Sacred as Liberty is sacred, it represents Tradition—that is to say, the sum-total of acquired truths—just as Liberty is the security for further progress along the paths of other truths, truths that shall constitute a basis for a new Authority. The fact

Buchez stood alone in seeing in the French Revolution
a product of Christianity. He was the founder of a
School that had glimpses of many great truths, but lost
their fruits by mixing them with serious errors. He
understood that the essence of the Revolution was
Christian; but believing as he did in the eternity of
Christianity, and not divining its slow death-agony,
believing too that the *initiative* had been given to France
for all time, he saw in the Revolution the *beginning* of a
new Era, in which a transformed Christianity would be
converted into a social religion, and would make a
reality of the *Kingdom of God* on earth. But this is to
will the impossible. A religion is never transformed; it
exhausts the possibilities of life contained in the *principle*
that created it, and then it dies, leaving that principle
among the number of acquired truths. A given *end* is
never reached by an instrument designed for another
purpose. A faith that has for its *end* the salvation of
the *individual*; for its *means*, the belief in a *mediator*
between God and the individual; for its condition,
Grace; for dogma, the *fall* and *redemption* through
another's works—such a faith can never found a Society
which, though it works for the same *end*, has for *means*
the belief in the *collective* life of Humanity, the sole
mediator between God and the individual; for its condition, the works that we have done on the earth; for its
doctrine, Progress. An attempt like that of the French
Revolution, and guided by a gigantic energy of purpose,
was made six centuries before. What Gregory VII.
attempted, however superficially others may judge him,
was to destroy the dualism between two powers, and the
organisation of a world living a *collective* life, with the
instrument supplied by Christianity; not finding in
Christianity sufficient virtue to reach his end, he was led

is, the world is always moving in search of *Authority*, and has neither
life nor progress save in and by it. Only, all *Authority*, representing,
as it does, a definite and limited sum of Truth, is exhausted and perishes
when it has fulfilled its mission; and to him who persists in upholding
it in its decay, Revolutions reply that they intend to bury it and win a
new one.

Louis Blanc may say—I cannot—on what foundation the Fraternity which
he desiderates can rest, when all *authority* is destroyed and *individualism*
condemned.

to try, like the Revolution, and with similar futility, a policy
of violence and terrorism, imposing celibacy by decree,
and inflicting death upon souls by excommunication.

Other writers—the latest and most important being
Michelet, the author, I will not say of the best book on
the Revolution in its *historical* aspect, but the book most
imbued with a moral standard of judgment that I know
of—struck by certain incidents of rebellion common to
all Revolutions, and neglecting for excrescences and
foreshadowings inseparable from all great national movements that which constitutes their essence and definition, saw in the French Revolution a great rejection of
Christianity, and hence the *beginning* of a new Era.
Christianity, in the opinion of those writers, is the reign
of *grace*; the Revolution the reign of *justice* and the
abolition of privilege.   And they appeal, moreover, to
Voltaire and Rousseau, to the inspirers of the Revolution,
who were all, as they say, anti-Christian.

I will touch presently on the course of ideas and
tendencies followed by Voltaire and Rousseau ; and how
far the Revolution waged war without truce against
privilege, and inaugurated the reign of justice, will, I
hope, appear from the whole of this work.   But I think
I must here make two observations to facilitate the
development of the question.

The first is, that to estimate clearly the historical value
of a Revolution, we must distinguish between the
opinions of individuals and the facts of the Revolution
itself.   Men, during Revolutions, almost always surrender
themselves to the impulses that dominate the multitudes,
and compromise with their own.   It matters little that
Mirabeau, and perhaps many others in the Assembly,
took their inspiration from the irreligious scepticism of
Voltaire; for when, with the view of overcoming the
opposition of the clergy to the confiscation of ecclesiastical
property, and proving that the existing religion ran no
risk, the Carthusian Gerle proposed in April 1790 that
the Assembly should declare the Catholic, Apostolic,
Roman religion the religion of the State, and its worship
alone authorised, and when the whole of the Right of

the Assembly applauded his motion, Mirabeau, pretending to be astonished by the doubt which it implied, asked, "whether it were necessary to decree that the sun shone," and another deputy, with equally sceptical opinions, quoted "the gates of hell shall not prevail against" Catholicism, wondering that those words should be confirmed by a poor human decree. It matters little that Robespierre derived all his views from Rousseau's writings ; for when, in November 1792, Cambon proposed that the State should cease paying the salaries of the clergy, Robespierre declared that every attack upon the Catholic religion was a menace to popular morality, and contested the right of the Revolution to take an initiative by stating that "it mattered little whether the religious opinions followed by the people were prejudices or not, it was necessary, in any case, to base their reasonings upon them." The character of the Revolution must, in the series of the stages of Progress, be measured by what it *did*, not by what the revolutionists thought.

The second point, which is almost always overlooked, is, that human effort along any stage of Progress is achieved *first* in the intellectual, *afterwards* in the practical sphere.

A religion begins to die in the *mental* sphere—that is, in its dogma and ritual—when the *practical* application of its informing principle is in the first stage of its development in the field of civil and political facts. Like all great ideas, each religious synthesis begins by being elaborated in the intelligence, in the sphere of *spiritual* activity. The consequences are not realised in the sphere of *material* activity until the intelligence has completely assimilated that principle and is master of it. But the continuity of Progress requires, that even before the work that centres round the vital idea of the religious system of the Age is fully completed, the mind should see yet another religion dawning on the far horizon, and begin a new task of development, either around or parallel to it. In the meantime, as I said, the logical deductions of the old system are translated into facts in actual civil life.

If this were not so, Progress could only move by fits and starts. The human intellect would remain stationary during the whole time that the idea is being practically applied; and practical genius, if the work of application is exhausted, would necessarily be stationary in its turn, until the new idea is fully evolved in the intellect. The periods of human progress, interrupted by these stationary periods, would, to re-connect themselves, need an impulse, some *initiative*, from a higher source. This is the theory of direct immediate *revelations*, which we reject as false, and contrary to all we can divine of the nature of God.

The anti-Christian tendencies of some of the precursors of the Revolution do not therefore contradict my assertion. These thinkers, placed on the confines of two worlds, already had glimpses, not of the future religion itself, but of its necessity and the insufficiency of the old one; while, on the field of civil and political facts, the Revolution summarised and concluded the Christian Age.

III

Christianity, setting aside its conception of heaven and its slow ingrafting of dogma, and considering it in its historical relation with other religions, is, as I have said, the religion of the *individual*; and this constitutes its vital essence, its mission.

In the slow and progressive development of the great formula of the Universe, the supreme word of which is UNITY, and which assigns to all of us for a final *end* the conquest of the moral Unity of Humanity, so that each one of us may one day reflect the conception of the Law given us,—in this development, Historical Tradition (when we regard it, not with the presumptuous ignorance of modern materialists, but with the reverent attention due to the representation of our collective life, the sole standard from which we can deduce and verify the conception of the Law that governs it) shows us a series of great ages, all hall-marked and defined by a religion, all intended to concentrate human activity on the evolu-

tion of one of the essential elements of the world's
problem, God, Nature, the Individual, Humanity. Every
age reveals, in part at least, a new term of the formula,
and points to a new goal for the forces of the intellect.
Every religion pours a fresh drop of the universal life
into the human soul.

Of the ancient religions of the East, some had conceived of God as solitary, supreme, beyond the reach
of human intellect, menacing as Fate; others, as sometimes blessing, sometimes cursing Nature. All of them
neglected man; none suspected the ray of the divine
ideal that is in him, the bond that joins him to the
Infinite. On one side was an immense, inscrutable force,
on the other, an immense, unconscious, passive weakness; and, between the two, Love had not yet traced
with its wings a bridge for possible union. The East
had expressed God alone; man lay crushed, a slave,
the sport of an inexorable Fate, or of the caprices of
the deified forces of Nature.

The polytheistic religions expressed *man*, and his
spontaneous nature. They rescued him from a pantheism
that oppressed him; they had glimpses of the fact that in
the scheme of the universe man had a part; but they did
not succeed in defining this part. Ignorant of the *unity* of
Life, and its double manifestation in man, *individual* and
collective; conscious only of the former, they focussed
the work of the intellect on the *individual*, and saw in him
only the subjective existence of the *ego*—that is, *liberty*.
But without conception of the mission of humanity, uncertain as to the *end*, and therefore as to the *means* to be
pursued, the work was arrested, powerless to attain its
purpose, in the face of a universal fact,—*inequality*; and
they accepted this fact, decreeing by an infallible dogma
the *two natures* in men. Greece and Rome nobly
developed the idea of *liberty*, but for one class of men
only. *Slaves* existed, by the doom of birth or conquest,
side by side with the citizens.

The Christian Age came to complete the work begun
by Polytheism, and to contemplate the *individual* in his
other aspect, in his *external*, objective, relative existence.

Its principal work was, therefore, to develop the idea of *equality*. The Mosaic religion had already established the vital dogma of the divine *unity*. Christianity appropriated this dogma, and, advancing a step further, withdrew it from the privilege of the *chosen* people in order to diffuse it among *all* peoples. The God of Moses was the God of Israel, of the Nation : the God of Christianity was the God of men, who were necessarily brothers in Him. The slow abolition of *slavery* was a consequence of the triumph of Christianity, of the evangelisation of the slave by the priests. The immediate completion of emancipation being impossible, except at the risk of grave dangers, so barbarised and so brutalised were the slaves, there arose under the feudal system an intermediate stage of *serfdom* ; but the Church itself represented in this respect the *ideal*. As the guardian of that portion of the Moral Law which the times permitted, she abolished in her own ranks the fatality of birth and the hereditary principle, and made *merit* alone the basis of every ecclesiastical.

Beyond this Christianity neither did, nor could, proceed. The prevalent conception of Life knew nothing of *collective* Humanity, of the Law of Progress that governs us, of the Historical Tradition that reveals it and explains its *method*, of the solidarity that exists between past, present, and future generations, of the unity that binds together earth and heaven, the ideal and the real, the infinite and the finite. With aspirations towards the future more potent than some think, with a worship of the *ideal* visible in Art, as in all the other Christian manifestations of the first thirteen or fourteen centuries, Christianity, placed between an *end* so tremendous and remote as salvation, or in other words, *perfection*, and on the other hand the feeble, unequal, isolated, fruitless powers of the *ego*, active only for a brief period of time, Christianity was driven to two conclusions : first, the impossibility of solving the problem with the conditions of this life as they were then known ; and next, the necessity for the intervention of a superior power independent of all law, in order to overcome the immense disparity between the *end* and the *means*.

Hence the *divinity* given to Jesus ; *grace* ; the contempt of earthly things ; the insufficiency of works ; the ardent longing for heaven, which is the source of prayer, of isolation, of renunciation of the visible world, not of association, or the progressive transformation of the elements in which we live, or self-sacrifice to incarnate so much of the *ideal* as is possible *here below* ; hence the divorce between the visible and the invisible world, between the life on earth and a kingdom of Justice and Love to be realised *only* in Heaven. Christianity received the idea of *liberty* that Paganism had worked out, added the idea of *equality*, and preached *charity* to the brethren ; but it was a liberty purely spiritual ; an equality of souls before God ; a charity to be exercised between individual and individual only, and a part of the renunciation of earthly goods rather than an attempt to suppress the causes of pain and evil. Religion was not life, but a reward promised for a life to be accepted on the earth such as it was.

I am speaking of Christianity, not of Catholicism, which was at first a form of Christianity, then a deviation from it. Even Protestantism, which was generally supposed to be a Revolution, and which many believed a progressive movement in Christianity, was practically nothing more than a protest in favour of intellectual *liberty*, that had been systematically violated by the Papacy ; and, in a higher sense, an evidence, little understood by the Reformers themselves, of the slow extinction of the Christian age. Sixteen centuries had exhausted the vigour of the Christian philosophy. The human spirit was bound to move again towards another and vaster philosophy ; hence the necessity for a strong assertion of the individual, and for that right of private judgment without which every attempt to pass the limits of the old belief would have failed. Protestantism unconsciously asserted it. And that was its sole mission in the world ; it did not pass beyond the boundary of the age. The *sovereignty* of the individual—arbitrarily confined within the limits of the Bible—was its last word, re-echoed in the Arts the Economics, the Politics that it inaugurated

France took on herself the task to conclude the Age of the *individual*, which was sterilised and moribund, by two more centuries of dissolution. She summarised its conquests, its principles, its characteristics, and translated them practically into the sphere of civil life.

Did she cross the boundary?

Did she initiate the new Age?

IV

Ideas rule the world and its events. A Revolution is the passage of an idea from *theory* to *practice*. Whatever men have said, material interests never have caused, and never will cause, a Revolution. Extreme poverty, financial ruin, oppressive or unequal taxation, may provoke risings that are more or less threatening or violent, but nothing more. Revolutions have their origin in the mind, in the very root of *life*; not in the body, in the material organism. A Religion or a philosophy lies at the base of every Revolution. This is a truth that can be proved from the whole historical tradition of Humanity.

Now, what were the ruling ideas in the period immediately preceding the Revolution? What were the doctrines that hovered over its cradle? What was it that inspired and baptized its development and the various parties that promoted it? Did they go beyond the confines of the Age of the *individual* and his *rights*? Did they initiate the Age of DUTY; and of *Association*, the only means of fulfilling Duty?

Three men, Voltaire, Rousseau, Montesquieu, comprehended the whole intellectual movement of the eighteenth century, and exercised a visible and predominant influence on the development of the Revolution : Montesquieu, on the ideas of the Constituent Assembly ; Rousseau, on the men of the Convention ; Voltaire, on the beginnings of the movement and certain general tendencies that reappear intermittently to recall his name, and the indefatigable war he waged for fifty years against the traditions of the Church and the caprice of despotism.

Voltaire's genius was quick, subtle, acute, analytic, encyclopædic, but not profound; he was moved by good and philanthropic instincts rather than by strong and reasoned moral beliefs; a warrior rather than an apostle; a hater of *evil* rather than a worshipper of *good*; too much extolled by some, too much depreciated by others, Voltaire founded no doctrine, but, as I have said, popularised tendencies,—tendencies that existed already, and were almost innate in the French genius, but to which he gave new force and clothed in noble language,—tendencies which leak out in a number of the events of the Revolution, and, excepting the more rigid puritans of the Mountain, from Camille Desmoulins to Barres, influence, one might say, every actor of the period. They were philanthropic tendencies, inspired by momentary impulses of kindness rather than by a conception of life, and of its law,—tendencies of a vague, sterile, superficial deism, which relegated God to heaven and sundered His undying connection with the world, and which was merely a compromise between the tradition still extant in the popular mind, and the scepticism that, however covertly, dominated Voltaire and his followers,—tendencies of antagonism to every imposed authority, to every form of superstition and fanaticism, but born rather of a sense of rebellion natural to one who *thinks*, than of faith in the destinies of those who have yet to *learn* to think,—tendencies that worshipped the rights of reason, but only for those individuals who by good fortune and education can share in them, and which were mingled with some spirit of contempt for the masses, a spirit which afterwards founded the fatal distinction between the popular and the bourgeois classes,—tendencies of equality, but confined, as in the philosophy of the ancients, to one order of men, regardless of the rest. I have mentioned the bourgeois class, and Voltaire was, in fact, consciously or unconsciously, the teacher and master of the *bourgeoisie*, and his influence was all-powerful in the acts that, in the period just before the Revolution traced the first lines of a division that has been more recently organised into a system, by Guizot and the French eclectic school : the *bourgeoisie* of the two Bourbon Revolutions idolised him. A man of impulses, of intuitions, rapid but short-lived, of enthusiasm, intellectual rather than moral, Voltaire, who displayed rare humanity in his efforts to clear the memory of Calas and the Sirven family, was flatterer at once of the Empress Catherine and King Frederic of Prussia. He sanctified their crimes ; he burlesqued, in low comic verse, the heroic resistance of the Poles to the dismemberment of their Fatherland. An apostle of toleration in religious matters, he was the type of intolerance towards all his enemies, and capable of using any weapon, even calumny, to their prejudice. He waged a relentless, rabid war against catholicism, and when threatened with death wrote a declaration of catholic faith and repentance. I write this as a debt to my own conscience, and because I see arising among our young men, who have neither studied all his works nor his life, an intemperate and dangerous admiration for him; but it is more important to my present purpose to note how Voltaire destroyed prejudices and errors, but neither built nor cared for the future. He had no perception (his historical works and his theory that great events depend upon little causes prove this) of a Law dominating the life of Humanity, no perception of Progress, of a human mission, of Duty, of Association, or of anything that constitutes the *end* and the *method* of the new Era that we invoke. He recognised no standard of good except in the *rights* of the *individual*. And like all who start from the idea of *right* alone, he could not help being forced to give the preference to rights already existing and recognised. He declared that "a State being a collection of lands and houses, those who possessed neither land nor house ought not to have any deliberative voice in the management of public affairs." In one of the most beautiful moments of his long life, he gave full expression to the idea that guided him, when he uttered, under guise of a blessing on Franklin's young son, the sacred but insufficient words—*God and Liberty*; a formula that opens the way to a possible *initiative*, but does not itself *initiate*. Liberty is a mere instrument of *good* or *evil* according to the path it chooses.

Montesquieu, a more profound thinker than Voltaire, though less profound than some say, was the chief of a political school that had for its disciples, in the first period of the Revolution, Monnier, Malouet, and many others in the Assembly; Rivarol,[1] Bergasse, Mallet Dupan,[2] and others in the periodical press. The influence of the ideas he expounded in the *Esprit des Lois* is visible in the acts of the Constituent Assembly.

His influence lay in his historical studies of antiquity, that would be thought superficial at the present day, but then appeared vast and almost unique. His intellect was acute, and swift in seizing the salient points of things; his aspirations were advanced; the expression of his thoughts vigorous. Montesquieu was at times unconsciously impelled, by his native logic, near to the unknown confines of the new Age; but he was hindered by his lack of any religious conception of the life of Humanity, by the prevailing theory of the ebb and flow of Nations, perhaps, too, by the inevitable influences of a semi-patrician birth and the conditions of office; and so he retreated ever more and more towards the old Age, and never, even in his most daring flights, crossed the limits of a period that began the transition. For an instant he caught a glimpse of the true definition of *liberty*, when he said that it consisted "in being able to do what one *ought* to will, and in not being constrained to do what one *ought not* to will" (Book XI. c. iii). But this was a momentary flash, an isolated saying, whose consequences he was unable to deduce. He suspected the existence of a general *end*, common to humanity, and a *special* end, belonging to each nation; but he was incapable of rising from that glimpse of an idea to the conception of a providential mission. He

---

[1] *Actes des Apôtres.*   [2] *Mercure Politique.*

notes "that the object of Rome was aggrandisement;
of Lacedemonia, war; of the Judaic laws, religion; of
Marseilles, commerce; of the barbarians, natural liberty";
but he never saw that those *facts* were only *means* to
reach the *end*, and that the appointed end is general
progressive civilisation, the slow formation of a collective
human *unity*. It is clear from twenty passages that
he feels in his soul the superiority of the republican
form of government to all others; and yet, finding no
body of *principles* that convert the intuition of the
moment into a demonstrated truth, he concludes by
labouring to teach how a monarchy may be durably
established. He too, in all his researches, starts only
from the individual, and so, like all who have no other
criterion of Truth, he can only grasp the notion of *right*.
For him, as for the other philosophic thinkers of the
time, there are *rights* consecrated by the *fact* of their
existence, by prolonged possession; and the political programme is reduced to efforts to find a place for them in
the social organism, and to seek an impossible equilibrium that shall preserve the peace among them, and
prevent one right from doing violence to another. Placed
between a monarchy that said "France is mine," an
aristocracy powerful by past domination and an exclusive
influence over the monarchy, and the first threatening
murmurings of the *Tiers État*, Montesquieu did not
pretend to pass judgment on those three forces, or
ascertain the sum of vitality that existed in each, and
which was doomed to early death, which destined to
long life in the future. They *existed*, and he accepted
them, consecrating the labour of his intellect to co-
ordinate their existence and functions in the organisation
of the State. His ideal was the English system, the
result, not of any conception of political philosophy,
but of a unique historical development of causes and
effects which existed nowhere else. His theory is that
which we have seen in practice for more than half a
century under the name of constitutional monarchy,
where the search for an equilibrium between the three
elements of Crown, and Nobility, and Commons, has

everywhere condemned the peoples to alternate between stagnation, reaction, and periodic revolution.

The problem, therefore, in the *Esprit des Lois* is vitiated by a fundamental error. Montesquieu labours heavily about the distinction between the three Powers, legislative, executive, and judiciary, and makes this the cardinal point of the whole question; he thus, by exaggerating this distinction, destroys the conception of National Unity. The real, the sole, the vital question should be, for him as for us all, the question of Sovereignty; what is its origin, and where its interpretation is to be sought with the least uncertainty and the greatest probability.

There does not, and ought not to exist more than one LAW; it is its application to the diverse branches of social life that implies a distinction in the higher branches of the administration between the different functions *delegated* to provide for its execution. Just as the exaggeration of the triple aspect of *life* in God changed little by little the three different *aspects* of divine action into Three Persons, and founded a Tri-theism in religion opposed to the conception of Unity, so the theory of rights, and hence of acquired rights, impelled Montesquieu to discover *powers* where they did not exist, and found a political Tri-theism which has survived even to this day, and impairs every conception of national organisation. Having raised these social elements to Powers, he confers on them attributes which suffice to break up the harmony of the State. He was confronted by the danger, either of antagonism between the three powers, or compulsory stagnation; but he replied with superficial carelessness, "that, as they were urged forward by the necessary movement of things, they would be constrained to move in unison."

Montesquieu abounds in false ideas respecting the hereditary nature of the aristocracy, the function of the monarchy, the rights conceded to the *executive* over the legislative, and many other questions. But it is not my task to notice them. It is sufficient for my purpose to have reminded my readers of the thought that dominates his conceptions. He has no *criterion* outside that of the *individual*. He reaches no formula of political organisation beyond that of *rights*. He has no scope, no mission to suggest for the State, except *liberty*, and by *liberty* he understands, in the general course of his work, nothing more than " the citizen's consciousness of his own safety, and of having nothing to fear from any other citizen." Political science is therefore narrowed to a science of *limits*, of mutual defence. And the government, deprived of any other mission, is to use the force of society to watch that those limits are not overstepped by violence. A Religious conception, the Law of Progress, Duty, Association, the *end* assigned to Humanity and to each People, collective Education, and the office of the Press to gradually promote the unity of the human family, everything, in short, that is characteristic of the Age we call for, is unknown to the man who inspired the Constituent Assembly.

Montesquieu was neither inspirer nor prophet of an Age.

He summarised, with singular acumen, the conditions and consequences of political laws as he found them, incomplete or in partial activity, in the period in which he lived. He sketched in outline, not always, but frequently exact, the existing tradition, but nothing more. When we point to him, at the present time, as the master of future legislation, we commit the same error as when we make poor Machiavelli the guardian of the cradle of reborn Italy—Machiavelli, who anatomised the dead body of old Italy and showed the wounds that caused her death ; when we take Adam Smith—who was but the wise exponent of the laws that governed the economic phenomena of his time—and make him the founder of an immutable science, the teacher of an Age in which the economic relations between class and class are hastening to an inevitable change.

Rousseau, the inspirer of the Convention, followed another road, but without passing the confines of the Age that France was preparing to summarise. A poor plebeian, without deep study of the past, abhorring the

times in the consciousness of his own superiority, and
for the exaggerated demands of Society as he found it,
he, on the great political questions of the day, questioned
only his own intelligence and the intuitions of the
heart. His intelligence was more powerful than that of
Montesquieu ; his heart was led astray by a leaven of
egotism that too often soured his natural inclination to
good ; and both together drove him to the principle that
takes its birth, if not its consecration, from him—the
principle of popular sovereignty. A true principle, if
considered as the best method of interpreting a supreme
Moral Law which a nation has accepted as its guide,
which is solemnly declared in its Contract and transmitted
by National Education ; but a false and anarchical principle
if proclaimed in the name of force, or in the name of a
Convention, and abandoned to the caprice of majorities,
uneducated and corrupted by a false conception of life.

For Rousseau, the popular sovereignty remained in
these last terms, uncertain, ineffective, shifting. He, too,
had no conception of the collective life of Humanity, of
its tradition, of the Law of Progress appointed for the
generations, of a common *end* towards which we ought to
strive, of *Association* that can alone attain it step by step.
Starting from the philosophy of the *ego* and of *individual*
liberty, he robbed that *principle* of fruit by basing it,
not on a Duty common to *all*, not on a definition of man
as an essentially social creature, not on the conception
of a divine Authority and a providential design, not on
the bond that unites the *individual* to Humanity of
which he is a factor, but on a simple *convention*, avowed
or understood. All Rousseau's teaching proceeds from
the assertion " that social right is not derived from
nature, but is based upon conventions." [1] He drives this
doctrine so far as to comprehend the family itself within
it. "Sons," he says, "do not remain united to their
fathers except so long as they have need of them for
their preservation. . . . From that time forth the family
is only maintained in virtue of a convention."

From the doctrine that recognises the rights of the

[1] *Contrat Social*, in the first chapters.

contracting *individuals* as the only source of social life,
nothing could result but a political system capable of
protecting, within the limits of a narrow possibility, the
liberty and *equality* of each citizen ; and Rousseau has
no other programme.   "The aim of every system of
legislation"—these are his very words—"reduces itself
to two principal objects, liberty and equality" (Book II.
c. xi.) ; and earlier, in c. iv. of Book I., "to find a form
of society that shall *defend* and *protect* with all the collective forces the person and the property of each associate,
and in which each one, uniting himself to all, shall obey
only himself and remain as free as he was before : this is
the fundamental problem."   Stated in these terms, the
problem contains neither the elements of normal progress nor the possibility of solving the social *economic*
question that is so prominently agitating men's minds
in our time.   An isolated sentence in the book seems to
lay down the principle that "no citizen ought to be rich
enough to be in a position to buy another ; none poor
enough to be constrained to sell himself"; this is just,
but it does not connect itself with the general bearing
of the *principles* he expounds, nor is there any indication
how it may be reduced to fact.   It is of little importance
that in many particulars he is superior to every other
thinker of that period.   The Society of Rousseau, like
that of Montesquieu, is a mutual insurance society, and
nothing more.

That first statement, the key of the whole system, is
by now proven to be false ; and, because false, fatal to
the development of the principle of popular Sovereignty.
It is not by the force of *conventions* or of aught else, but
by a necessity of our nature that Societies are founded
and grow.   Each of us is a part of Humanity, each of us
lives its life, each is called upon to live for it, to aid the
attainment of the *end* assigned to it, to realise, as far as
possible in each one of us, the ideal type, the divine
thought that guides it.   Law is one and the same for
individual and collective life, both of which are the expression of a single universal phenomenon, differently
modified by space and time.   And life, we know now,

is Progress. If you throw over Moral Authority, our
natural tendencies, our mission, and substitute the merely
human authority of *conventions* as the source of social
development, you risk arresting that development, or
subjecting it to arbitrary caprice. And since you need
the consent of all the contracting parties to dissolve these
conventions and make a change for the better, you are
threatened, on the one hand by the power of every
minority, logically indeed of every individual, to stop
you ; on the other hand, inasmuch as the prolonged
existence of a *fact* pre-supposes, at all events, a tacit
convention, you are threatened by the necessity of perpetuating rights and powers that are not founded on
justice, or conducive to the common good. No " man "
has, you say, " natural authority over his fellows : Might
cannot create right ; therefore conventions are left as the
only basis of legitimate authority." But is there not an
authority higher than any man, in the True, the Just,
the *end* which we have set before us and which we are
bound above all things to discover ? Is not some of that
authority passed on to the people or to that fraction of
the people which is its best interpreter ? And, to discover that *end*, do we not possess the double criterion
supplied when the Tradition of Humanity and the
conscience of our times both harmonise ? And for a
method of practical verification, can we not examine
whether this item of discovered truth profits or not the
common progress ? Rousseau believed in God, but in
his study of human phenomena he continually forgot
Him.

Rousseau believed in God. He believed—and it is
well to remind of this those republican materialists who
venerate the *Contrat Social*—that a State could not be
established without having religion for its foundation.
And he pushed this belief to the fanaticism of intolerance,
declaring (Book IV. c. viii.) that the Sovereign power
could exile from the state all who disbelieved in God and
Immortality, and condemn any citizen to death who,
after publicly confessing his belief in those dogmas, by
his subsequent conduct convicted himself of deliberate

falsehood. But he confined himself within a narrow deism that placed God far off in heaven, and never understood his universal, never-dying life manifested in Creation ; he was ignorant of the Law of Progress—the sole but potent and living mediator between God and Humanity ; he was fettered by the individualist philosophy; he had no glimpse of any religion besides Christianity; and so he was incapable of deducing and applying the logical consequences of his faith to Society.

Like Voltaire and Montesquieu, Rousseau was not the intellectual herald of an Age. His conception, though more daring, more explicit, more advanced than theirs, never passes the limits of the individualist world, elaborated by the Pagan-Christian Age. The influence of the three schools with which these names are associated could not push the Revolution beyond those limits, to the World of Progress and Association for which we are now fighting.

V.

Did France collectively effect what these three great and influential thinkers failed to effect ? Did she, by virtue of enthusiasm, cross the boundaries of that world within which their doctrines were confined ? Often, like intuition in the individual, Insurrection (which is the intuition of a people, the concentration of all the faculties harmoniously directed to a given point), advances further than the slow, peaceful, solitary labour of the intellect. The electric spark, set free when the masses are kindled by a common aspiration and suddenly rise to self-sacrifice and victory, flashes more strongly through the darkness, and illumines a horizon more distant than what the pale, steady light of the sage's lamp reveals. Let us see if this was so.

The best method of gauging the value of a Revolution is to thoroughly scrutinise the series of solemn declarations made in its name by the collective authorities, freely chosen by the people to represent the movement, or by the extra-legal movements of the people itself, when they announce a determined end, and leave a mark that points in the direction of the future. Every revolution has, by the very nature of things, isolated geniuses outside its own orbit. They are the aerolites of the moral world, and give indications of important eccentric phenomena, but teach us nothing as to the path of the planet. To select, as some do, from a speech of Claude Fauchet or St. Just, a chance unconscious phrase, in contradiction with the whole, and argue from it the spirit of the Revolution, is to falsify the historic significance of great events; it is to mistake the aerolite for the planet.

The first solemn declaration of the spirit of the Revolution is seen in the Instructions given by the electoral colleges to the deputies that represented the three orders, Clergy, Nobles, and Third Estate, in the States-General. The members elected numbered 1200; 600 for the Third Estate, 300 for each of the privileged orders. The electors, who voted indirectly, in two removes, for the Third Estate and the lower Clergy, and directly for the remaining members, reached the total of six millions.[1]

Since the time of Louis XIV. France had been suffering a material and moral decadence. Morally, the insolent, brazen corruption of the Court under the Regency of Philip of Orleans and Louis XV. had infected the nobility and the higher *bourgeoisie*. The luxury, the decay in morals, the arbitrary rule of the Government and men of position was unbounded; one would be tempted to say that the details given us were lies invented by historians, were they not confirmed by contemporary documents. It is not my purpose to repeat them here; but the squandering of money, which, from the time of Louis XIV. to the Regency, had run up the debt of France to three milliards, explains how a hundred servants were often collected in a single palace, how 150,000 francs were spent annually in dinners alone by a financier, Samuel Bernard, just as the seraglio

[1] France—I could wish that the Italians, to-day bowed down before her because she was able to fight and vanquish Europe, should remember this —numbered then twenty-five millions of inhabitants.

of young girls, bought or kidnapped for the king,[1] since
the days of Pompadour, explains the private life of the
nobles, of whom fifteen out of twenty did not live with
their wives; and as the fifty State prisons, nearly all
governed by Jesuits, into which the inmates entered
for an indefinite time, without trial, and in virtue of
a royal or ministerial order that the minister often gave
away in blank or sold, explains the custom of fathers to
imprison at times sons to be rid of the annoyance of
a projected marriage, or of wives who thus escaped the
over-watchful eyes of unloved husbands. Just as a lesion
of the brain afflicts the whole organism with disease,
so a corrupt monarchy, slowly but inevitably, corrupts
the whole country. In the meantime, in contrast with
this life in high places, poverty and misery had increased
among the people, and most markedly among the cultivators of the soil, to a degree that would appear in-
credible, if we had not at hand the testimonies of men
of all classes, men who were more than moderate in
their views, from Bossuet to Fénélon, from Vauban to
Bois-Guillebert, from the reports of the Intendants of the
Provinces to those of the Minister Argenson. Specu-
lators, seconded by the Government and the more
covetious courtiers, traded on this misery, and had
organised what was termed by contemporaries the *Pact
of Hunger*. By a series of market operations the whole
corn of the country was exported, and when the
premium paid on exportations had been received, the
whole stock was accumulated in Jersey or Guernsey
and other depots, and sold again, when the needs of
the people had reached their greatest extremity, at very
high prices, as though it had arrived from America.

From such conditions, with these causes for indignation long repressed, there arose unexpectedly, suddenly,
by the convocation of the States-General, which the
urgent need of money had wrested from the king, a
people of six millions, that gave voice to its wants in
the Instructions. The frenzied, tortured soul of France
and the character of the movement then beginning,

[1] *Parc aux Cerfs.*

were bound to be plainly revealed in them. And the Instructions—the *Cahiers* as they were termed in France —did reveal them. The Revolution, irritated by the many-sided opposition, developed a prodigious energy in the *means* it adopted to obtain satisfaction for the popular demands, but in substance, hardly, if at all, advanced beyond them.

The Instructions express an immense aspiration for *liberty* and civil *equality*. The individual, violated, repressed, downtrodden for centuries, panted for life, and asserted itself in the popular Programme given to the Revolution. But that Programme does not contradict the fundamental proposition of my article. It is not the programme of the new Age, that we who love, fight, and hope foresee to-day. It is not based on a new definition of Life. It does not *initiate* ; it reasons out, and summarises previous acquisitions of the intellect, which had been left sterile and inoperative in the sphere of facts. It does not escape from the circle of Christian inspirations ; it only demands, like the Hussites, the *cup for all* that the rewards promised in heaven shall be realised upon the earth, that the dogma of the salvation of the *individual* by means of *individual* works shall have an application in this world.

The Instructions of the Nobility are naturally inferior to the others. A breath of equality is, however, felt at times in their pages. They demand an equal distribution of taxes, the abolition of exceptional tribunals, uniformity of penalties for all, the abolition of ferocious punishments, the publicity of criminal trials. Some few among the localities suggest that all men of worth should be admitted to public offices. Three, Peronne, Montdidier and Roye, suggest that judges should be nominated by the king from lists drawn up by the people. But the old spirit shortly afterwards turns up, dominant, in the demand for the maintenance of seigneurial justice, of the exclusive right of hunting in feudal lands, of the exclusion of the non-noble from the higher military ranks, etc., and by these exceptions cancels their scanty instincts for good.

The Instructions of the Clergy, of the lower Clergy

especially, are better; more frequently, so powerful is
the influence even of worn-out and corrupt religion,
inspired by a love of the people and a sense of more
advanced equality.   In many localities they demand a
system of National Education, not to be left to local
caprice, but based on uniform principles approved by
the States-General, and also free schools for both sexes
in every commune.   In some they demand the erection
of hospitals in the richer communes, and, what is of more
importance, the exemption from taxation of men who
live by their daily toil; in others, measures in favour
of public morality, a most righteous suppression of publications tending to corrupt it, and the repression of
prostitution; in others again, the emancipation of the
negroes.   Politically they demand the permanency of
the States-General, or their convocation at least every
five years, ministerial responsibility, the abolition of all
exceptional tribunals, the foundation of Boards of
Arbitration, the inviolability of the secrecy of the Post,
municipal freedom, and the election of communal magis-
trates by the people, the codification of the law, publicity
of justice, the mitigation and equalisation of punishments,
the abolition of judicial torture, of confiscation and
banishment; next—from a spirit of antagonism to the
nobility, which the latter reciprocated—the abolition of
feudal rights, of caste privileges, and every monopoly of
public offices.   In religious matters the clergy confessed
the decay of discipline and the need of reform; and
some of them indicate as a remedy the convocation
of a National Council and Provincial Synods; others,
that plurality of benefices should be abolished, that the
clergy should be compelled to reside in their cures, that
all titles to office should be derived from merit and virtue;
some few recall the old popular elections and prefer the
restriction of episcopal authority.   None the less, the
exclusive Catholic conception betrays itself and entirely
dominates the Instructions, destroying at once the good
results of the measures they ask for.   The clergy demand
that education shall be entrusted solely to the religious
orders, that the University shall not receive professors

unless proved to be adherents of the Catholic faith, that
the censorship shall be maintained for all publications,
that an ecclesiastical committee shall have the power
to condemn any books opposed to the teaching of the
Church, and that the Government shall then proceed to
suppress them, that Catholicism shall be recognised
as the sole and dominant religion, that certain provisions
be made to the prejudice of non-Catholics, that the concessions of civil rights and marriage given to the
Protestants by the edict of 1787 be revoked.

But the two privileged orders could not express the
feeling of the Nation : the Third Estate alone could
do that.   And, taken generally, the Instructions of the
Third Estate affirm the sovereignty of the Nation, the
necessity of a Declaration of Rights, of the convocation
of the States-General independently of the will of any
individual, the inviolability of the Deputies, and the
responsibility of Ministers ; next, freedom of conscience,
freedom of the Press, freedom of internal trade, individual liberty, suppression of State prisons and of
exceptional jurisdictions.   Jurors are to be the judges
of *fact*, indemnity is to be made to any prisoner
declared to be innocent, the law is to be codified,
property is to be equally divided among children,
entail to be abolished.   Such are the demands of the
several localities.   Others claim an equal distribution of
taxation, assessment by the provincial Estates, journey-
men being exempt ; others, the uniformity of weights
and measures, the establishment of discount banks
wherever the commercial conditions are favourable
boards of arbitration, free justice, a commercial code ;
others, the organisation of a public health department,
hospitals, foundling asylums, the direction of education
to the double purpose of developing in the pupils
a strong physical constitution and a knowledge of the
principles necessary to man and the French citizen ;
some few demand that ecclesiastical offices be filled
by popular election, that the religious orders shall be
totally or partially suppressed, that tithes shall be reduced, lotteries and gaming establishments abolished ;

they ask for the erection of country hospitals, offices for charitable relief, work for the able-bodied, aid to the sick, loans on easy terms to workmen and to cultivators of the soil.

On this magnificent programme, of which I only give a rapid sketch, was superimposed, in the Instructions of the three orders, the twofold dogma of the Christian world—Catholicism and Monarchy. The former was declared the religion of the State,—the latter asserted to be inseparable from the life of the Nation, hereditary and inviolable.

But not one of the reforms they indicated advances beyond what I call the doctrine of the *individual* and of the Age from which we are trying to escape to-day. The conception of Life from which all those Instructions emanated was identical with that which I have already shown as inspiring the Encyclopædists, and Montesquieu, and Rousseau. The *end* of human existence is for all of them material *well-being*, the means to reach it, *liberty*. They desire the inviolability of conscience, of the expression of thought, of action, of private correspondence, because "the natural liberty of *each* man, his *personal* security, his absolute independence from *all authority* except that of the written law, require it." *Liberty* in the Instructions given by Nemours and other localities is stated to be "the right of each man to do without hindrance whatever does not injure his fellow-men." "Men," say the Instructions of Nivernais and Rennes, "have only renounced the use of private force that they may be more effectively protected by public force, and this is the only source of the reciprocal obligations of citizens ; of citizens towards Society, of Society towards them." From Paris, Marseilles, Nemours, Mérindol, Aurons, St. Vaast, Rosny, St. Sulpice, Villers-Cotterêts, from twenty other places there appears with one voice the ruling principle of the Instructions, that "natural rights" shall constitute the "basis of the Government of France," that the "preservation of rights" is the "sole object" of political societies.

This idea is so universal that it induces them to reject

conscription in the organisation of the army, and to substitute *voluntary* enlistment, thus destroying, from reverence for the rights of the individual, one of the most sacred duties of a citizen, the duty of defending the Fatherland by arms ; and it impels them to propose the abolition of the oath to defendants, to speak the Truth, from respect for the right of defence in the individual, forgetting that it is the *duty* of every man, whether accused or not, to speak the Truth.

The acts of the Revolution will, I hope, demonstrate how this conception condemned it, in its first long stage, to waste its forces in the search for an impossible harmony between two opposing principles, and in a system of *guarantees*, ineffectual in *practical* organisation, instead of the *positive* and educational function of the Government.   Now, this is the only vital point to be noted.   The Instructions, important as they are, and based in great part on truth, show a consciousness, neither of the *mission* of life, nor of a collective *end*, nor of the law of Progress as a *method*, nor of *association* as a *means*, nor of aught else that passes beyond the horizon dimly viewed from the Christian heaven, or the science of the individual.

FROM THE COUNCIL TO GOD

This essay was translated by Miss L. Martineau, and published in the *Fortnightly Review*, June, 1870. "After Mentana he (Mazzini) left London again for Lugano to be nearer his work, and was constantly passing backwards and forwards between there and Genoa, finding time among it all to write his great religious apology, the sum of all his teaching, 'From the Council to God.'"—*Mazzini*, by Bolton King, page 213.

FROM THE COUNCIL TO GOD

A Letter to the Members of the Œcumenical Council

I

ONE thousand five hundred and forty-four years ago, the first Œcumenical Council of believers in the religion of Jesus met together at Nice. You are now met together in a new Council—your last—in Rome. The first Council was the solemn and venerable consecration of the triumph and organised unity of the religion needed by the age. The present Council—whatever you intend by it—will proclaim the great fact of the death of a religion, and, therefore, of the inevitable and not distant advent of another.

Thirty-seven years ago I wrote certain pages entitled, *From the Pope to the Council.* In those pages—misunderstood, as usual, by superficial readers—I declared the Papacy to be morally extinct, and invoked the meeting of a Religious Council to declare that fact to the peoples. But the Council I desired was not yours. It was a Council convoked by a free people, united in worship of duty and of the ideal ; to be composed of the worthiest in intellect and virtue among the believers in things eternal, in the mission of God's creature upon this earth, and in the worship of progressive truth ; who should meet together for the purpose of religiously interrogating the pulsations of the heart of Collective Humanity, and to demand of that prophetic but uncertain instinct of the future which exists in the peoples :

What portions of the old faith are dead within you ?
What portions of the new faith are wakening into life
within you ?

At a later period (in 1847), when the same Pope who
now bids you declare him Infallible was hesitating
between the suggestions of vanity flattered by popular
applause and the inherent tendencies of despotic power ;
when all the Italians, both learned and unlearned,
frantically endeavoured to make of him their leader in
their struggle for nationality and liberty ; I alone—in a
letter also misunderstood—frankly declared to him the
truth : *that a new faith was destined to take the place of
the old : that the new faith would not accept any privileged
Interpreter between the people and God:* and that, if he
desired to avail himself of the enthusiasm by which he
was surrounded, and become himself the initiator of the
new epoch and the new faith, he must descend from
the Papal throne, and go forth among the people an
apostle of truth, like Peter the Hermit preaching the
Crusades.   I quote myself, reluctantly, that you may
know that, in thus addressing you, I am neither moved
by the hasty impulse of a rebellious soul, nor by foolish
anger at the Pope's withholding Rome from my country.
We shall have Rome—even before your fate is sealed—
so soon as the republican banner is again raised in
Italy.   It is from a profound conviction, matured by
long and earnest meditation, and confirmed by the
study and experience of more than a third of a century,
that, in the face of a Pope who, by his syllabus, has
thrown his gauntlet of defiance to the idea of the
progressive mission of humanity in the face of a
Council composed of the members of one Church only,
without the intervention of any possible representatives of the dawning Church of the future, I declare
to you :

That your faith is irrevocably doomed to perish : that,
whether as promoters of a new schism, if you separate
on the question of the Pope's pretensions, or as suicidal
destroyers of the primitive conception of your Church,
if you submerge it in the arbitrary will of an individual,

you are and will be inevitably cut off from, and excommunicated by, humanity ; and that we, who are believers more than you, and more than you solicitous of a religious future of the world, reject beforehand your decrees, and appeal from your Council to God ; to God the Father and Educator of man ; to the God of life, not of things dead ; to the God of all men, not of a caste.

II

The three hundred and twenty bishops who met together at Nice did lawfully represent the multitude of believers : they were the issue of a democratic inspiration, which is the soul of every rising faith : they were the elect of the clergy and the people.

You are but a pitiful aristocracy, created and consecrated by power ; and, like the elements of all falling institutions, without root in the heart of the Church, the people of believers. You represent nothing but a hierarchy, the reflex of the thought of others, in which every spontaneous thought is regarded as rebellion.

The majority of the first Council bore upon their brows the signs of sacred sorrow felt for the numberless races of slaves disinherited of every human right, and the traces of persecutions undergone for the sake of the faith that promised them emancipation ; the greater number of them were poor.

You make display of luxury and wealth—there is no sign upon your brows of the sorrows that purify and refine ; nor pallor, save that of constant *inertia* and idle ease of indifference to the miseries of millions of brothers given to you by God, and to the vital questions by which our hearts are tormented.

In the face of the brute force of the corrupt and tottering empire, whose frontiers echoed to the threatening footsteps of the barbarians, those bishops raised the banner of a moral idea, of a spiritual power,

*L 224

destined to save civilisation, and win over the barbarians to its rule.

You worship Force; force which, from Prometheus to Galileo, has ever sought to enchain the revealers and precursors of the future to the motionless rock of present fact.   Before this force do you bow down and preach to the peoples blind submission, even when it violates the moral law; as you invoke its aid, whether proffered by infidels to your faith or not, whensoever you are threatened in your usurped temporal power.

The believers of Nice initiated an era, and blessed the peoples congregated at its threshold.   You are struggling to recommence a worn-out and exhausted past, and you curse the generation which will not, cannot, follow you in your labour of Sisyphus.

I am no materialist.   Young men of narrow intellect and superficial education, but warm-hearted and irritated to excess against a dead past which still would dominate the present; whose vanity is flattered by an idea of intellectual daring; who lack capacity to discover in that which has been, the law of that which shall be, are led to confound the negation of a worn-out form of religion, with denial of that eternal religion which is innate in the human soul; and in them materialism assumes the aspect of a generous rebellion, and is often accompanied by power of sacrifice and sincere reverence for liberty.   But when diffused among the peoples, materialism slowly but infallibly extinguishes the fire of high and noble thought, as well as every spark of free life, through the exclusive worship of material well-being, and finally prostrates them before successful violence, before the despotism of the *fait accompli*.   Materialism extinguished every spark of Italian life amongst us three centuries ago; as, eighteen centuries earlier, it had extinguished all republican virtue in Rome; as it would—should it again be infused among our multitudes—extinguish every germ of future greatness in our newborn Italy.

Morally, materialism is disinherited of all criterion of

right, or principle of *collective* education.   Between the
idea of an intelligent, preordained law, which assigns
to human life an *aim*, and the idea of a blind, unreason-
ing, fatal force of *facts*, or transitory phenomena, there
is no middle path ; and materialists, by ignoring the first,
are necessarily driven to the worship of the second, and
prostrate themselves, sooner or later, before the despotism (whether its *method* be Bonapartist bayonets or
republican guillotines is of little matter) of force.   Admitting neither a providential conception regulating the
existence of collective humanity, nor the immortality of
the individual *Ego*, they may, illogically, utter the holy
words *progress* and *duty* ; but they have deprived the
first of its basis, and the second of its source.   The
senseless, brutal doctrine cancels from men's minds the
only real virtue, sacrifice ; for, although individual
followers of that doctrine may be urged by a religious
instinct within them to *fulfil* it, they cannot teach it.
What avails martyrdom for a holy idea, when all pledge
of future benefit to the race, or even to the individual
himself, is destroyed ?   Amid the darkness of a world
deprived of all ideal ; in a brief, tormented existence,
ungoverned by any law save sensation and the appetites
to which it gives rise, the answer of mankind to every
moral lesson will be, *Egotism.*   Such has, in fact, been
their answer in all those periods when a common faith
has passed away, and given place to the anarchy of cold
and sterile negations : *panem et circenses* : *each for himself:
Interest, lord of all.*

Scientifically, interest is based upon a periodical
confusion in men's minds of the instruments of life
with life itself ; of the manifestations of the *Ego*, with
the *Ego* itself ; of the consequences and applications of
thought, with the thinking being itself ; of the secondary
forces revealed in the operation of the organism, with
the initial force which excites, moderates, examines,
and compares those operations ; of the limited, transitory,
relative, and contingent phenomena which alone are
accessible to the organism, with the life which links
them all to that absolute and eternal truth which alone

gives value and significance to those phenomena ; of the application of the human faculties to the eternal world, with the faculties themselves ; of effects, with causes ; of the real, with the ideal ; of facts, with the law by which they are governed.

That *Ego* which reflects upon the phenomena of the organism, is not that organism ; that life which forms the harmony and unity of the whole, which consciously and mindfully directs the special functions towards a given aim, is not those functions themselves ; the being which ponders of the future, of providence, of God, of immortality, of the infinite, of choice between good and evil ; which resists the impulse of the senses and denies their sway—now in Athens and now on Golgotha ; now in the prison of Petroni [1] and now on the national battle-field, in sacrifice of self—is not those senses themselves.

The *experimentalism* of those children lisping science who call themselves materialists, is but one fragment of science ; it simply verifies, through as many facts as it can muster, the discoveries of intuition ; those sudden, spontaneous discoveries made by the rapid, intense concentration of all the faculties upon a given point. And the facts themselves which, being embraced and explained by hypothesis and discovery, demonstrate truth, require, in order to be usefully observed, interpreted and classified, the guidance of a *principle*, a pre-accepted conception of law. Synthesis, the innate supreme faculty of the human soul, illumines the path of analysis from on high ; without its aid analysis could but stumble uncertainly and impotently along a labyrinth of facts, of aspect and bearing constantly differing according to their relation to other facts.

There is a harmony between the order of things and the human mind, pre-existent to all experiment, which does but ascertain and define that harmony. Equally inaccessible to experiment are man's con-

---

[1] Petroni, a distinguished lawyer of Bologna, had languished in the Papal dungeons since 1853. He was offered a means of escape, but as his fellow-prisoners were not included, he decided to remain with them.

sciousness of himself, the mode of transmission between the inert, inorganic matter and the living and thinking matter; the universal, perennial, and dominating intuition which exists in a limited and imperfect world, ruled (according to the materialist theory) by chance, or the blind unconscious sequence of facts, of an ideal, a conception of indefinite perfectibility; the power of free activity which exists in man; the undeniable existence within us of a something which is not enchained in any special organ, but passes from one to another, examining, deciding upon, and connecting their operations; and the hourly visible influence of moral force, of *will* upon the material world.

Experiment may give us the accidents, not the essence of things; to reach that essence, science must maintain its connecting link with religion. Without a theory or *method*, all real, true, and fruitful science is impossible. The *method* is furnished by our conception of the *aim* of life; the aim, once ascertained, affirms the relation between man and humanity, between humanity and the universe, the universe and God—law and life. Now the *aim*, which is the discovery and progressive realisation of the design according to which the universe is evidently organised, and of which material laws are the means, can only be found through a philosophical religious conception.

Science reveals and masters the material and intellectual forces given to man wherewith to realise the aim; but the aim itself is determined by the religious synthesis of the period; and the religious synthesis is the sanction of the duty of each man to avail himself of those forces in furtherance of the aim, according to his faculties. To break this union is to render science sterile. Humanity pursues a different course, and when the history of science shall be rightly written, it will demonstrate that to every great religion is attached a corresponding epoch of fruitful scientific progress; and that, although during the periods of transition between the fall of one religion and the rise of another, Science may discover phenomena and collect facts which offer materials for the new synthesis, she will misconceive alike their value and their law, as is the case at the present day.

Historically, materialism is inexorably, invariably representative and characteristic of a period of transition between one religious faith and another, when all unity of conception and of aim being lost, and lost every sense of a common doctrine and true philosophic method, human intellect invariably falls back upon the mere anatomy of facts, refuses the guidance of synthesis, and is left with one criterion of truth only—the *Ego* disjoined from Collective Humanity and God—negation and anarchy.   It is but a funeral lamp that dimly illumines a bier, and is only extinguished when, inspired by the breath of the future, the bier is transformed into the cradle of the new faith, not ascertained, but invoked by the majority, and forefelt to be inevitable and near. This moment is approaching more rapidly than is generally believed, in spite of all that you men of the past, and true prolongers of the disastrous period of transition, can do to prevent it.

Meanwhile materialism denies humanity, in which the religious sense, like the artistic and philosophical, is an alienable element of life : it denies tradition — the harmony of which with the voice of individual inspiration and conscience is the sole criterion of truth we possess on earth : it denies history, which teaches us that religions are transitory, but Religion is eternal : it denies the solemn witness borne in adoration of God and the Ideal, by the long series of our greatest minds, from Socrates to Humboldt, from Phidias to Michel-Angelo, from Æschylus to Byron : it denies the power of revelation innate in man, in order to date the discovery of truth from the meagre labours upon a fragment of creation studied by one single faculty of the mind of a Moleshott, Buchner, or other.

Not for you do I write this—you are nearly all of you practical materialists—but for my young fellow-countrymen, good, but misled ; and, because I hold that no man who assumes to speak of the future of our rising Italy has henceforth a right to keep silence as to his own

religious belief, or to abstain from uttering his protest
against the irruptions of the Barbarians of thought who
rave amid the ruins of an epoch.

I am not ungrateful to that epoch, nor irreverent to
those grand ruins. I am not forgetful of the gigantic
step taken by humanity towards its destined aim, through
the religious faith in the name of which you are met
together. Neither have I forgotten that we owe to it,
not only the idea of the unity of the human family, and
of the equality and emancipation of souls, but also the
salvation of the relics of our anterior Latin civilisation,
and the recall of my fast-expiring country to the life half-
extinguished by her barbarian invaders, by awakening
her to the consciousness of her second mission in the
world.

The salvation of Christianity, and through it of European civilisation, through the unity of your hierarchy
during a period of darkness and anarchy—the spirit of
love towards the poor and afflicted outcasts of society,
which inspired your early bishops and popes—the
severe struggle sustained by them in the name of the
Moral law against the arbitrary power and ferocity of
feudal lords and conquering kings—the great mission
(misunderstood in our day by those who know nothing
or comprehend nothing of history) fulfilled by that giant
of intellect and will, Gregory VII., and the fruitful
victory won by him in aid of the rule of mind over royal
arms, of the Italian over the German element—the
mission of civilising conquest you fulfilled among semi-
barbarous peoples, the impulse given to agriculture by
your monks during the first three centuries, the preservation of the language of our fathers, the splendid epoch
of art inspired by faith in your dogma, the learned works
of your Benedictines, the commencement of gratuitous
education, the foundation of institutions of benevolence,
your sisters of mercy,—I remember all these things, and
bow down in reverence before the image of your past.

But wherefore do you, in a world wherein all things,
by God's decree, die and are transformed, seek to live
for ever? Why pretend that a past, which has been

extinguished for ever beneath five hundred years of inertia and impotence, should live again in the future? How is it that, in the face of three centuries of dismemberment into an infinitude of Protestant sects, and of a century of philosophical incredulity; amid the reappearance of all those signs and warnings which characterised the intermediate period between the fall of Paganism and the rise of the Christian era, you see not that your mission is concluded; that the world is urged onward in search of a new heaven and a new earth? Wherefore, in the face of the grand tradition of humanity, throughout the course of which God reveals to us the Law of life he gave to all; which teaches you through its succession of religions the gradual continuous revelation of a Truth of which each historic epoch acquires a fragment, and none the whole, do you persist in believing, or asserting—you, whose religion had its beginning, and who represent but one epoch among many—that you hold that entire truth within your grasp? How dare you strive to violate alike the Providential design and the free conscience of mankind, by restricting within a given narrow, the limitless ascending spiral traced by the finger of God between the universe and the Ideal it is destined slowly to attain?

III

I do not accuse you, as do our copyists of other (French or German) copyists of the eighteenth century, of having—impostors from the earliest times—built up a religion in order to attain to power. Humanity does not tolerate a lying Fable for eighteen hundred years. If the majority amongst ourselves were believers as fervent and sincere as were the men of your faith during the first thirteen hundred years, God's new truth—of which at present we have but faintest glimpses—would already unite the multitudes in harmony of belief.

I do not accuse you of having disseminated errors, which for long years past have impeded or misled mankind upon questions which have become of vital moment at the present day. Every religion is the issue of the times, and the expression of an essentially imperfect stage in the education of the human race; but each contains a truth destined to live for ever, although overshadowed by passing error; and that amount of truth which it was possible for the age to accept and to incarnate in action, was widely and beneficially diffused by you.

I do not accuse you—though I might with better foundation—of having been the inexorable persecutors of all who differed from you. I remember how terror was erected into a system, only sixty years back, by the advocates of liberty; and I know, moreover, that every religion founded upon the belief in an immediate, direct, and superhuman revelation, cannot fail to be intolerant.

I do not accuse you of persisting in the attempt to nail us down to a conception of God and of the relation between God and man belied by science, and against which every faculty of heart and mind granted to man for the discovery of truth, and matured by eighteen hundred years of aspiration, study, suffering, and victory, protest at the present day.

I do accuse you of maintaining a divorce between faith and science—the two wings given to the creature wherewith to elevate himself towards the divine Ideal—which must inevitably result in mental slavery or materialism.

I do accuse you of insanely pretending that a beacon kindled eighteen hundred years ago to illumine our journey across a single epoch, is destined to be our sole luminary across the path of the infinite.

I do accuse you of destroying the unity of Collective Humanity, by dividing mankind into two arbitrary sections; one devoted to error, and the other sacred to truth; and of blaspheming against the eternally creative and revealing power of God, by imprisoning the Word within an insignificant fraction of time and space.

I accuse you of having utterly misunderstood the

holy soul of Jesus—superior to every other in aspiration
and fraternal love—by transforming Him, in despite of
His sublimest presentiments, into an eternal and vulgar
tyrant of souls.

I accuse you of having closed your eyes in vanity
and lust of power, and refused to perceive that, even as
one existence succeeds another, so does one mission
succeed another, and each and all are governed and
sanctified by a religious synthesis.

And, above and before all, I accuse you of living no
real life; of having no other existence than that of the
phantoms seen wandering among tombs to delude
mortals into superstition, or degrade them by terror,
but doomed to vanish at the first blush of dawn.

Life is love. You know no longer how to love. The
voice of your chief is only heard in groans of discouragement; the formula of your declarations is an
anathema.

Life is movement, aspiration, progress. You deny
progress; shrink in terror from all aspiration; crucify
humanity upon Calvary; reject every attempt to detach
the idea from the symbol, and strive to petrify the living
Word of God. You reduce all history (which is the
successive manifestation of that Word) to a single
moment; you extinguish free will (without which no
consciousness of progress can exist) beneath the fatalism
of hereditary responsibility, and cancel all merit in
works or sacrifice by the omnipotence of grace.

Life is communion: communion with nature and
with man, wheresoever he loves, struggles, or hopes,
and with God. You have attempted, by denying the
continuity of creation, and the universal diffusion of
the creative spirit, to imprison the Deity in one sole
corner of the universe, and one brief period of the
immensity of time. You seek even now, by the immoral
antagonistic dualism you establish between earth and
heaven, to banish from men's minds all reverence for
nature (which is a form of the divine thought); and
you refuse, in the name of an individual salvation to be
achieved through faith and prayer, all communion with

the great *collective* sorrows, the holy battles, and the emancipatory hopes of mankind. Kepler, when he taught mankind how the universe opened upon the field of the infinite on every side, felt God more than you; and Byron—whom you condemn as a sceptic—worshipped Him more truly than you, when he sacrificed wealth, genius, and life for the cause of liberty in Greece.

Life is production: increase of that already gained; and you have for upwards of five centuries been struggling, with ever lessening power, merely to conserve.

When a religion no longer either creates, determines or directs action; when it rouses no power of sacrifice; when it no longer harmonises and unites the different branches of human activity; when its vital conception ceases to inform new symbols, or new manifestations in art, science, or civil life—that religion is expiring. You may still, by help of the deceptions of your ministers and the pomp of your rites, gather a numerous concourse of apparently devoted followers around you, and you will continue to do so, so long as their sole choice lies between the records of a faith once grand and fruitful of good, and the arid negations of a brutalising materialism; but demand of these followers that they should die for you and for the faith you represent, and you will not find a martyr among them. You did not find one when we confronted your banner with our own in Rome, upon which was inscribed the Word of the future, *God and the People*, and proclaimed—through the unanimous vote of the very men who, the day before, declared themselves believers in you—the abolition of your temporal power and the Republic.

Your Pope fled in disguise, and all of you vanished utterly; the constant intrigues with which you endeavoured, when at Gaeta, to raise up internal enemies amongst us, were fruitless. You were reduced to beg the aid of bayonets, the instruments of the tortuous policy and ambition of a vulgar pretender, whom you well knew to be as infamous as he was unbelieving in

your doctrines. Our men died—they still die for the
sake of the glimpse vouchsafed them of that new faith
which, ere it has enlightened their intellects, has fired
and warmed their hearts—in dungeons, or upon the
scaffold or the battle-field, with a smile of defiance upon
their lips; but around you I see none but mercenaries
greedy of rank or gold.

Be not deceived: faith is perishing around you. Even
as lingering sparks still issue from a dying fire, the
expiring faith of the day finds its expression in the
prayers muttered before your altars through the force of
habit at stated brief moments; it evaporates at the
church door, and no longer rules or guides men's daily
life: they give one hour to heaven and the day to earth
—to its material interests and calculations, or to studies
and ideas foreign to every religious conception.

Science proceeds onward; regardless of your doctrine,
heedless of your anathema and of your councils, destroying at every step another line of the Book you declare
infallible. Art wanders in the void; now retracing its
steps towards the pagan ideal, now doubtfully pursuing
religious aspirations other than yours; and now, as if
in despair of finding any other God, reduced to worshipping itself; but always apart from the Christian synthesis,
always irresponsive to the conception which inspired
your architects and painters in ages past.

The iniquitous Governments of the day, to whom it
is a necessity to maintain your authority in order to prop
the tottering foundations of their own, deny it, none the
less, in the practical exercise of their power: " the law "
for them "is atheist,"—the separation of the temporal
from the spiritual power is their supreme rule of guidance;
and the very king who implores your benediction in secret,
affects before his subjects to despise it the day after.

The men of highest power, whether of intellect or
eloquence, belonging to your creed, from Lamennais
down to Père Hyacinthe, detach themselves from you
one by one. Not a single one of the vast strides made
upon the path of progress in our age was either suggested
or consecrated by your faith.

Two nations, once sisters—the Greek and Italian—
have burst asunder the walls of the tomb wherein they
had lain buried for ages, and they have neither asked
nor could obtain one holy word of baptism from
you.

Four millions of black slaves have been emancipated
—in pledge of other emancipations—across the Atlantic,
in the name of the immortal human soul within them,
and they owe it to no crusade of yours, but to a war
of an exclusively political character, fought by men whose
sole idea was one of national unity.

Like the great German family at the downfall of
paganism, and as if as a warning of the approach of a
similar epoch, the Slavonian family is in movement
upon a zone extending from the North Sea to the
Adriatic, and eager to proffer its word at the fraternal
European banquet; while you—the sometime distributors
of distant lands among the monarchs—appear scarcely
conscious of the fact. They ask for aid in their work,
not from you, but from us.

Mute, and disinherited alike of inspiration and affection, having abdicated all power of intervention in the
events that transform and improve God's earth, you,
who were once the world's centre, are gradually being
driven back to its extremest orbit, and are destined to find
yourselves at last alone in the void beyond. Motionless
sphinxes in the vast desert, you inertly contemplate the
shadow of the centuries as they pass. Humanity, whom
you should have guided, has gone otherwhere. Faith
is perishing among the peoples, because the dogma that
inspired it no longer corresponds to the stage of education
which they, in fulfilment of the providential plan, have
reached.

IV

The Christian dogma is perishing. The arch of the
Christian heaven is too narrow to embrace the earth.
Beyond that heaven, across the fields of the infinite, we
discern a vaster sky, illumined by the dawn of a new

dogma ;[1] and on the rising of its sun your own heaven will disappear. We are but the precursors of that dogma : few as yet, but earnestly believing ; fortified by the collective instincts of the peoples, and sufficiently numerous to convince you—had you sense to comprehend it—that when the tide of materialism shall recede, you will find yourselves confronted by a far other foe.

We worship not anarchy : we worship Authority ; but not the dead corpse of an authority, the mission of which was concluded in a now distant past, and which can therefore only perpetuate its power through tyranny and falsehood.

The authority we revere is founded upon the free and deliberate acceptance and popular worship of the truth conquered by our epoch ; upon that conception of life which God reveals to mankind in time and measure through souls devoted to Him and to His Law.

Your dogma may be summed up in the two terms, FALL and REDEMPTION; our own in the terms GOD and PROGRESS. The intermediate term between the Fall and Redemption is, for you, the Incarnation, at a given moment, of the Son of God.

The intermediate term for us, between God and His Law, is, the continuous and progressive incarnation of that law in Humanity, destined slowly and gradually to discover and to fulfil it throughout the immeasurable, indefinite future.

The word PROGRESS, therefore, represents to us, not a mere scientific or historic fact, limited, it may be, to one epoch, one fraction, or one series of the acts of humanity, having neither root in the past, nor pledge of duration in the future. It represents a religious conception of life radically different from yours ; a divine Law, a supreme formula of the eternal, omnipotent, creative force, universal as itself.

[1] By this word dogma—now generally misunderstood, because usurped and accepted exclusively in the Christian sense—I mean a truth of the moral order, which, usually perceived in the first instance by philosophy, or prepared by the progress of science, and still more by the civil condition of one or more peoples, becomes incarnate in the life of one or more individuals privileged in love and virtue, and wins over the mind of the multitude and gradually transforms itself into a religious axiom.

The root of every religion is a definition of life and its mission. For you that definition of life is the doctrine of Original Sin, and of resurrection to God through *faith* in a Divine Being, who descended upon earth to sacrifice Himself in expiation of that sin.

Our definition of life asserts the *imperfection* of the finite creature, and its gradual self-correction by virtue of a capacity of progression, given to all men, through *works*; through the sacrifice of the egotistic instincts for the sake of the common improvement, and through faith in a divine Ideal, which each is bound to incarnate in himself.

God, the Father and Educator; the law prefixed by Him to life, the capacity, inborn in all men, to fulfil it; free will, the condition of merit; Progress upon the ascent leading to God, the result of right choice—these are the cardinal points of our faith.

In the dogma of Original Sin, which is the keystone of your edifice (except the *presentiment* it contains of that human solidarity which you do not comprehend), we see nought but Evil profanely made the baptism of life: the absolute impossibility of accounting for the inequality of evil tendency manifested among men, and an hereditary *doom* which denies alike human free will and responsibility.

In the Redemption through the incarnation of the Son of God (except the symbol it contains, by you neglected, of that aspiration which impels the finite towards union with the infinite) we only see subtraction made of the divinely educating force; the substitution of an arbitrary fact for the majesty of a divine law; a solution of the continuity of the collective life of humanity, and the sanction of an unjust dualism between the generations anterior and posterior to the Cross.

From this diversity in the foundations of faith, follows a series of consequences which affect both heaven and earth—the Dogma and the Moral Code.

You believe in the divinity of Jesus. I can well understand the origin of this belief in times when it alone was able to secure the doubtful victory of Christianity; when the idea of Progress was unknown, and consequently unknown the conception of the gradual manifestation of God through His Law. You could not avoid attributing to the Announcer of truth a character which would compel mankind to obey His precepts.

We, who at the present day believe in the continuous revelation of God throughout the collective life of humanity, have no need of a sole immediate *Revealer* to teach us either to adore His power, or to feel His love.

The divine incarnation of both these attributes is perennial in the great facts which bear witness to the collectivity of life; in the great intellects, sanctified by virtue, who prophesy or interpret that universal life; and in the grand aspirations of individual conscience, which foretell or accept truth.

We venerate in Jesus the Founder of the epoch that emancipated individual man; the Apostle of the unity of the divine law, more largely understood than in times anterior to His own; the Prophet of the equality of souls: we reverence in Him the Man who loved more than any other; whose life—an unexampled instance of harmony between thought and action—promulgated as the eternal basis of every future religion, the sacred dogma of Sacrifice; but we do not cancel the Woman-born in the God; we do not elevate Him to a height whereunto we may not hope to follow Him: we love Him as the best of our human brothers; we do not worship and fear Him as the inexorable Judge, or intolerant Ruler of the future.

You believe—thus depriving yourselves of every basis of intellectual certainty and criterion of truth—in *miracles*; in the supernatural; in the possible violation of the laws regulating the universe.

We believe in the Unknown; in the Mysterious—to be one day solved—which now encompasses us on every side; in the secrets of an *intuition* inaccessible to analysis; in the truth of our strange presentiment of an Ideal, which is the primitive fatherland of the soul; in an unforeseen power of action granted to man in certain rare moments of faith, love, and supreme concentration of all the faculties towards a determinate and virtuous aim—deserved therefore—and analogous to the power of revelation which the increased concentration of rays in the telescope communicates to the human eye : but we believe all these things, the pre-ordained consequence of laws hitherto withheld from our knowledge.

We do not believe in the miraculous, as you understand it ; in the infringement of laws already known and accepted by arbitrary will ; in facts in contradiction *to* the general design of the creation, which would, we consider, simply testify to a want of wisdom or of justice in God.

You appeal in support of your theory to an idea of divine Free Will. We deny it. We are free, because imperfect : called to ascend, to *deserve*, and, therefore, to choose between good and evil ; between sacrifice and egotism. Such free will as ours is unknown to God, the perfect Being, whose every act is necessarily identical with the True and Just ; who cannot, without violation of our every conception of His nature, be supposed to break His own law.

You believe in a God who has created and reposes. We believe in continuity of creation ; in a God the inexhaustible source of the Life diffused perennially throughout the infinite ; of thought, which in Him is inevitably identical with action ; of conceptions, realised in worlds.

You believe in a heaven extrinsic to the universe : in a determinate portion of creation, on ascending to which we shall forget the past, forget the ideas and affections which caused our hearts to beat on earth. We believe in *One Heaven*, in which we live, and move, and love ; which embraces—as an ocean embraces the islands that stud its surface—the whole indefinite series of existences through which we pass. We believe in the *continuity* of life ; in a connecting link uniting all the various periods through which it is transformed and developed ; in the eternity of all noble affections, maintained in constancy until the last day of our existence ; in the influence of each of these life-periods upon the others ; in the pro-

306 From the Council to God

gressive sanctification of every germ of good gathered by
the pilgrim soul in its journey upon earth and otherwhere.

You believe in a divine hierarchy of natures essentially
distinct from our own and immutable. From the solemn
presentiment enfolded in the symbol of the angel you
have deduced no better conception than that of a
celestial aristocracy—the basis of the conception of aristocracy on earth—and inaccessible to man. We recognise
in the *angel* the soul of the just man who has lived in
faith and died in hope ; and in the inspiring, or guardian
angel, the soul of the creature most sacredly and constantly loving and beloved by us on earth, having earned
the recompense of watching over and aiding us on earth.
The ladder 'twixt earth and heaven of Jacob's dream
symbolises, for us, the ascending and descending series
of *man's* transformations on the path of initiation in the
divine Ideal, and the beneficent influence exercised
over us by the beloved beings who have preceded us
upon that path.

You believe in an Eden surrounding the cradle of
mankind, and lost through the fault of our first parents ;
we believe in an Eden towards which God wills that
humanity—traversing the path of error and sacrifice—
shall constantly advance. You believe that the soul can
pass at one bound from its human existence to the
highest beatitude, or to absolute, irrevocable perdition.
We believe the human period of our existence too distant
from the highest ideal ; too full of imperfections to allow
that the virtue of which we are capable here below can
suddenly deserve to reach the summit of the ascent
leading to God. We believe in an indefinite series of re-
incarnations of the soul, from life to life, from world to
world ; each of which represents an advance from the
anterior ; and we reject the possibility of irrevocable perdition as a blasphemy against God, who cannot commit
self-destruction in the person of the creature issued from
himself ; as a negation of the law prefixed to life, and as
a violation of the idea of love which is identical with
God. It may be that we shall retraverse the stage over

which we have already passed, if we have not deserved to ascend beyond it, but we cannot, spiritually, either retrogress or perish.

You believe in the resurrection of the body, such as it was at the termination of our earthly existence ; we believe in the *transformation* of the body (which is naught other than an instrument adapted to the work to be achieved) in conformity with the progress of the *Ego*, and with the mission destined to succeed the present.

All things are, in your creed, definite, limited, immediate, bearing the stamp of a certain immobility, which recalls the characteristics of the materialist conception of life. In our creed all is life, movement, succession, and continuity.

Our world opens upon the infinite on every side. Your dogma *humanises* God: our dogma teaches the slow, progressive *divinisation* of man.

You believe in grace ; we believe in justice. You, by believing in grace, believe—more or less explicitly, but inevitably—in predestination, which is but a transformation of the pagan and aristocratic dogma of the two natures of man. Grace, according to you, is neither granted to all, nor to be achieved through works ; it is arbitrarily bestowed by the Divine Will, and the *elect* are few. We believe that God called us, by creating us ; and the call of God can neither be impotent nor false. *Grace*, as we understand it, is the tendency and faculty given to us all gradually to incarnate the Ideal ; it is the law of progress which is His ineffaceable baptism upon our souls.

That law must be fulfilled. Time and space are granted to us wherein to exercise our free will. We can—through our action and endeavour—hasten or delay the fulfilment of the law in time and space ; multiply or diminish the trials, struggles, and sufferings of the individual ; but not, as the dualism taught by your dogma would do, *eternise* evil, and render it victorious. Good only is eternal: God only is victorious.

Meanwhile, that dualism which dominates your doctrine of *grace*, of *predestination*, of *hell*, of *redemption* half-way upon the historic development of humanity, and every portion of your Dogma inspires and limits your Moral Code, and renders it irremediably imperfect and inefficacious to guide and direct human life at the present day.

V

Your dogma is expiring. Your moral code is therefore rendered sterile and expires with it. It is deprived of its origin and its sanction; of that faith in the duty and necessity of regulating human life by its precepts, whence it derived its power to govern men's individual instincts, passions, and free will. You have but to look around you in order to perceive this.

The moral code is eternal you say, and you point to the precepts of love towards God and man, of sacrifice, of duty, of preference given to the salvation of the soul over the desires and interests of a day.

Yes; those precepts spoken by the lips of Jesus do live, and will live; they are as undying as our gratitude towards Him. His cross, as symbol of the sole enduring virtue—sacrifice of self for others—may still be planted, without any contradiction, upon the tomb of the believer in the new religion; but a moral code which is to have a fruitful, active influence upon mankind requires far more than this.

The precept of love, which is inborn within the human soul, is the basis, more or less apparent, of all religions; but each religion gives a different value and larger interpretation to that general formula of Duty. The moral problem, the solution of which progresses with the epoch, is the problem how we are to worship God, how we are to love man, how we are to work out the soul's salvation; and it is the mission of the religion of each epoch to give the force of a law, supreme over all and equally binding upon all, to the definition of the How, and to compel the fulfilment of the duty thus defined by linking it with heaven, tracing it back to the Divine conception of the creation. Even if your moral code were sufficient for the intelligence and aspirations of the epoch it would still remain sterile ; a mere inert, inefficacious dead letter, because this link is lost. Your heaven exists no longer, your conception of creation is proved false. The telescope has destroyed it for ever in the fields of the infinite ; geology has destroyed it on earth ; the recently recovered tradition of the past of humanity has destroyed it in the kingdom of intelligence, and the presentiment within us of a new law of life has destroyed it in our hearts. But your moral code, holy as it was before it had become adulterated by your corruption, intolerance, and cowardly compromise with the atheistic powers of the world, is unequal to the obligations imposed upon us by God.

The dualism of your dogma, transferred into your moral code, generated that antagonism between earth and heaven, matter and spirit, body and soul, which, no matter to what grade of the doctrine you belong, essentially narrowed your conception of the unity of life, and of its mission here and elsewhere, rendering it impossible that the great social questions of the day should be solved through help of your religion.

In the face of an empire believed to be omnipotent, and founded upon the prestige of material force placed between a religion which sanctioned the dogma of the two human natures (freeman and slave) and a philosophy which consigned mankind to the dominion of fatality, in a world of which there existed no conception of the collective life of humanity, or of an innate faculty of progress in individual man—having to address himself to men either intoxicated with tyranny and lust, or crushed by poverty and the abject servility induced by despair of a better future—it was impossible for Jesus to conceive any other mission for the benefit of the brother-men He loved so well, than that of effecting their moral regeneration, or any other consolation for their wretchedness on earth than that of creating for them a country of free men and equals in heaven. It was His purpose to teach men how to save, to redeem themselves, in spite of, and against, the earth.

From the legend of the temptation, in which the earth is evidently the heritage of the evil spirit, down to the " render unto Cæsar the things that are Cæsar's " of the three first Gospels; from the opposition between the law of God and the flesh, of Paul (Rom. vii.), down to the "love not the world," of John (2 Ep. ii. 15), the teachings of Jesus and the Apostles constantly insist upon our divorce from all terrestrial things, as a condition of moral improvement, of salvation. In their eyes our earthly abode is overshadowed by the curse of sin and temptation; and our sole hope of salvation from this curse lies in our suicide of the man within us. As Tell, even in the midst of the tempest, spurned from him the bark that bore the oppressor, each of us is held bound to spurn from him the earth, to cast loose every tie that binds him to it, in order to raise himself on the wings of faith to heaven.

The result of these teachings is a moral code which may be thus summed up:—Adoration of God, and faith in Christ, as the necessary intermediate to our salvation; renunciation of every natural desire; abdication of every aim of social transformation; indifference to every earthly good; resigned acceptance of every existing evil, either as a means of expiation, or of imitation of the sufferings of Jesus; war to the body and to the senses; submission to the powers that be; exclusive importance given to the work of internal purification, especially to the realisation within ourselves of faith in heavenly grace.

The holy nature of Jesus's own mind diffused a breath of love over the whole of his teachings, and generated a spirit of charity and disposition to good works in his hearers; but it was the love of men who, despairing of vanquishing the evil existing in the world, sought only to alleviate the more immediate sufferings of individuals. Christian charity was rather a means of purifying one's own soul, than the sense of a common aim which it was God's will that man should realise

here below. It did not overpass the limits of benevolence, and led the believers in the new religion to feed
the hungry, clothe the naked, and heal the sick with
whom they came in contact; but to no attempt to
destroy the causes of human hunger and misery. Even
as the earth itself was despised, so were all the good
things of the earth to be despised as a perennial source
of temptation, and the gifts to the poor and to the
Church testified to this belief. Poverty itself was
preached by the majority of Jesus's followers as a
blessed mortification of the flesh, and regarded by all
as an incontestable necessity. Love of country, and
that love which embraces the generations of the future,
and is devoted even unto sacrifice for their sake; that
love which will not tolerate the brand of inequality or
slavery on the brow of a brother-man, was unknown to
Christian morality. The true country, the real home of
Christian free men and equals, was heaven; every man
was bound to direct his course thither; and the greater
his sufferings on earth, the stronger the hope he might
entertain of his soul's future, and of celestial joy. The
world was abandoned to Satan. Religion taught man to
renounce it; religion, which was alike his isolation
and his refuge; it imposed no mission of earnest and
resolute struggle, and of slowly progressive but certain
victory.

Such was, such is, your Moral Code. Solitary contemplation and monastic life were its first logical
consequences. At a later period, when you were
triumphant, when the necessity, which all religions
undergo, of transforming society in their own image,
compelled you to mingle in social and political life, you
frequently (with immense advantage to civilisation)
obeyed that uncertain and instinctive sense of right and
equality which lies at the root of your religion; but it
was simply as a fact, not as a doctrine, and did not in
any way alter the educational principle of your Moral
Code; which was incarnated historically in the dualism
of the temporal and the spiritual powers—the Papacy
and the empire. The greatest of your Popes, Gregory VII.,

attempted to crush this dualism beneath the omnipotence of moral force; but he failed, and died in exile.
The greatest of your philosophers, Thomas Aquinas,
attempted to destroy the antagonism between the soul
and the body, through a definition of man borrowed
from Aristotle; but it was too late; not even the decrees
of your Council of Vienna, in support of his attempt,
could transform a moral code which had been identified
with the Christian Conception of Life for thirteen
centuries.

Your religion was the religion of individual man.   It
did not—it could not, at its origin, contemplate collective
humanity.   It aspired towards the ideal, the divine, and
would, had it been possible, have sought to realise its
ideal on earth.   But the instrument failed it.   The
short, imperfect life of the individual (beyond which
this conception did not extend) is incapable of its
realisation.   Your religion, as if to avenge its own
impotence, cried anathema upon the terrestrial world,
and referred the solution of the problem to the world
of grace—to heaven.

Herein lies the secret of all you have achieved, and
of all you have failed to achieve.

Christianity is the religion of individual man.   The
vast religious synthesis through which we are gradually
advancing towards the realisation of the ideal, is resolved
like an equation containing an indefinite number of
unknown quantities.   Every religious epoch disengages
one such unknown quantity, and classes one more term
of the problem among the known quantities, never more
to be disputed.   Two grand primary epochs—the
gigantic Aryan religions of the East—concentrated their
intelligence, inspiration, and labour upon the two terms
—God and Nature.   But in both these epochs, the ideal
man (crushed by spiritualist or materialist pantheism)
was absent.   While Mosaism elaborated the idea of the
divine unity, and preserved the sacred deposit for
futurity by incarnating it in a people, a third great epoch
assumed (in Europe) the office of disengaging the human
unknown—beginning with the individual—and adding

it to the number of known quantities. As the human
individual manifests life under two aspects, personal and
relative—represented by the two terms, liberty and
equality—so that epoch was divided into two long
periods.

In the first period, polytheism affirmed the individual,
and elaborated his emancipation within certain narrow
limits, evolving—in the Greco-Roman world—the idea of
liberty. During the first labour of elaboration, however,
and in the intoxication of rebellion against Oriental
pantheism, the conception of the Divine unity was
broken up into fragments, and all basis of durability
was thus destroyed.

In the second period, your religion, having inherited
from Moses its belief in the Divine unity, replaced the
Deity at the apex of the pyramid, and fulfilled its mission
with regard to the problem of the individual, by defining
his relative life, proclaiming the equality of souls, and
declaring all men the children of one Father.

Such was the historic mission of Christianity; nor
was it possible that the epoch, when—as it invariably
happens—it deduced its political and economic constitution from its religion, should advance beyond the
limits of the doctrine of the individual, and the two
terms (liberty and equality) by which that doctrine is
represented. When the Protestant sects—moved by the
corruption of Catholicism—sought to recall the multitudes to initial Christianity, they were unable to discover
any other criterion of truth than individual conscience.
The great political and social revolutions which, towards
the close of the last century, attempted (knowingly
or unknowingly) to realise the Christian principles in
practical life, summed up their whole labour and
endeavour in a declaration of the rights common to
every individual, and prefixed as sole governing law of
the development of the double life—moral and material
—of mankind, the insufficient rule of liberty.

God; God and Nature; God, Nature, and Man—
three cantos of the gigantic religious Epopea which has
the ideal for its subject and the generations for its poet.

Wherefore do you pretend that God and the generations shall now be dumb? Wherefore should we bury in your sepulchre an inspiration inseparable from life itself, and silence the new canto rising to the lips of creation, which has for its theme—God, Nature, Man, and Humanity? Wherefore should not the new heaven, of which we already have dim prevision, be represented by a new earth? the new dogma, by a new Moral Code?

VI

The earth is of God; it cannot be accursed. Life, like the God from whom it springs, is One and everlasting; it cannot be broken up into fragments, or divided into periods of a character radically opposed. There is no antagonism between matter and spirit. Matter gives forms to thought; symbols to the idea; means of communication between being and being. The body, given by God as the earthly tenement of the individual, and the means of communication between His life and that of the external world, is not the seat of evil or temptation. Evil and temptation, wherever they do exist, exist in the Ego: the body is the instrument which translates either good or evil into action, according to our free choice. The dualism between the temporal and spiritual power is an immoral conception, without any basis in the nature of things. The moral law—once recognised and accepted—ought to be supreme; and the mission of the temporal power is its application to the civil and economic realities of life. Wherever such is not the case, either the moral law is—as yours is at the present day—the corpse or lying phantom of law, or he whose duty it is to translate it into action is false to it and is immoral.

The earth is of God. It is a step upon the infinite ascent that leads us to heaven: our sojourn during one of our existences, wherein we are bound to prepare ourselves for the next. It is neither a dwelling of expiation nor an arena of temptation. The necessity of purification from sins committed, and the temptations to evil which are conditions of our free will, exist in ourselves; and will accompany us in every ulterior evolution of the life of the Ego. The earth is the sphere wherein we have an appointed mission to perform, with instruments of labour furnished by it; and we are bound to regard it with love and reverence, as the seat of our possible sanctification. In the ascending series of worlds, separate stages of the long pilgrimage of the Ego, the earth also has its appointed place; it also is— within prescribed limits—the cradle of the ideal; an incarnation—in time and space—of the eternal world; a note in the immense concord which harmonises and embraces creation; an essential link of the chain which unites the universe with the throne of God.

Life is a mission: human existence that portion of it which we have to accomplish here on earth. To discover, comprehend, and intellectually to master that fragment of the divine law which is accessible to human faculties, to translate it in action (as far as human powers allow), here, where God has placed us, is our aim, our duty. We are each and all of us bound to strive to incarnate in humanity that portion of eternal truth which it is granted to us to perceive; to convert into an earthly reality so much of the "kingdom of heaven"—the divine conception permeating life—as it is given to us to comprehend. Thus doing, we are slowly elaborating in man the angel; failing to do this we shall have to retrace our path.

The moral code deduced from our dogma preaches therefore to man:

"Seek not to isolate yourselves: imprison not your soul in sterile contemplation, in solitary prayer, in pride of individual purification, in pretending to a grace which no faith not realised in works can enable you to deserve. Be not deceived by the doctrine that salvation may be achieved in spite of, and in opposition to, the earth. You can only achieve it through the earth. You can only save yourselves by saving others. God asks not, What have you done for your soul? but, What have you done for the brother souls I gave you? Think of

these : leave your own to God and His law.   Labour
unweariedly for others' good : such action is the holiest
prayer.   In God, thought and action are one.   Seek to
imitate Him from afar.   Aim not at contemplating God
in Himself : you cannot do it.   Contemplate Him in
His works.   Say not in dismay, the works of God are
great, and I am nothing.   God, by breathing into you a
breath of His life, has decreed that you also are of
worth.   His works are your teachers ; were it not so,
would He have spread them around you ?   Seek in
them His design, a syllable of the conception which is
the soul of creation.   Study that conception without
foolish pride or hypocritical modesty, in the history of
collective humanity, throughout which He gradually
reveals to us the law of progress prefixed by Him to
life.   Study Him—purifying your heart as a sanctuary
from every base passion, guilty desire, or idolatrous
superstition—in the secret aspirations of your own soul ;
in those instincts of truth which spring up within you
in supreme moments of devotion or affection ; then
when you have mastered that syllable of the law, caught
that ray of the divine conception, rise, calm in conviction, and strong in will, priests and apostles of that
which you know to be the aim of life.   Let every word
speak faith in it, every act represent it.   All that is in
harmony with it is good ; all that tends to divert from it,
evil.   Help the first earnestly, combat the last openly.

"Avoid alike the vanity which makes display of duty,
and the resignation that shrinks from its fulfilment and
submits to evil.   Evil is here to be fought against ;
that we, who have free choice, may deserve.   When
victory is impossible, count martyrdom a benediction of
God.   The angels of martyrdom and of victory are
brothers ; both extend their protecting wings over the
cradle of your future life.

'Hold in honour your body, your faculties, and the
material forces that surround you in nature.   Instruments given to you by God for the discovery and
fulfilment of your appointed aim, they are good or evil
according as they are used for others' benefit, or for

your own; for egotism is the root of all evil, as sacrifice is the root of all virtue, and he who cries anathema on them, cries anathema on God.

"Say not that wealth and material power are of Satan. Wealth is blessed when employed to relieve sorrow and suffering; accursed, when employed to minister to selfish passion, pleasure, or pride: blessed, when it emancipates a people; accursed, when it builds up the dominion of a single man, and denies God's law of progress. All that exists is given for use and aid, and you sin equally by neglect or misuse.

"You are bound to endeavour to transform the earthly dwelling assigned to you for a time into a visible temple of the law: a gem of the crown the worlds are fashioning for the Eternal; and each of you may do this according to his sphere, if he look beyond the limited horizon of self. Look from the family to the commune; from the commune to the nation; from the nation to humanity; from humanity to the universe; from the universe to God. Let every act be such as, if accepted as the rule by the whole generation, would increase the actual sum of good, or decrease the actual sum of evil; and be you an unlettered peasant or a ruler of men, your merit will be equal, and your tomb the cradle of a new life, higher upon the scale of progress than your own.

"Love God in your fellow-men: men in the progress to be achieved for them and with them. Hold as offensive to God all that offends the dignity of the human being bound to worship Him; all that hinders the intellectual development of the being bound to comprehend Him gradually through his design; all that violates the liberty of the being bound to attune his life to that design; all that contaminates by corruption, materialism, superstition, or falsehood the being destined progressively to incarnate the ideal in itself. Combat such evils by example, word, and deed, and call upon your brother men to combat with you. Evil is not eternal; but the battle against it must be a crusade, for the conquest of the ideal demands the effort of entire humanity, the sum of all the faculties vouchsafed to it by God. Develop these faculties by association as intimately and widely as possible. Association, the sole method of progress, is—substituted for charity—the religious word of the epoch. Let help, given to individual suffering and consolation to him that weeps, constitute for you the joys of life. Let the sorrows of those who suffer afar off be equally sacred ; be your life's duty a watch in the night. Your battle is not with the effects, but with the causes of evil : wheresoever those causes are sustained by law or opinion, wheresoever you behold upon God's creature the stamp of inequality or slavery, there is the sign of Satan ; and be that sign on the brow of the negro, the working man, or the woman, you are bound to raise, with deeper meaning than of yore, the old Hussite cry, 'The Cup for all !' and either conquer or die, that others may.

"The earth's hymn to God can only be worthily sounded by the lips of freemen united in a common aim. Wrest from Satan the kingdoms of the earth with which he tempted Jesus ; then may you stand erect in conscious duty done and raise that hymn. Let the banner of the new faith, God, Progress, Humanity, head the crusade. God, the origin and end of all; progress, the law He gave to life; humanity, the interpreter, in God's own time and throughout all time, of that law. Deduce your rule of action from that faith, combat for the earth on the earth, but with eyes raised to heaven. Be your love the love that gives and receives support upon the ascending path of life. Hate the sin, but never the sinner : he bears within him (though stifled now by egotism) germs of the same virtues that are in yourselves, and destined yet to be developed. Love in him your brother of the future. Punish not : protect the society in which you live, and educate the erring members of it. Preach not, labour not, in the name of rights which do but represent the individual ; but in the name of duty, which represents the aim of all. You have no rights, save as the consequence of duties fulfilled; they may all be summed up in the one right, that others should fulfil towards you the duty you fulfil towards them. Say not the sovereignty is in us. The sovereignty is in God. The will of the people is sacred only when it interprets and applies the moral law. It is impotent or null when it departs from it, and represents naught other than tyranny.

" Transform not yourselves from believers into idolaters by accepting any privileged interpreters between yourselves and God. The sun of God shines on all, the Word of God must illumine all. Earth's mists arise between you and the sun, and clouds of error, superstition, and egotism intervene between the human soul and God; but you can chase those clouds from the soul by educating it to religion, sacrifice, and love, and between you and God extend the links of the long and sacred chain of martyrs of thought and love, who still remember and love the earth whereon they accomplished a mission.

" Be your priests and counsellors in all the doubts and agitations of conscience those whom long years of tried virtue, and study of things eternal, have proved worthy to be such. Prophets and guides upon the weary pilgrimage of humanity are the men upon whose brow God has set the seal of genius sanctified by virtue; but forget not that the Divine element exists also in yourselves; never yield up the liberty of your immortal souls into the hands of your brother-man. Love, honour, and follow, but serve not. Respect in yourselves that human unity which is a reflex of the unity Divine. The false philosophy of the day has, in the absence of a religious faith, broken up that unity, by parcelling it out into faculties of reason, sentiment, and sensation, and some have worshipped one and some another of these faculties; but remember that neither thought, aspiration, nor economic fact constitutes life: they are but the instruments of life, equally necessary and equally sacred when united in action towards the realisation of its aim, the progressive incarnation of the ideal; and respect alike the inviolability of thought, the sanctity of aspiration, and the organised development of the material faculties, without which the development of the rest is impossible.

"Let labour be the basis of civil society, and let the distribution of its fruits be according to works. Let him who will not labour possess naught.

"Hold sacred the religious faith which unites the millions in a common part of love and action, but hold sacred also the heresy wherein, it may be, lies the germ of the faith of the future. Represent the first in your rites and fraternal associations, but fail not to protect the second from all intolerance.

"You owe to all men education founded upon your religious synthesis, but forget not that the supreme conception of that religion is progress, and let the last words of that education be these : we have made known to you the moral law, in the name of which the brothers amongst whom you are called to live and labour are associated ; but remember that life is given to you in order that you may endeavour to improve the society in which you live, to purify and enlarge its faith, and to urge forward on the path of eternal truth the men who surround you, and who will bless your work."

You may cast your dying anathema on this moral code, but, humble individual as I am, I declare to you that the time is not far off, when it will take the place of that which you, while daily violating it in your actions, proclaim eternal.

VII

No; the Book of God is not closed. And you who blaspheme against the Omnipotent by declaring yourselves the depositaries of its last page, give the lie to the sublimest previsions of Jesus, to the prophetic words recorded in the divinest of your four Gospels, words which alone would suffice to constitute the superiority of Christianity over all anterior religions.

"God is a Spirit, and they that worship Him must worship Him in spirit and in truth."—John iv. 24.

"And I will pray the Father, and He shall give you another Comforter, that He may abide with you for ever."—John xiv. 16.

"Even the Spirit of truth; . . . for He dwelleth with you, and shall be in you."—*Ibid.* xiv. 17.

"I am the true vine and My Father is the husbandman."—*Ibid.* xv. 1.

"Every branch in Me that beareth not fruit He taketh away : and every branch that beareth fruit, He purgeth it, that it may bring forth more fruit."—*Ibid.* xv. 2.

"It is expedient for you that I go away : for if I go not away, the Comforter will not come unto you."—*Ibid.* xvi. 7.

"I have yet many things to say unto you, but ye cannot bear them now."

"Howbeit when He the spirit of truth is come, He will guide you unto all truth : for He shall not speak of Himself ; but whatsoever He shall hear, that shall He speak : and He will show you the things to come."—*Ibid.* xvi. 12, 13.

All the greatest thinkers, from Prometheus to Socrates and Plato, and from them down to our own time, have prophesied the fall of one belief and the rising of another. None had prevision, like Jesus, of the characteristics of the future faith. One of those rare intuitions, which make of Him a type hitherto unique amongst men, inspired the words above quoted, linking His own faith to the faith to come. It seems as if the symbolic forms of religion, the transformatory work of time upon them, the sanctity of universal tradition, and the continuous revelation of the Spirit of God through humanity, were all foreseen by Him, on the eve of the sacrifice He had accepted ; when the darkness of the future was illumined by the immense love He bore to His fellow-men. You are no longer capable of love or sacrifice, and, therefore, those words have no meaning for you ; unintelligible as the warning at the banquet of Belshazzar.

You will die, then—fate so wills it—but instead of dying in love, like Jesus, and invoking the coming of the Comforter to mankind, you are doomed—as I formerly declared to you—to die the saddest of all deaths, with curses on your lips.

The Book of God is not closed. The coming generations are not disinherited; they who preceded Jesus were not accursed. Children of God all of them, identical in faculties and tendencies, they transmit from each to each, in brightness growing with the growth of time and their own endeavour, the lamp of life kindled by Him, and fed and nourished by His Spirit. Revelation, which is, as Lessing says, the education of the human race, descends continuously from God to man; prophesied by genius, evoked by virtue and sacrifice, and accepted and proclaimed from epoch to epoch, by the great religious evolutions of collective humanity.

From epoch to epoch the pages of that eternal gospel (which Italians, neglected by us and persecuted by you, were the first to foretell) are turned; each fresh page, disclosed by the ever-renovating Spirit of God, indicates a period of the progress marked out for us by the providential plan, and corresponds, historically, to a religion. Each religion sets before mankind a new educational idea as its aim; each is a fragment, enveloped in symbols, of eternal truth. So soon as that idea, comprehended by the intelligence, and incarnated in the hearts of mankind, has become an inalienable part of universal tradition, even as the mountain traveller on reaching one summit beholds another rising above him, so is a new idea or aim presented to the human mind, and a new conception of life, a faith, arises to consecrate that idea, and unite the powers and activity of mankind in the fulfilment of that aim. Having accomplished its mission, that religion disappears; leaving behind the portion of truth it contained, the unknown quantity disengaged by it from its symbol, a new immortal star in humanity's heaven. As the discoveries of science have revealed, and will reveal, star upon star, until our knowledge of the celestial system, of which the milky way is zone, and the earth a part, be complete, so the religious faculties of humanity have added, and will add, faith to faith, until the entire truth we are capable of comprehending be complete. Columns of the temple which the generations are building to God, our religions succeed and are linked with one another, sacred and necessary each and all, but having each and all their determinate place and value, according to the portion of the temple they sustain. You who seek to support God's temple on a single column seek the impossible. Could mankind follow you in the insane attempt, column and temple would fall together.

The world is athirst of God, of progress, and of unity. You substitute for God an idol, an infallible Pope. You oppose to progress the impotent, barren negations of your canons. You impede unity by accepting—on condition that a fraction of the State be preserved to you by force—the dualism between the temporal and spiritual power, represented by the Papacy and monarchy. The hideous idolatry will be answered by God, the destroyer of all idols, past, present, and to come. Your wretched negations will be answered by humanity, which will look upon you, smile, and pass on. The dualism you perpetuate will be answered by the people—the sole power destined to increase—who are hourly acquiring that consciousness of their own strength which alone is needful for their victory.

The epoch of individuality is exhausted. The epoch of association has begun, and is destined—perhaps through the very Rome you desecrate and profane—to sweep away monarchy and the Papacy together.

I remember vaguely, while I write, a short poem of Byron's called "Darkness." Amid the ruins of a world expiring in icy cold, two beings alone are left. They also are doomed to perish, but they persist in struggling against the approaching dissolution. Groping amid the darkness, they reach the ashes of an expiring fire, and strive, with all the anguish of one who seeks to prolong existence, if only for a day, to revive it with their breath. When at last they succeed in raising a feeble flame they turn to gaze upon each other, to discover, with rage and terror, that they are enemies !

I know not what idea inspired these lines to Byron ;

but my thoughts, as I recall them, turn involuntarily to you. The last, doomed representatives of a world, from which all life is withdrawn, you, Papacy, and Monarchy, have sought to dominate humanity more surely by dividing it in twain. Conscious of your incapacity of re-uniting it, and yet jealous in your impotent ambition of each other, you have striven to found an impossible alliance between the powers you have disjoined, and from time to time have embraced each other upon the tomb of some once free and dreaded nation ; but hating and despising each other in your hearts, and seeking to injure each other so soon as freed from any imminent danger. Now groping onwards, solitary and suspicious, amid the darkness, and vainly seeking to rekindle the fire irrevocably consumed, you bend your dying gaze upon each other in rage and fear.

Descend into the tomb you have dug for yourselves. Had you loved, forefelt the future, and adored in time the Spirit of truth announced by Jesus in dying, you might have made of that tomb an altar. It is now too late. The Angel of Death will inscribe upon that tomb the condemnation you have forgotten :

" And whosoever speaketh a word against the Son of Man, it shall be forgiven him : but whosoever speaketh against the Holy Ghost, it shall not be forgiven him, neither in this world, neither in the world to come."
—Matt. xii. 32.

APPENDIX

NOTE ON THE REVOLUTION OF 1831

THE Revolution of Central Italy in 1831 was a sequel of the July Revolution in France. The Parisian Carbonari had been industriously connecting the threads of revolution in North and Central Italy. Early in February it broke out in Modena and Bologna, and within a fortnight all but a fraction of the Papal States and the Duchies of Modena and Parma, the mass in fact of Central Italy, with the exception of Tuscany, were in full revolt. The temporal power was abolished ; a National Assembly was decreed ; the Pope was on the point of flight. The Bolognese Government had relied on French promises to protect them against Austrian aggression. One of the formulas of the July Revolution had been, that no nation should be allowed to interfere in the domestic concerns of another. The French ministers had protested that France would never allow the principle of non-intervention to be violated, and had promised to fight if Austria sent troops into the revolted provinces. At the same time they were sending Metternich private assurances to the contrary, and soon afterwards, throwing off the mask, they declared that "the blood of Frenchmen belongs to France alone." Free from French opposition, the Austrians easily overran Parma and Modena. When the Modenese forces retired into Romagna, the

Provisional Government at Bologna, in pedantic observance of the non-intervention formula, still hoping against light that France would insist on its observance by Austria, regarded them as belligerents entering a neutral territory, and disarmed them. "None of our people," they said, "shall take part in our neighbours' quarrels." Their fears gave the lie to their high-sounding phrases of Italian unity and nationality, and took the life out of the struggle. A feeble retreat to Ancona, varied by some spirited fighting on the part of the volunteers at Rimini, was followed by complete surrender, and, though the Revolution broke out again at the end of the year, it was easily suppressed by the Papal troops.

The revolution has been, perhaps, over-hardly criticised by Mazzini and others. The irresolution and incompetency of its leaders, their pedantic belief in phrases, their incapacity to guide, admit of no defence. The lawyers and professors who directed it had small experience of public life. They thought they could sway men by maxims, and despised the spiritual forces that are the life-blood of a revolution. And so the people welcomed the revolution, but after the first few days had no enthusiasm for it. They chose their deputies for the Assembly, but were never made to feel their own responsibility and place in the new order. Men who under good leadership would have fought and perhaps conquered found themselves isolated and paralysed, and resigned with hardly a struggle to the old hated rule. And yet it was in advance of the revolutions of Naples and Piedmont ten years before. In some respects it went ahead of popular feeling, and the abolition of the temporal power scandalised the masses outside the great cities. It accentuated, though with a somewhat uncertain voice, the nationalist bearings of the democratic movement. Italian liberalism too had broadened since 1821. It had spread from the army to the lawyers and tradesmen and artisans. Democracy no longer paraded in military full-dress : it had become bourgeois and unostentatious, and if it lacked

capacity and enthusiasm, it had gained in a certain plain
solidity. There was a disinterestedness and probity about
it that testified to the new spirit. Social reform had been
absent from the programmes of the earlier revolutionists ;
it had now, *pace* Mazzini, come to the front, and the first
days of freedom had been signalised by a long list of
practical improvements in law and taxation and social
rights.

COSIMO CLASSICS

COSIMO is an innovative publisher of books and publications that inspire, inform and engage readers worldwide. Our titles are drawn from a range of subjects including health, business, philosophy, history, science and sacred texts. We specialize in using print-on-demand technology (POD), making it possible to publish books for both general and specialized audiences and to keep books in print indefinitely. With POD technology new titles can reach their audiences faster and more efficiently than with traditional publishing.

> ➤ **Permanent Availability:** Our books & publications never go out-of-print.

> ➤ **Global Availability:** Our books are always available online at popular retailers and can be ordered from your favorite local bookstore.

COSIMO CLASSICS brings to life unique, rare, out-of-print classics representing subjects as diverse as *Alternative Health, Business and Economics, Eastern Philosophy, Personal Growth, Mythology, Philosophy, Sacred Texts, Science, Spirituality* and much more!

COSIMO-on-DEMAND publishes your books, publications and reports. If you are an Author, part of an Organization, or a Benefactor with a publishing project and would like to bring books back into print, publish new books fast and effectively, would like your publications, books, training guides, and conference reports to be made available to your members and wider audiences around the world, we can assist you with your publishing needs.

Visit our website at www.cosimobooks.com to learn more about Cosimo, browse our catalog, take part in surveys or campaigns, and sign-up for our newsletter.

And if you wish please drop us a line at info@cosimobooks.com. We look forward to hearing from you.

Printed in the United States
71434LV00001B/1-60